The Business Francis Means

Other CUA Press Titles on
Business, Catholic Social Teaching

A Catechism for Business: Tough Ethical Questions and Insights from Catholic Teaching. 2ⁿᵈ edition. Edited by Andrew V. Abela and Joseph E. Capizzi.

Translated into Spanish by Francisco J. Lara as *Un Catecismo para los Negocios: Respuestas de La Enseñanza Católica a Los Dilemas Éticos de la Empresa, Segunda Edición*

Handbook of Catholic Social Teaching: A Guide for Christians in the World Today. Edited by Martin Schlag. Foreword by Peter K. A. Cardinal Turkson.

Free Markets with Sustainability and Solidarity: Facing the Challenge. Edited by Martin Schlag and Juan A. Mercado.

Church, State, and Society: An Introduction to Catholic Social Doctrine. By J. Brian Benestad.

THE BUSINESS FRANCIS MEANS

UNDERSTANDING THE POPE'S MESSAGE ON THE ECONOMY

MARTIN SCHLAG

THE CATHOLIC UNIVERSITY OF AMERICA PRESS

Washington, DC

Library of Congress Cataloging-in-Publication Data

Names: Schlag, Martin, 1964- author.
Title: The business Francis means : understanding the pope's message on the economy / Martin Schlag.
Description: Washington, D.C. : Catholic University of America Press, 2017. | Includes bibliographical references and index.
Identifiers: LCCN 2017031835 (print) | LCCN 2017034422 (ebook) | ISBN 9780813229744 () | ISBN 9780813229737 (alk. paper)
Subjects: LCSH: Economics—Religious aspects—Catholic Church. | Francis, Pope, 1936– | Christian sociology—Catholic Church.
Classification: LCC BX1795.E27 (ebook) | LCC BX1795.E27 S36 2017 (print) | DDC 261.8/5088282—dc23

LC record available at https://lccn.loc.gov/2017031835

Contents

Preface   vii

1. Business in Catholic Social Thought   1

General Perspectives on the Development of Catholic Social
   Thought   2

The Paradigm Shift at the Second Vatican Council   5

The Principles of Catholic Social Teaching   7

Specific Topics   12

2. Pope Francis's Spiritual and Cultural Context   48

Change of Hermeneutics   50

Cultural Transfer   55

Francis the Jesuit: The Renewal of the Society of Jesus under
   Fr. Pedro Arrupe and the Social Dimension of Faith   57

Francis the South American: The Latin American
   Experience   71

3. Pope Francis's Message on Business and the
Economy   98

The Distinctiveness of Pope Francis   99

Reading Pope Francis Positively   111

Strong Moral Messages to Business   127

4. Contemplation and Business   156

Bibliography   173

Index   187

Preface

Americans pledge to be one nation under God, indivisible. In reality, however, the country is deeply divided over fundamental moral issues like abortion, contraception, gender, immigration, war, inequality, climate change, race relations, the scope of the right to privacy, property rights, and the list could go on. Catholic social thought has something to say on all of these topics, and strives to apply the Gospel message over their whole breadth in a balanced way. In contrast, groups on both sides of the divisions over these social issues tend to focus their attention on one or a few of them, disregarding the others.

Pope Francis, generally speaking, has thus far chosen to concentrate his papacy on evangelization and social justice issues, as opposed to doctrinal or liturgical ones. This has led to Francis being hailed as a hero by many on the left, while it has made some conservative supporters of St. John Paul II and Pope Emeritus Benedict XVI disappointed and uncomfortable, even though they may love Francis personally and appreciate his gestures of mercy and compassion. Some find his teachings difficult to embrace, and many turn away, especially from those concerning business and the economy. Pope Francis has spoken of building bridges as part of what it is to be Christian, but aspects of his message seem to be constructing walls between the Holy Father himself and groups of the faithful.

In this book I hope to break through some of these walls and show that Pope Francis has a lot to say to Christians on all sides. His message, taken as a whole, prevents us from dividing the "seamless garment" of Christ: he reminds conservatives

of the problems of inequality and poverty, and liberals that
social justice is not enough because the Church is the bride
of Christ, not a social institution or an NGO. In writing these
pages, I have in mind especially those Catholics and Christians
who, in general, feel more at home with St. John Paul II and
Benedict XVI, and who, like me, are conservative on doctrinal
questions, but at the same time want to rise to the demands of
the Gospel that we serve the poor among us.

This book summarizes and explains Pope Francis's message
on business and the economy. This implies a twofold limit
readers should be aware of: first, I do not present the whole
of his social message—much less all of his pastoral program
and teaching—but only the part related to business and the
economy. I myself am not an economist but a theologian with
a background in jurisprudence. Thus my expressions are the
thoughts and reflections of an interested priest who is a lay-
man on economics. Second, I do not deal with these topics in
general, but only as they are presented by Pope Francis. This
is therefore not a book on business ethics, poverty, inequality,
or economic matters generally, but instead on what Francis
thinks and says about these themes.

Francis has frequently repeated that he is not adding anything to Catholic social teaching. I have thus chosen to begin
with a chapter on business and finance in the tradition of
Catholic thought in order to analyze the truth of this claim,
and to examine what might be new and original in Francis.
After providing this background, I undertake in Chapter Two
the task of translating the Pope's statements into the Western
cultural context, which is a much more challenging exercise
than translating texts into another language. Cultural transfer is possible only through transformation of ideas; literal
translation of ideas does not get us far, and can even be damaging. Francis has said himself that he has not changed his
style from when he was an Archbishop in Buenos Aires. His
ideas are thus shaped by his specific cultural and spiritual
experience, which I seek to uncover so as to shed light on

the issues at hand. Finally, it is important to remember that Francis does not pretend to present an economic theory but rather a strong moral message. This I explain and summarize in Chapter Three, and then I finish in Chapter Four with a meditation on the importance of contemplation as a spiritual source of social renewal.

I thank The Catholic University of America Press for suggesting the idea for this book, and for all the editorial support along the way, especially that of Gregory Black, who thoroughly corrected the text. I acknowledge the valuable observations of the two anonymous peer reviewers who substantially improved the contents of the book. The remaining errors are completely my own. As always, Elizabeth Reichert has done a wonderful job of editing my text and researching some of the footnotes. A big thank you to her!

Rome, April 23, 2017. Sunday of Divine Mercy.

1

Business in Catholic Social Thought

WHY DOES CATHOLIC THEOLOGY address business and markets so extensively? Shouldn't Catholic theology remain in its field of competence (as is true of all other sciences), treating religious and spiritual questions only? The short answer to these questions begins with recalling that God is the Creator and final cause of all that exists. In all we do we should aspire to live according to God's will and love Him, including in our economic relationships. Thinking about the moral dimension of business means thinking about God as the aim of all our activities. The Catholic tradition reflects on the economy from a viewpoint of faith because Christian faith has a public, or, as one might say, a cultural dimension, as John Paul II wrote: "A faith that does not affect a person's culture is a faith 'not fully embraced, not entirely thought out, not faithfully lived.'"[1] Catholic reflections on the economy and on society have generally taken place on three levels. The hierarchy of the Catholic Church has published documents on social issues that form its body of Catholic social *teaching*. These documents were and are prepared following theological discussion, and the documents in turn lead to more discussion after their publication. These theological reflections, taking place both before and after the publication of a document, are denominated Catholic social *thought*. Catholic social thought, however, comprises not only reflections on Church documents, but also independent theories gravitating around the Catholic faith as well as reflections on the Church's practical service to the poor and needy. Both Catholic social teaching and Catholic social thought form the Catholic social *tradition*[2] that has evolved over the centuries. Catholic social teaching, thought, and tradition thus relate to each other in the manner of widening concentric circles.

General Perspectives on the Development of Catholic Social Thought

For anyone coming from a non-Catholic religious tradition, it might be important to understand the differences between the course taken by the Catholic tradition as compared to that of the Christian communities that emerged from the Reformation. Both the Catholic and Protestant traditions have attempted to resolve an inherent tension in Christianity—the tension between temporal power and spiritual authority, a distinction that has its root in Christ's injunction to give to God what belongs to God and to Caesar what belongs to Caesar.[3] In a religious context where those who wield political power are also entrusted with religions questions (as was the case in pagan Rome), or in a context in which the spiritual authority also regulates temporal affairs, there is theoretically no intrinsic tension between the two because religious and political functions are exercised by the same people belonging to one and the same system. Even when these traditions, ideally, distinguish the profane from the sacred sphere, the people who are in charge of the vertical relationship with God are also in charge of horizontal earthly affairs. There might be different interpretations or political alignments among these people, but in principle, any tensions are not between "Church and State." This system is referred to as "monism." Christianity, in contrast, presents a universalized "dualism," beginning with the Old Testament distinction between royal and prophetic institutions. In the name of God, the prophets of the Old Testament raised their voices in defense of justice against abuses by the civil power. Christ's injunction about God and Caesar reinforces the dualism of the prophetic tradition. In a dualistic system, both functions, the spiritual and the temporal, serve the same people, but are entrusted to two different sets of institutions in the same society: the Church and the civil power structures. They can oppose one another. This "Christian dualism" thus opens a field of tension; however, as Pope Benedict XVI stated: "Unlike other great religions, Christianity has never proposed a revealed law to the State and to society, that is to say a juridical order derived from revelation."[4]

Despite this, the Christian Church has been and continues to be challenged to make its faith fruitful for social life. In its quest to foster social orders compatible with Christ's Revelation in every specific historical circumstance, the Church over the centuries up to the Reformation strove, with varying degrees of success, to maintain two principles: first, the distinction between and institutional separation of temporal power and spiritual authority; but at the same time, second, the primacy of Christian moral law over politics. This second principle expresses the conviction that the State is not the supreme authority in the universe, or in other words, that God is the Lord of history and of all things, and that therefore God's moral law also binds politicians. The second principle is a common heritage of all Christian denominations,[5] but not so the first. Since the Reformation, the social thought of Protantism and Catholicism have taken different roads in defining the relationship between these two principles.

In contrast to Luther's Two Kingdoms Doctrine[6] and the tendency in Protestant countries to entrust the secular sovereign powers with responsibility for the visible and external affairs of the Church,[7] the Catholic tradition developed the theory of "*potestas indirecta.*" This theory is linked to late Scholasticism, in particular to the School of Salamanca. It was made known to a wide public by Francisco de Vitoria[8] and Robert Bellarmine, SJ.[9] In a nutshell, *potestas indirecta* meant that popes had the right to teach Catholic moral principles to Christian princes, who were in turn obliged to put them into effect through their exercise of civil power. The doctrine implies a limitation on papal power, as it denies the pope *direct* political power. Popes, taught Bellarmine, usually had no right to interfere in the political affairs of Christian monarchs, and obviously none at all in the affairs of non-Christian princes. On the other hand, in contrast to the Reformers, the Catholic Church has taught and teaches that she is at the same time the visible and the invisible Church, and that the pope is sovereign over both the temporal and spiritual spheres. The Church is called to speak out on temporal matters as well as spiritual ones, and Christian behavior in temporal matters, not just grace by itself, is decisive for salvation. The moral principles applicable to politics and the social order, including the economy, taught by the Catholic Church, are not based on Revelation but rather on reason, and are, taken together, referred to as "natural law." In the words of Benedict XVI, the Catholic tradition "has pointed to nature and reason as the true sources of law – and to the harmony of objective and subjective reason, which naturally presupposes that both spheres are rooted in the creative reason of God."[10]

The *potestas indirecta* doctrine posed a problem in cases of conflict. What happened if the Christian monarch did not obey, stalled, or even acted in a way that contradicted a pope's injunctions? In that case, says Bellarmine, political power devolved to the pope, and he could legislate, proclaim legal judgments, exercise administrative powers, and even depose kings and queens.[11] This problem was one of the reasons the doctrine was only partially successful in practice.

By the time of the Second Vatican Council (1962–65), the doctrine's function as a guide for the Church had become completely untenable. By 1962, pluralist democracies had replaced monarchies in most countries, and after the terrible experience of totalitarianism the Holy See had become very wary of the assurances of authoritarian governments that they would defend the interests of the Church. However, for our present purposes, it is important to know that during the first half of the twentieth century, the *potestas indirecta* doctrine was the "default position taken by bishops in Catholic countries: the Church was the guardian of moral and spiritual values that the government should uphold and implement, while respecting the Church's freedom to Christianize society."[12] This was the situation in Pope Francis's Argentina during his youth.

The Paradigm Shift at the Second Vatican Council

In the Second Vatican Council's Pastoral Constitution *Gaudium et Spes*, the Catholic Church adopted a paradigm shift. This shift is already expressed in the council's designation of the Constitution as a "Pastoral Constitution on the Church in the Modern World," which does not represent a mere change in terminology. While Leo XIII had defined the relationship between faith and society as one between Church and State, the Second Vatican Council envisioned the Church "in the world." What this implies is a change in the way in which the mission of the Church and her evangelization are conceived. Whereas before the council there was a tendency toward a "top-down" approach, this was replaced by a "bottom-up" orientation; in other words, whereas before the council the stress was put on facilitating the conformity of society to the moral law through the aid of political instruments (laws, decrees, concordats, etc.), after the council the Church's emphasis was placed on the apostolate of the laity and culture. This process has been called the "voluntary disestablishment" of the Catholic Church,[13] which opted for a new habitat in civil society, proclaiming the hour of the lay Christian. Laypeople too are called to holiness, and through their personal apostolate from within the world, to bring about the evangelization of the societies in which they live. This implied the Church's recognition of spheres of earthly affairs with their own laws and logic. If Christians are supposed to be true citizens of this earth, sharing the joys and sorrows, the hopes and anguish of all other humans, then they must also embrace the rules according to which earthly affairs, including economic affairs, function. *Gaudium et Spes* refers to the "autonomy of earthly affairs,"[14] and thus implicitly accepts their emancipation from clerical tutelage, or, put differently, accepts modern secularity.[15]

Being centered and anchored in civil society and having renounced its political privileges, however, does not mean that the Catholic Church has ever or could ever accept the privatization of the Christian faith. This would be secularism, or in other words the imposition of public non-belief through governmental coercion. The autonomy of earthly affairs in reality is merely relative; that is, it is relative to God's law and subject to it. This means that Christians individually and collectively must raise their voices to defend unborn life, social justice, marriage and family, and other Christian values. The Christian faith has a public dimension. Pope Benedict XVI formulated the position of the Church on several occasions. He called the duty of the Church's hierarchy and teaching authority in regard to the State and politics "indirect" (in Latin: *officium intermedium*). This means that her social teaching "has no intention of giving the Church power over the State. Even less is it an attempt to impose on those who do not share the faith ways of thinking and modes of conduct proper to faith. Its aim is simply to help purify reason and to contribute, here and now, to the acknowledgment and attainment of what is just."[16] The Church's hierarchy itself does not intervene in party politics as the lay faithful may and should do, but through its "intermediate service" makes humane and just politics possible.

The Second Vatican Council was born out of a great optimism and filled with a desire for a new Christian humanism.[17] This stance was supported by the almost-total post-World

War social consensus on questions of natural law. There was hardly any consensual divorce, abortion was legally prohibited in most countries, there was no experience of experimentation on embryos, and there was no gay marriage, among other things. This consensus lasted only a short time after the conclusion of the council, however. In the late 1960s the sexual revolution broke out, a phenomenon which directly attacked Christian anthropology while at the same time using the language of human rights in which the modern ethos of liberation had been written, a language which the Church had opened herself to at the council. Seemingly overnight, the existence of "human rights" to abortion, contraception, divorce, etc., was postulated in Western societies. Pope John Paul II referred to this development as a betrayal by Western civilization of its own constitutional principles and cultural roots.[18]

The Catholic reaction to this new situation was to summon Christians to a "New Evangelization" in all fields of human life and activity, including but not primarily that of the economy. This undertaking evoked many questions: What role do Catholic faith and morality play in the world? Is the Christian faith only a reinforcement, an eschatological horizon for secular ethical rules? Is there anything specifically Christian? And if there is, is it only to be sought in the field of individual ethics? Is there nothing specific in Christian social and moral theology that speaks to human efforts to structure society?

The Principles of Catholic Social Teaching

The *Compendium of the Social Doctrine of the Church*, which summarizes the papal social encyclicals up to 2004, refers to charity as "the highest and universal criterion of the whole of social ethics." As from an "inner wellspring," the values of truth, freedom, and justice are born and grow from love.[19] "Charity is at the heart of the Church's social doctrine," said Benedict XVI in his social encyclical *Caritas in Veritate*.[20] The revelation that God is love and the centrality of the commandment of universal love, even of enemies, is the distinctive hallmark of the Christian religion. It is a demanding goal that we more often than not do not achieve in practice. The Gospel is the story of Jesus Christ who through His death and resurrection in humility calls us into His kingdom, which consists not in food and drink but in "righteousness, peace, and joy in the Holy Spirit."[21] Righteousness, the Biblical "*sedaqa*," is a concept whose meaning goes beyond mere justice in the classical legal sense—*sedaqa* combines God's justice with His grace and mercy. It is a form of justice that, out of mercy and compassion for the poor, actively takes up their cause. As a consequence of our being made in the image of God, believers are expected to imitate God in exercising this particular blend of justice and mercy. *Sedaqa* unites the religious dimension with the social one: God protects the weak, the poor, the widows, and the orphans. We are obliged to help them out of justice, not out of condescending generosity or beneficence.[22] Jesus requires this "greater righteousness" of His disciples (Mt 5:20). He did not send His disciples out to found cities or states but to be witnesses to His resurrection, and in the joyous light of this truth to recognize Him in the least of His brethren. In this endeavor, Christians must avoid fideism and fundamentalism: the Gospel is not a socioeconomic program that can be applied immediately and ready-made without the mediation of philosophy and science. Charity as the Gospel's heart needs reason and human skills, justice, institutions, and law in order to become manifest in the social order. Religious enthusiasm without reason can be very dangerous.

Since the first social encyclical, Leo XIII's *Rerum Novarum* in 1891, Catholic social thought has developed principles and values that serve as stepping-stones on the great road of charity. Leo XIII spoke out to improve the plight of workers (the "labor question"), demanding just wages, fair and moral treatment, and property and freedom for workers. He also called for their legal protection and their right to organize in worker associations. In the next social encyclical, *Quadragesimo Anno* in 1931, in the middle of the Great Depression, Pope Pius XI broadened the scope of the Church's social doctrine, addressing not only the plight of workers, but also the proper ordering of society (the "social question"). He called for social justice and social charity, proposing Catholic social teaching as an alternative to both materialistic socialism and libertarian capitalism. He re-asserted the Church's endorsement of private capital and introduced the principle of subsidiarity. During the Cold War and immediately after the Cuban crisis, Pope John XXIII published *Pacem in Terris* on peace and human rights. In it he referred to the values of justice and love, freedom and truth, but also to institutions like the separation of powers, the independent judiciary, and others, as essential elements of social improvement. This positive appraisal of institutions finds its magisterial conclusion in John Paul II's encyclicals *Sollicitudo Rei Socialis* and *Centesimus Annus*, in which the Pope defined solidarity as an essential virtue for international development, and explained the structural advantages of liberal constitutional democracies based on the rule of law and a free economy, while at the same time highlighting the risks that these present when they are not based on an adequate anthropology.[23] The recognition of the decisive role of institutions is of great importance for the social teaching of the Church—in the Catholic tradition there had been and to some extent still is a certain blindness on this topic.[24]

From this development of the social teaching (sketched only very cursorily here) have emerged the four *principles* of Catholic social thought—human dignity, common good, solidarity, and subsidiarity—and its four *values*: justice, love, freedom, and truth. The principles form the foundation of society and the points of departure for reform, whereas the values are the aims that should be reached.

Catholic social teaching applies its principles and values in three modes that exercise three different functions.[25] These "modes" correspond to the three offices of Christ that every

Christian receives in baptism and exercises through a holy life: the prophetic, the regal or pastoral, and the priestly. First, the Church denounces social injustice, the violation of human rights and dignity, and structures of sin. This is the prophetic tradition (mode) inaugurated by the prophets of the Old Testament, such as Amos, Isaiah, Jeremiah, and others, who in the name of God and with divine authority criticized abuses of economic and political power (function). From the first social encyclical onward, the Church has prophetically raised her voice to defend the weakest and those most in need of help. Thus Leo XIII in *Rerum Novarum* denounced "the utter poverty of the masses" and the fact that workers had been "surrendered, isolated and helpless, to the hardheartedness of employers and the greed of unchecked competition." He deplored "rapacious usury" and the injustice that a "small number of very rich men have been able to lay upon the teeming masses of the laboring poor a yoke little better than that of slavery itself."[26] However, denunciation helps the poor only if constructive and positive remedies are offered to counterbalance the criticism. It is relatively easy to criticize what does not work. The much more challenging task is to build a humane and happy society that works.

The second function of Catholic social teaching therefore consists in proposing considerations for a beneficial organization of society through economic models and institutions that might answer the question of how to overcome the social injustices, which have been rightly denounced. This corresponds to the second mode, in which Christians exercise their baptismal calling: the regal or pastoral office. For example, Leo XIII rejected socialism as a mistaken solution because it violates property rights and runs contrary to the true nature and mission of government.[27] Catholic social teaching has promoted property rights and the rule of law as institutional arrangements that protect workers; however, even the best institutions falter if they are undercut by poorly-formed individual consciences and a lack of social virtue.

Thus, thirdly, Catholic social teaching also repeats demands for virtuousness (pertaining to the priestly mode or office): structures and institutions alone are not capable of solving the problems that beset society. We need social virtues. This is one of the reasons why Pius XI did not trust competition to be the sole rule of markets but instead demanded that the virtues of social justice and social charity also regulate the economy.

Each pope has his specific accents. Pope Francis has thus far strongly emphasized his prophetic mission and the need for virtue (prophetic and priestly mode or office); in contrast, he has not emphasized the constructive function of the Church's social teaching about institutional ethics. It will become apparent in the pages of this book that Francis forcefully denounces injustice and demands virtuousness from all members of society. He has also shown a preference for a particular economic model, specifically the social market economy or social economy of the European tradition,[28] and has never endorsed the American economic model. His reference to the social market economy was, however, not in a major document, but rather in a short speech. He called for moving from a "liquid economy... directed at revenue, profiting from speculation and lending at interest, to a social economy that invests in persons by creating jobs and providing training... [and] that guarantees access to land and lodging through labor."[29] The term "liquid economy" must not be understood to refer to "financial liquidity," without which no modern economy could work, but to a type of economy that devalues stable human relationships and defined ethical roles, an economy "prepared to use corruption as a means of obtaining profits."[30] Francis is the first pope in history to explicitly endorse the social market economy. However, we must not attribute too much importance to this fact—he mentions it only once, and he might not be fully acquainted with its implications or its roots in post-World War II Germany. In addition, the tone of his speech and the aims he mentions in it are of the prophetic type, without any emphasis on the dimension of institutional ethics. This prophetic emphasis prevails in all of his messages about business. This means that although Francis has a great deal to say to us no matter what economic system we live under, he has not yet developed his own discussion of institutional ethics, a discussion which is a traditional part of Catholic social teaching.[31]

Certainly, the principles and values of Catholic social teaching are broadly stated and thus sometimes tend to be somewhat vague. They were not, however, formulated in isolation from real Christian life by obscure academics. These principles and values are the result of a deep theological reflection on specific topics, which are essential for the proper ordering of the economy, and over the millennia have challenged the Christian faith. These specific topics include private property, wealth and profit, markets, and money (finance). In the following sections, I will briefly present the Catholic tradition concerning these subjects.

Specific Topics

Private Property

The *Compendium of the Social Doctrine of the Church* states:

> Private property is an essential element of an authentically social and democratic economic policy, and it is the guarantee of a correct social order. *The Church's social doctrine requires that ownership of goods be equally accessible to all,*[32] so that all may become, at least in some measure, owners, and it excludes recourse to forms of "common and promiscuous dominion."[33] *Christian tradition has never recognized the right to private property as absolute and untouchable*: "On the contrary, it has always understood this right within the broader context of the right common to all to use the goods of the whole

of creation: the right to private property is subordinated to the right to common use, to the fact that goods are meant for everyone."[34]

Questions concerning private property; that is, whether property may belong to individual persons, and whether these persons are allowed to use and dispose of property as they deem fit, are decisive for any discussion of economics. As with other topics, Catholic teaching on private property is a blend of the Christian tradition as established by the Bible and the Church Fathers, the liberal system of Roman law, and modern influences.

The Church Fathers treated the institution of property not from a juridical, but rather from a theological and moral perspective based on the Bible. In the texts of the Old Testament, one can distinguish both a vertical and a horizontal dimension of property. The vertical dimension refers to the concept of property in the relationship between man and God. God, as the proprietor and overlord of the Holy Land, commands that this land be distributed among the tribes of Israel.[35] Only after the land is distributed does a horizontal dimension of property come into being. It consists of the juridical distribution and defense of private property among men, referring to the distribution of the land among the tribes and their individual members. The seventh commandment, "Thou shalt not steal," is a clearly stated protection of the institution of private property in this horizontal sense. Private property in the Old Testament was understood to be limited by moral and social considerations. The limitations on private property were apparent in the manifold legal prescriptions regarding society's care for the poor, widows, orphans, and foreigners. There was also positive legislation meant to protect slaves. In part, these protective norms were contained in the rules for the Jubilee. Even though they were probably never fully put into practice, the social measures of the Jubilee year were intended to institutionalize a fair economy: every fifty years, real estate that had been sold was to return to the original owner, family, or clan, and the Hebrews who had been sold as slaves were to be released. The Jubilee year provided a "reset" of economic equality in order to restore fairness to economic relations. These various limitations on private property provided for in the Old Testament were very difficult to put into practice, but the prophets severely criticized Israel for not doing so.

The New Testament presupposes the existence of private property, but at the same time urges believers not to put their hope and trust in material treasures that rot and pass away. Jesus demands a complete freedom of heart and detachment from all possessions in order to follow Him.[36] Property in the New Testament has the character of a means, and the attitude required of owners is that they should "buy as though not owning."[37]

In the following centuries, the Church Fathers concentrated upon the vertical dimension of property, underscoring the universal destination of goods, whereas the horizontal dimension was developed by the Scholastics in the Middle Ages in accordance with Roman law. In addition to the Bible, the Church Fathers were influenced by Hellenistic ideals of communal use and possession of goods. Augustine combined all of these influences in a theological perspective on issues of property—in accordance with Hellenistic moral philosophy, and following our Lord's teachings,[38] Augustine distinguished between goods we should enjoy (*frui*: God, virtue, *honesta*), and others we should only use (*uti*: material means, health, strength, power, etc.). For Augustine, to own something meant to use it rationally and justly, in a detached manner made possible only by interior freedom. Otherwise, an owner becomes enslaved to his possessions.[39] In his *Commentary on the Gospel of St. John*, Augustine argued that by divine law all things belong to God, and that God created the world for everyone. It was human law that effectively divided things and attributed property individually to owners.[40] The later medieval reception of this text reduced the Augustinian position to the idea that private property was not derived from divine law, but was a result of positive human law alone. This interpretation omits the important fact that for Augustine human law pertaining to property is based on a divine origin.[41] Augustinianism, as the medieval reception of Augustine is called, held that property was a consequence and necessity of sin, not of nature.

The various Christian traditions related to property resulted in the conviction, still present in Catholic social teaching, that "in need all things are common."[42] This idea must not be confused with collectivism or communism. The Church Fathers argued from a moral perspective, concentrating on the vertical dimension of property. In the eyes of God, human beings do not own anything, but instead God has created all things for the common use of the entire human race. Utz called this concept "negative communism,"[43] as things by nature belong to nobody in particular, but are meant by the Creator to serve all. In this sense, for instance, St. John Chrysostom wrote: "Not to share one's wealth with the poor is to steal from them and to take away their livelihood. It is not our own goods which we hold, but theirs."[44] This was spoken in a certain socioeconomic context—at that time a few families owned vast expanses of farmland that was tilled by poor, dependent settlers. Like the later serfs, they were obliged to deliver a portion of their products to the landowners, who, as we know from the results of archaeological excavations, lived in magnificent palaces. In times of famine and dearth, the situation of the individual farmers became unbearable. The rich families always had abundant food, receiving it from the poor. That is why John Chrysostom affirmed that the goods of the well-off, among whom he also identified himself, actually belong to the poor workers. This must not be interpreted in a contemporary context as advocating collective ownership or condemning private property, but rather as a wake-up call to our social conscience.

The morality of private property is confirmed by the universal teacher of the Catholic Church, Thomas Aquinas, who followed Aristotle in founding private property on natural reason. From Aristotle's arguments for property, Thomas developed three arguments in favor of private property: (1) the argument from efficiency, (2) the argument from order, and (3) the argument from peace. First, people tend to take better care of what is their own. Holding goods in common is inefficient, because when dealing with what is not their own, people leave the work to others. Second, without a division of property, there would be confusion. If everyone knows exactly which things are in their care, things are treated better, and order results. Third, with private property, every person has his or her own property and can be content with it. Undivided communal goods among sinful men lead to frequent quarrels and disturbances of the peace.[45] Division of property was not originally established by natural law, Thomas notes, because by nature nothing, absolutely speaking, is ascribed to anyone in particular; this division was a rational addition for the better cultivation and peaceful use of possessions.[46] It is noteworthy that it is the common good that justifies the institution of private property, not the right of individuals. Something similar was taught by the other major Catholic theological school, the Franciscan School, whose greatest scholar was the Scotsman John Duns Scotus.

In contrast to the Aristotelian Dominican School, founded by Albert the Great and Thomas Aquinas, the Franciscan School more closely followed the Augustinian tradition, stressing that private property was a consequence of sin and an institution belonging solely to civil law. Duns Scotus taught that before original sin, there was no private property, but instead communism.[47] In the present state of fallen nature, however, communism was revoked because the strong and mighty would not leave the poor and weak their share.[48] Private property is thus necessary to defend the poor. Duns Scotus does not go on to conclude that the institution of private property is therefore part of natural law; on the contrary, for his school, private property was instituted by mere human law, and can therefore be modified, confiscated, or transferred by law.[49] The ideas of Thomas Aquinas were to prevail over time, and the conviction that private property is an institution mandated by natural law is the opinion shared by most theologians nowadays.[50]

It is important to understand, however, that in the Catholic tradition up to the encyclical *Rerum Novarum*, the common good was prior to individual rights. The latter existed only insofar as they served the common good of the community. As we have seen, the medieval teachers justified private property because it contributes to the general well-being and peace of society. Under the medieval view, there was no need to reconstruct the notion of societal common good in light of individual interests, because the common good had not been fragmented into individual rights understood as potentially antagonistic to the common good. The common good came before the individual good. Modern political philosophy overturned this approach—for John Locke, for instance, the first right before any other right, before the common good, is private property: man, through his work, appropriates the objects he produces, and the fruits of those objects. With the creation of a surplus of production, men begin to exchange goods and come together in commonwealths to better ensure the protection of their property (understood as life, safety, and material goods).[51] Thus, in Locke's view, the good of the individual turns out to be not only prior to but also at the origin of the common good. The paradigm shift of modernity took us from natural law as ordering society as a whole to natural rights as individual entitlements against the whole. This paradigm shift also affected Catholic social teaching on private property, though not so radically. It was Leo XIII in *Rerum Novarum* who chose the modern approach and language: he postulated a natural right to property that is prior to the formation of society.[52] In this change he was undoubtedly (albeit indirectly) influenced by classical economists like Adam Smith. Having established private property as a natural right, Catholic social teaching undulates between formulations that stress its individual character and others that are more inclined toward the common good. Pope Francis is closer to the medieval Franciscan tradition, giving priority to the common good and the universal destination of goods.[53] He sees private property as an institution of natural law, but not as an individual right prior to the common good.

Wealth and Profit

> The Church acknowledges the legitimate *role of profit* as an indication that a business is functioning well. When a firm makes a profit, this means that productive factors have been properly employed and corresponding human needs have been duly satisfied. But profitability is not the only indicator of a firm's condition. It is possible for the financial accounts to be in order, and yet for the people — who make up the firm's most valuable asset — to be humiliated and their dignity offended. Besides being morally inadmissible, this will eventually have negative repercussions on the firm's economic efficiency. In fact, the purpose of a business firm is not simply to make a profit, but is to be found in its very existence as a *community of persons* who in various ways are endeavoring to satisfy their basic needs, and who form a particular group at the service of the whole of society. Profit is a regulator of the life of a business, but it is not the only one; *other human and moral factors* must also be considered which, in the long term, are at least equally important for the life of a business.[54]

The message of the Bible regarding wealth and profit is linked to the concept of poverty and the poor.[55] In the Old Testament, wealth and riches are initially presented as God's blessing for a righteous life, whereas poverty, need, and misery are seen as a curse and a punishment for sin. It was the experience of the "scandal" of the rich and the well-off sinner, as well as that of the suffering of the innocent that provoked a change of perspective.[56] Additionally, it was the experience of collective humiliation and poverty during the Exile, as well as that of post-exilic Judaism and the incessant vexations suffered by the Jewish people that peaked during the wars of the Maccabees, which provoked an awareness that poverty could be a sign of loyalty to God's covenant. The Jews who remained faithful to God's commandments preferred poverty to wealth if the latter was achieved at the price of betraying the covenant. Israel was God's "poor people." Although it is a matter of debate whether or not there was a political movement or social group that identified itself with the "poor of God" ("*anawim Jahve*"),[57] the great value attached to poverty of spirit in intertestamental Judaism, such as was characteristic of the Qumran community, is significant.[58] However, it should be also be noted that poverty resulting from laziness was decried in the Bible, especially in the Wisdom literature.[59]

True to its characteristic inclination toward individual ethics, the New Testament deals with poverty and wealth mainly in terms of voluntary poverty, the renunciation of material means as a virtue in following Christ. The parables of the camel able to pass through the "eye of a needle,"[60] and of the hidden treasure and the precious pearl,[61] express the need for complete interior detachment and freedom of heart. At the same time, Jesus, in word and deed, cared for the poor and taught His disciples to address the needs of their neighbors. In His discourse on the Final Judgment, the works of mercy practiced on the poor and needy are presented as the law by which we shall be judged.[62]

However, our Lord's words should not be interpreted in a modern political sense, as if the poor of the Bible were the proletarians of Marxist doctrine. Even less can one justify violence and class struggle by means of Christian revelation. Jesus Himself dealt with rich people, accepting and praising their services.[63] Encountering Christ allowed the rich to discover their social responsibility and the joy of sharing.[64]

In the epistles of the New Testament, which reflect the reception of Jesus's teachings among the first generation of Christians, we discover two attitudes toward the rich: one is represented by 1 Timothy,[65] the other by James.[66] The difference between the two is striking. The harsh condemnation expressed in James finds no parallel in 1 Timothy, which understands wealth as an opportunity to do good. The two quotations seem to reflect two general moral attitudes, one of severity, austerity, and peremptoriness toward the rich; the other of social realism, conciliation, and motivation to good. In any case, it is significant that both lines remain in an unresolved tension bequeathed to Christian theology.

Turning to the Church Fathers, it is necessary to take into consideration the cultural context in which they taught. In Greek, the poor were divided into the *ptochoi* and the *penetes*. *Ptochos* was a person who lived in misery and was physically incapable of fending for himself, either because he was sick (e.g., a leper) or because he had no material resources whatsoever. A *penes* was someone who had to work in order to survive. He might possess health, tools, a house, even some slaves, but he had to work on a regular basis. This person was considered "poor" in antiquity. The "rich" in ancient parlance were the *eleutheroi*, the free men, representing a very small portion of society, whose material means were of such abundance that they had the leisure of not having to work (*negotium*), and could dedicate themselves to philosophy, politics, warfare, and related matters (*otium*).[67] The ancient concept of poverty, and thus also that of the Church Fathers, was linked to the concept of work, reserved for the poor and considered unworthy of the rich.[68] The Church Fathers had to overcome this attitude, especially in the budding monastic communities in which the sons and daughters of rich families desired to abstain from manual work in order to dedicate themselves solely to prayer, study, and teaching. Augustine is quite clear: all must work, in obedience to Paul's injunction that he who does not want to work shall not eat.[69]

In their writings, Basil, John Chrysostom, Ambrose, and others defend the poor (*penetes*) against exploitation.[70] They demand that the rich invest their money in productive activities instead of keeping their wealth locked away.[71] Stoic philosophy was helpful in this respect. Wealth was one of the preferable *adiaphora* (things that as such are not necessary to a moral life but are advantageous to it); its moral quality depended upon its virtuous use. It was not the possession of wealth that was evil, but its abuse—wealth could and should be used for a good cause. Clement of Alexandria summed this up in the question: if nobody had anything, who could help the poor?[72] The concern of the Fathers was not the formulation of an economic theory, but aid being provided to the poor (*ptochoi*) and the organization of charity in the churches.

This is the ethical heritage of Catholic social thought, in the light of which it sought to understand the role of profit in commercial society.[73] The search for profit as an aim in itself has been seen over the centuries as avarice, one of the capital vices. However, in economic life, the quest for material wealth is a prime motivation, a fact Catholic theology could not ignore. The general trend of medieval Scholasticism was therefore to justify a moderate profit, not as an end in itself, but insofar as it was needed for the merchant's sustenance and that of his family and for maintaining (but not improving) his social position, for the common good, and for almsgiving.[74] Modern Catholic social thought still more or less moves along the same lines. Of course, with the emergence of social mobility and particularly of the commercial society replacing the feudal system, the social implications of the faith had to unfold in a changed context, and the wish to improve one's social position was no longer seen as avarice. The concept which best expresses the contemporary position of Catholic social teaching is "integral development."[75] This is a combination of economic growth and the moral, spiritual, and cultural aspects of human life. Economic growth, material prosperity, and wealth are without doubt necessary conditions for living in dignity and freedom, but they are insufficient. Health care, education, faith, and family life are values without which happiness cannot be attained. In this sense, Pope Francis has demanded:

> nourishment or a "dignified sustenance" for all people, but also their "general temporal welfare and prosperity." This means education, access to health care, and above all employment, for it is through free, creative, participatory, and mutually supportive labor that human beings express and enhance the dignity of their lives. A just wage enables them to have adequate access to all the other goods which are destined for our common use.[76]

Together with all other Christian traditions, Catholic social thought has therefore throughout the centuries made present Christ's healing love among the sick, the hungry, and the miserable, not only alleviating the effects of immediate privations, but also struggling to overcome their causes. This is also the best way to secure internal and external peace. Paul VI put it this way with the iconic phrase: "Development, the new name for peace."[77] At the same time, Catholic social thought stresses interior detachment from all material wealth, also within the Church. One of the hallmarks of Pope Francis's goals for reform of the Church is his attack on any form of "spiritual worldliness."[78]

Markets, exchange, value, and just price

> It would appear that, on the level of individual nations and of international relations, the *free market* is the most efficient instrument for utilizing resources and effectively responding to needs. But this is true only for those needs which are "solvent", insofar as they are endowed with purchasing power, and for those resources which are "marketable", insofar as they are capable of obtaining a satisfactory price. But there are many human needs which find no place on the market. It is a strict duty of

justice and truth not to allow fundamental human needs to remain unsatisfied, and not to allow those burdened by such needs to perish.[79]

That the exchange of goods is a necessity of everyday life, as well as the core and essence of economic activity, is accepted without question in the Catholic tradition of social thought. Catholic social teaching does not attempt to explain the economy analytically in the scientific sense but strives to imbue it with ethical and spiritual values. However, in order to do so it must understand and accept the laws and logic of markets. The Catholic tradition of reflection on economic exchange emphasizes the *justice* of prices and wages. What makes a price or a wage just is not easy to establish; usually it simply means the competitive market price. However, as has already been stated, Catholic social teaching is based not on economic but rather on moral theory. The concept of a *just* price and a *just* wage conveys the idea that there exists a measure besides and beyond money. In medieval economic ethics, for instance, reference to the estimation of the market or to what we would call the market price was understood as a standard of justice (not merely as an economic outcome of negotiations), meant to protect the buyer from economic coercion: a special need or urgency of the buyer or the seller should not cause the price to rise above the usual market average.[80] The Catholic tradition over the centuries has also consistently and unanimously condemned market manipulations in the form of monopolies or oligopolies.[81]

Exchange regularly takes place in markets created by commercial dealings among merchants. The Church Fathers, although they wrote quite infrequently about the theme, had a positive or neutral attitude toward commerce and trade, presupposing its moral admissibility. The social concerns of the Church Fathers centered upon the protection of the poor from exploitation, and social aid to the sick, widows, and orphans, as well as foreigners. Consequently, they preached against irresponsible luxury and wealth, and against usury, understood as oppressive interest rates on loans to the poor. This attitude simply echoes the Bible itself.[82]

St. Augustine, the greatest authority of Latin Antiquity, defended commerce against wholesale condemnation; according to him, the vices observed in commercial dealings were to be blamed on the individual merchants, not on commerce as such.[83] It was in the feudal period that a negative view of commerce entered the Christian tradition. The feudal society was ordered according to a principle of "hierarchical representation": the knights fought for and defended all, the monks and nuns prayed and did penance for all, and the farmers worked for and fed all. The cultural value horizon created by such a social order had little space for merchants, who seemingly did nothing for others, and only put money in their pockets. Thus a commentary on Matthew from the sixth century says that just as Jesus expelled the merchants and money changers from the temple, the Church had to be liberated from businesspeople! This idea was reinforced when it was introduced in the *Decretum Gratiani*, an eleventh-century collection of Church laws.[84] Such a harsh judgment could not be maintained for long.[85] The general attitude in the Catholic tradition of social thought is that commerce and markets are necessary and useful social realities, and are thus seen in a positive light. The same is not true of capitalism—the European Catholic tradition (as opposed to the the Anglo-American tradition) tends to distinguish "markets" from "capitalism." In the European tradition, capitalism is generally regarded negatively as a system of exploitation.

When Pope John Paul II published his encyclical *Centesimus Annus* after the collapse of the Communist bloc, he was well aware of these different interpretations and traditions. His encyclical is a critical endorsement of the free market economy and of Western liberal and social constitutional democracies based on the rule of law. His distinctions and definitions are still worth repeating:

Can it perhaps be said that, after the failure of Communism, capitalism is the victorious social system, and that capitalism should be the goal of the countries now making efforts to rebuild their economy and society? ...
... If by "capitalism" is meant an economic system which recognizes the fundamental and positive role of business, the market, private property and the resulting responsibility for the means of production, as well as free human creativity in the economic sector, then the answer is certainly in the affirmative, even though it would perhaps be more appropriate to speak of a "business economy," "market economy" or simply "free economy." But if by "capitalism" is meant a system in which freedom in the economic sector is not circumscribed within a strong juridical framework which places it at the service of human freedom in its totality, and which sees it as a particular aspect of that freedom, the core of which is ethical and religious, then the reply is certainly negative.[86]

Eighteen years later Benedict XVI approached the topic of markets quite differently. The circumstances had changed. Not only had the Western world just been through its worst financial and economic crisis since 1929, but the intellectual context had become dominated by post-modernism. Post-modernism rejects all universal narratives of meaning: all meaning and sense in life is subjective and of one's own choice. As it were, each one of us sits on his or her own cloud, without connection to others because there is no sky in common. Post-modernism thus also implicitly rejects the notion of *essential* differences between people in the strong sense of the word, accepting only the notion of diversity as the result of individual choice. Personal identity, for example, has become fluid. People have no stable personal profile anymore; it can change continuously because no objective limits on self-definition are accepted, a fact which can be seen in the ever-growing number of genders.

Without *difference* in the strong sense of the word, true duality and thus relationship are not possible because they both presuppose objective difference. In such a cultural context, Benedict XVI proposed rethinking the Holy Trinity in its social dimension and rediscovering the human person as relationship. According to Benedict, personhood does not consist in mere individuality, as personality might, but in a communion of relationships that make possible what is typically human in us: love, comprehension, dignity, freedom, etc. Benedict XVI thus rethinks the markets as engendering relationship:

> In a climate of mutual trust, the *market* is the economic institution that permits encounter between persons, inasmuch as they are economic subjects who make use of contracts to regulate their relations as they exchange goods and services of equivalent value between them, in order to satisfy their needs and desires. The market is subject to the principles of so-called *commutative justice*, which regulates the relations of giving and receiving between parties to a transaction. But the social doctrine of the Church has unceasingly highlighted the importance of *distributive justice* and *social justice* for the market economy, not only because it belongs within a broader social and political context, but also because of the wider network of relations within which it operates. In fact, if the market is governed solely by the principle of the equivalence in value of exchanged goods, it cannot produce the social cohesion that it requires in order to function well. *Without internal forms of solidarity and mutual trust, the market cannot completely fulfill its proper economic function.*[87]

These considerations fit into the overall project of Benedict XVI of serving the political and economic society indirectly by helping to broaden the concept of reason: faith and reason, religion and society, need each other and "should not be afraid to enter into a profound and ongoing dialogue, for the good of our civilization."[88] For this reason too, Benedict XVI wrote that the social problem has become a radically anthropological one.[89] The human person has become an object of technical manipulation, economic exploitation, and political and military subjection, as has become apparent in the appalling mass migration that is taking place on the European doorstep. With science we know *what* man is, but we do not know *who* he is, or what he is here *for*. For Benedict XVI, love is central to answering the anthropological question. Only love is credible; the central element of the new evangelization of society is Christian love. The challenge of charity is the principal legacy that Benedict XVI left to Catholic social teaching on markets. It is formulated as a challenge, leaving the answers to the question of how to insert charity into normal business dealings to those operating in the field:

> The great challenge before us, accentuated by the problems of development in this global era and made even more urgent by the economic and financial crisis, is to demonstrate, in thinking and behavior, not only that traditional principles of social ethics like transparency, honesty and responsibility cannot be ignored or attenuated, but also that in *commercial relationships* the *principle of gratuitousness* and the logic of gift as an expression of fraternity can and must *find their place within normal economic activity*. This is a human demand at the present time, but it is also demanded by economic logic. It is a demand both of charity and of truth.[90]

Gift, gratuitousness, and fraternity are concepts that at first glance have little to do with business, but the fact that they are employed by Benedict provides us with a number of important insights[91] that also highlight the continuity between Benedict XVI and his charismatic successor Francis. We will return to them later on.

Pope Francis is pursuing a program of "radical evange-lism." For professors of hard-core economics, the Pope's eco-nomic statements sound too much like easily-stated claims of absolute truth, insufficiently technical to be taken seriously as a scientific contribution to defining and understanding the markets. I think the Pope would agree with this: he does not pretend to be, nor does he want to be an economist. However, there are economists who are open to social concerns and who want to go beyond a merely technical comprehension of their subject, and who therefore agree with the aims proposed by the Pope. These economists have joined forces with him in con-ducting research that focuses on topics such as the inclusion of the poor in the market economy, the importance of ethics in economics, the struggle against any form of corruption and cronyism, and related topics.

The Latin American pope has brought new vigor, life, and joy into Catholic social teaching. But the Anglo-American tradition can also make a valuable contribution to Catholic social thought: the positive experience of inclusive political and economic institutions that are just as necessary as indi-vidual virtues like charity and mercy, if not more so.

Finance and Financial Markets

> Finance . . .needs to go back to being an *instrument directed towards improved wealth creation and develop-ment.* Insofar as they are instruments, the entire economy and finance, not just certain sectors, must be used in an ethical way so as to create suitable conditions for human development and for the development of peoples. . . . Financiers must rediscover the genuinely ethical founda-tion of their activity, so as not to abuse the sophisticated instruments which can serve to betray the interests of savers. Right intention, transparency, and the search for positive results are mutually compatible and must never be detached from one another. . . . Both the regulation of

the financial sector, so as to safeguard weaker parties and discourage scandalous speculation, and experimentation with new forms of finance, designed to support development projects, are positive experiences that should be further explored and encouraged, highlighting *the responsibility of the investor.*[92]

Money existed in primitive societies in the form of seashells, cattle, pieces of metal, and finally coins and the forms of money we use today. Since its invention money has played a decisive role in exchange economies. Why is money so attractive? Be it in the form of metal coins or banknotes, of book money, non-cash money, or digital bitcoins, we can neither eat it nor immediately use it as a tool. It is a symbol, and yet, political power is at its command, nations are under its sway, armies march at its behest, and we all scramble after it. What is it that makes money so powerful, that overcoming its temptation is practically a miracle? St. Thomas Aquinas comments on the passage of Matthew in which Jesus asks Peter to catch a fish, take the coin he would find in its mouth, and pay the temple tax with it: Thomas says that whoever constantly talks of money and wealth has a coin in his mouth. Whoever converts such a person and removes his overweening desire for money has miraculously caught a fish and fulfilled Christ's command. He has freed the person from slavery to money.[93] Mary L. Hirschfeld has pointed out that "money mimics God as the object of human desire for the genuine infinite good [God], diverting that desire to the simulacrum of an indefinite accumulation of finite goods, or, even worse, of money itself."[94] The only true infinite good is God, who alone can fulfill our desire for infinite good. When a human being turns away from God, and thus also away from his or her true happiness, surrogates fill God's place. Among these money beckons with its appearance of unlimited possibilities. It contains a false promise that ignites in us the "greed for gain, which knows no limit and tends to infinity."[95] Money is therefore dangerous.

On the other hand, we need money. Any good project in this world—for instance a university—needs money. A colleague at my university once jokingly (but also half-seriously) described to me its (fictitious) coat of arms: a hippopotamus in a river with its mouth wide open, and a man standing on a bridge over it, pouring a sack of gold into its mouth! I will leave the interpretation of this image to the reader's imagination; however, one thing is clear: at some point, the hippopotamus has had enough. More would be greed; more would damage, not serve. Money is a two-faced Janus: it has a good side but also a very dangerous one.[96]

In his pastoral speeches, Pope Francis reflects this ambiguity. Speaking to representatives of Italian cooperatives the Holy Father said:

> It takes money to do all these things! Cooperatives in general are not established by large capitalists, but rather it is often said that they are structurally undercapitalized. Instead, the Pope tells you: you must invest, and you must invest well! In Italy of course, but not only, it is difficult to obtain public funds to compensate for a shortage of resources. This is the solution I propose to you: bring good means together with determination in order to accomplish good works. Collaborate more among cooperative banks and businesses; organize resources to enable families to live with dignity and serenity; pay fair wages to workers, investing above all in initiatives that are truly necessary.[97]

On the other hand, the Pope has warned against the idolatry of money time and again. With St. Francis, he has called it the "devil's dung," and cries: "Money must serve, not rule!"[98] Accountancy, which is an important service for any business, seems to cause an allergic reaction in Pope Francis,[99] and he is not alone in this difficulty.

Today, when we refer to finance we mean not simply money but financial capitalism as it has developed in the

Western world. The financial sector has grown enormously over recent decades due to globalization and the reduction of international barriers to exchange. In financial capitalism, financial assets acquire a prevailing importance to the point of determining the performance of the economy. This, as such, is not bad; rather, it is typical of advanced or developed economies.[100] Finance is an *indispensable* element of modern free market economies. In order to function well, the financial market must be liquid—meaning that the owner of a financial position can trade it with ease, if for example he or she wishes to diversify his or her portfolio to reduce risk. Liquidity is important because it reduces transaction costs and the costs of capital in general, thereby encouraging investment, generating more profits, raising wages, and creating wealth that can be used to address social and environmental needs.[101]

Across the political spectrum, thinkers agree that well-functioning, ethically sound financial markets, systems, and institutions are integral to economic growth and well-being.[102] Economic research provides empirical evidence that finance fosters growth, promotes entrepreneurship, supports education, alleviates poverty, and reduces inequality.[103] Developmental economists share the conviction that poverty is more often caused by an absence of financial institutions rather than their existence.[104]

So, why the aversion to finance in some quarters? Perhaps because, despite all its positive effects, recent decades have also brought out some sobering consequences of financial capitalism—the fragility of the financial system has unequivocally come to the fore in bank runs, moral hazards, boom-and-bust cycles, systemic distress, bank failures, and currency crises.[105] Within the last fifteen years there has been an excessive expansion of credit and excessive monetary expansion in general. There has also been a terrifying amount of unethical conduct in the financial sector: "not a day passes without news of a fresh financial scandal."[106]

Furthermore, the findings of Piketty on the re-emergence of a class of rentiers—that is, of people who live off the rent of capital—is hardly surprising.[107] Academics who clearly support capitalism have affirmed that:

> The link between the size of the financial sector and economic growth weakens—or even reverses—once countries become rich and reach the technological frontier. Now rent seeking in financial markets can lead to great private gains but have little impact on economic growth. Growth is actually harmed to the extent that talented risk takers are drawn into the financial sector to engage in rent transfers, rather than starting businesses and engaging in rent creation.[108]

These authors acknowledge that "there is no theoretical reason or empirical evidence to support the notion that all the growth of the financial sector in the last forty years has been beneficial to society," because a major component of this growth has consisted of "pure rent seeking," that is, activities that have only profited individuals without any attendant work or service to others.[109]

The dark side of finance alone, however, does not suffice to answer the question as to why something so clearly useful is viewed by some in such a dubious ethical light. Many other industries, like the pharmaceutical or the chemical industries, not to mention politics, have endured terrible scandals without anyone doubting the justification for their existence. Why is the case of finance different? Although people might not like Bill Gates, they can immediately appreciate the advantages of the PC. They do not, however, immediately feel the same way about the benefits of a liquid financial market, especially when it is working well. And when things go awry, the public usually blames the bankers. The reputation of finance is very low because it is seen as serving private interests and not the public good. This creates "envy and public resentment…There is a natural public dislike towards finance."[110] This is dangerous because "without public support, the best form of finance – the competitive, democratic, and inclusive finance – cannot operate."[111]

There is also diffused skepticism about finance in the Christian tradition, especially the Catholic tradition. St. Josemaría, for instance, had to overcome great difficulties in convincing the Holy See that lay Christians who earnestly strive for holiness can work in business and finance.[112] This should not surprise us: St. Josemaría was up against molds of spirituality that viewed the holiness of religious as the only model. Thomas Aquinas, for example, taught that clerics and religious should refrain from commerce because they should not only avoid what *is* evil but also what *seems* to be evil, as was—according to him—the case for business because of the vices frequently connected with it.[113] However, this attitude does not have its source in Scripture or the Church Fathers, who, as noted above, had either a positive or neutral attitude toward commerce. The Church Fathers for instance expressed the history of salvation in the monetized language of the ancient commercial society in which they lived—"redemption," the "economy of salvation," and other expressions and parables are taken from financial and business language. The deepest reason for the Church's wary stance toward commerce and finance in the past was her concern about avarice or greed, defined as "immoderate love of possession."[114]After Gregory the Great systematized the capital vices,[115] there was an ongoing debate among the Scholastic teachers concerning whether pride or avarice was the worst sin of all. The Bible offered support for both positions.[116] In any case, in Scholastic eyes merchants and especially financiers were in constant danger of avarice because they worked for profit. They wanted to increase their wealth. The profit motive as such was condemned as avarice.

Nonetheless, there is no condemnation of money either in the medieval Dominican or Franciscan Schools. Following Aristotle, these Schools saw money as a measure of value, a means of exchange, and a store of wealth.[117] Nor was there any condemnation of money and finance as such in the School of Salamanca, which incorporated the positive elements of Renaissance humanism into the Catholic tradition.[118]

This latter point is important for the topic at hand because a semantic shift regarding avarice had taken place in the civic humanism of the Renaissance, particularly in Florence. The new upward mobility in society had justified the profit motive and the desire for greater wealth. The boundaries of permissible growth had been expanded, and the answer to the question when enough was enough had become gray.[119] In this new cultural horizon, finance could be seen in a slightly more positive light, albeit still fraught with moral peril. Domingo de Soto (1494–1560), the author of the first textbook of moral theology as an independent discipline, explained that the reason for his literary endeavors was the complexities of finance and the need to guide the Christian conscience in the field of contemporary business.[120] Because of this, finance is at the origin of modern moral theology.

There is, however, one significant, decisive difference between the Scholastic view and some modern views of money. In the medieval tradition, money is placed at the service of the so-called "economic cycle": goods are exchanged for other goods with the help of money as a means of exchange and as a measure of value between disparate commodities. The economic cycle thus is Goods (G)—Money (M)—Goods (G). Goods are the aim and measuring stick of money. Money is measured and limited by goods. There is no need for more money than the value of the goods that are available for purchase.

This explains why just price and just wage were and are so central to the Catholic tradition. I am aware of the great difficulties attached to these notions and of the debates on the various definitions of value. However, as has already been stated, the notion of justice in business fundamentally expresses the idea that there is a measure of value beyond money: goods should be truly good and services truly serve.

Thus, the Scholastics, following Aristotle, opposed the so-called "chrematistic cycle" in which money in itself is the aim. In this cycle, money is exchanged for goods in order to acquire more money, which is a reversal of the scheme described above: M—G—M. For the Scholastics, there is no objective end to this cycle. In the economic cycle, goods are measured by needs or at least wants, and there is an objective limit to what a person can physically consume or possess. In the chrematistic cycle, in contrast, money is pure potentiality and is infinitely expandable.

The rejection of the chrematistic cycle is one of the reasons for the canonical and theological condemnation of usury. For nearly a thousand years of Church history, any form of interest on loans was condemned as intrinsically evil.[121] A thorough discussion of the historical development of, and the debates surrounding, this prohibition is beyond the scope of the present chapter. However, this much must be said: when Thomas Aquinas and the other Scholastic teachers came to reflect on the matter, the condemnation of usury was already a centuries-old tradition in the Church, as confirmed by the pronouncements of popes and councils.[122] It thus had become a question of faith, which medieval theologians supported rationally from a natural law perspective. In his book *De Malo*, Aquinas, for instance, lists twenty-one arguments against the charging of interest.

For practical commercial and financial reasons, for example, the creditor's evident opportunity costs of holding onto liquid funds and the default risk of the debtor, the Catholic tradition developed a distinction between mere money and capital.[123] When a merchant invested money it acquired a seminal character: it became an instrument, grew, and bore fruit. When the merchant extended a loan from his capital, he was thus entitled to interest (not usury). This typically "Catholic" form of finance was employed until the end of the eighteenth century, and as late as 1745, Pope Benedict XIV re-affirmed it in his encyclical *Vix pervenit*.[124]

I am not arguing for a return to such a regime, but for the wisdom of the insight into the difference between money and capital. Benedict XVI called for a renewal of the entire financial system in the hope that it could once again be "an instrument directed towards improved wealth creation and development."[125] This requires a sober intention of putting financial capital at the service of productive activity. Francis has similarly complained that the "lessons of the global financial crisis have not been assimilated," and that "finance overwhelms the real economy."[126] Both recent pontiffs are in line with the medieval skepticism of increasing wealth through purely monetary operations, and both agree about the evils of consumerism.

In view of the potential moral dangers of finance described here, a Christian might feel inclined to avoid getting involved in it. However, this attitude would miss an important point: following the logic of Christ's Incarnation, Christians must not withdraw from the world, but rather should engage with its temporal structures, sanctifying them from within through the light of truth and the warmth of love.[127] Christ has redeemed the whole of reality, including finance, and continues to do so through the efforts of Christians. Christians today should therefore be leaders of social innovation joined to moral improvement. This implies avoiding investments in unethical activities (for instance, abortion, contraception, illicit drugs, and child labor, but also socially unjust or ecologically damaging production), and requires the moral strength to reflect on the avoidance of foolish private and public debt. In many cases, the correct moral decision will not be clear. The color of the markets is often not black and white but gray: frequently investors will have to apply the principle of double effect or the moral rules governing material cooperation in evil. Christian behavior should also put the central Christian commandment into effect: love of God and neighbor. Along this line, Benedict XVI posed the challenge of introducing love into social macro-relationships, thus expanding its limits beyond the sphere of family or friends.[128] One way of doing this, for example, is charitable investment decisions (not donations but impact investments). Christians have a lot to contribute by advocating for the anthropological dimension of money as a medium of virtuous relationships. The cardinal virtues—practical wisdom, justice, temperance, and courage—are all extremely necessary in order to correctly assess whether particular financial products are means to good ends, to rein in greed, and to control our "animal spirits" and "irrational exuberance." The possibility of leading a virtuous life can encourage Christians who are active in finance to evangelize in their walk of life. Evangelization, so dear to Pope Francis, is a program of cultural transformation that starts with the affirmation of the goodness of what exists. It then proceeds to cleanse it of its sinful elements.[129] This second step, the cleansing process, unfolds in three actions: the proclamation of values (or practical truths), offering exemplary practices (virtues, best practices), and the creation of institutions.[130]

As I will try to show in the following pages, Pope Francis has sent strong moral messages to business and finance following Catholic social thought but with his own particular style and accent. The Pope's messages, I think, can give important positive stimuli to a Christian business leader's vocation, but they have not always been perceived as positive by quite a number of people in the United States. On the basis of traditional Catholic social thought, I will now specifically analyze Pope Francis's message on business.

Notes to Chapter One

1.　John Paul II, Apostolic Exhortation *Christifideles Laici* (December 30, 1988), 59, quoting himself from multiple prior occasions.

2.　On the following pages I also call the Catholic social tradition the "tradition of Catholic social thought" or the "Catholic tradition of social thought." See Johan Verstraeten, "Re-thinking Catholic Social Thought as Tradition," in *Catholic Social Thought: Twilight or Renaissance?*, ed. Jonathan Boswell,

Francis P. McHugh, and Johan Verstraeten (Leuven: Leuven University Press, 2000), 59–77.

3.   See Mt 22:21 and parallels in Mark and Luke.

4.   Benedict XVI, *Address in the Reichstag Building on His Visit to the Bundestag*, September 22, 2011. To this quotation one might add that there have been peripheral Christian groups that have tried to implement a revealed social order in a fundamentalist way.

5.   See Hugo Rahner, *Church and State in Early Christianity* (San Francisco: Ignatius Press, 1992); Martin Rhonheimer, *Christentum und säkularer Staat* [Christianity and the secular state] (Freiburg: Herder, 2012).

6.   Luther taught that God ruled the whole universe in the form of two kingdoms: the secular kingdom He ruled through law and coercion; the heavenly one through Gospel and grace. See Robert Kolb, "Two-Kingdoms Doctrine," in *The Encyclopedia of Christianity*, vol. 5, ed. Erwin Fahlbusch et al. (Grand Rapids: Eerdmans–Brill, 2008), 569–75; Reiner Anselm, "Zweireichelehre I," in *Theologische Realenzyklopädie*, vol. 36, ed. Gerhard Müller (Berlin: De Gruyter, 2004), 776–84; Wilfried Härle, "Zweireichelehre II," in ibid., 784–89; Max Josef Suda, *Die Ethik Martin Luthers* [The Ethics of Martin Luther]. (Göttingen: Vandenhoeck & Rupprecht, 2006), 117–37; Harold J. Berman, *Law and Revolution II: The Impact of the Protestant Reformations on the Western Legal Tradition* (Cambridge, MA: Harvard University Press, 2003), especially 40–42, 177.

7.   See especially Thomas Hobbes, *Leviathan*, ed. J. C. A. Gaskin (Oxford: Oxford University Press, 2009), 3.42.

8.   Francisco De Vitoria developed his theory of *potestas indirecta* in connection with the Spanish conquest of America, of which he is deeply critical, in "Relectio De potestate Ecclesiae prior," in *Obras de Francisco de Vitoria: Relecciones teológicas*, ed. Teofilo Urdanoz (Madrid: BAC, 1960), 242–327. For more information see Luciano Pereña, "La Escuela de Salamanca y la duda indiana," in *Francisco de Vitoria y la Escuela de Salamanca: La ética en la conquista de América*, ed. Demetrio Ramos (Madrid: CSIC, 1984), 291–344.

9.   See Robert Bellarmine, "Controversiarum De Summo Pontifice Liber Quintus (De potestate Pontificis temporali)," in *Roberti Bellarmini Opera Omnia*, vol. 2, ed. Justinus Fèvre (Paris: Vivès, 1870); a partial English edition of various writings can be found in Robert Bellarmine, *On Temporal and Spiritual Authority*, ed. Stefania Tutino (Indianapolis: Liberty Fund, 2012).

10. Benedict XVI, *Address in the Reichstag Building*.

11. Cf. Bellarmine, "Controversiarum," 5.6.

12. Austen Ivereigh, *The Great Reformer: Francis and the Making of a Radical Pope* (New York: Holt, 2014), 27.

13. See José Casanova, *Public Religions in the Modern World* (Chicago: The University of Chicago Press, 1994), 62–63.

14. See Vatican Council II, Pastoral Constitution *Gaudium et Spes*, December 7, 1965, 36.

15. Modernity has been characterized as a process of "secularization" by Ernst-Wolfgang Böckenförde, "Die Entstehung des Staates als Vorgang der Säkularisation," in *Recht, Staat, Freiheit: Studien zur Rechtsphilosophie, Staatstheorie und Verfassungsgeschichte* (Frankfurt: Suhrkamp, 2006), 92–114. See also Ernst-Wolfgang Böckenförde, *Der säkularisierte Staat: Sein Charakter, seine Rechtfertigung und seine Probleme im 21. Jahrhundert* (München: Carl Friedrich von Siemens Stiftung, 2007), 75; Josef Isensee, "Die katholische Kritik an den Menschenrechten: Der liberale Freiheitsentwurf in der Sicht der Päpste des 19. Jahrhunderts," in *Menschenrechte und Menschenwürde*, ed. Ernst-Wolfgang Böckenförde and Robert Spaemann, (Stuttgart: Klett-Cotta, 1987), 138.

16. Benedict XVI, Encyclical Letter *Deus Caritas Est* (December 25, 2005), 28a; see also Benedict XVI, *Address in Westminster Hall*, September 17, 2010.

17. Pope Paul VI summarized the spirit of the Council with these two concepts in his *Address During the Last General Meeting of the Second Vatican Council*, December 7, 1965.

18. John Paul II, Encyclical Letter *Evangelium Vitae* (March 25, 1995), 20. See also Russell Hittinger, "Introduction to Modern Catholicism," in *The Teachings of Modern Roman Catholicism on Law, Politics, and Human Nature*, ed. John Witte Jr. and Frank S. Alexander (New York: Columbia University Press, 2007), 1–38, 32.

19. Pontifical Council for Justice and Peace, *Compendium of the Social Doctrine of the Church* (Vatican City: Libreria Editrice Vaticana, 2005), 204–5. Henceforth CSDC.

20. Benedict XVI, Encyclical Letter *Caritas in Veritate* (June 29, 2009), 2.

21. See Rom 14:17. Unless otherwise noted, this and all other Scripture quotations are taken from the New American Bible, Revised Edition (NABRE).

22. See John Ziesler, "Righteousness," in *The Oxford Companion to the Bible*, ed. Bruce M. Metzger and Michael D. Coogan (Oxford: Oxford University Press, 1993), 655–56; Pinchas Lapide, *Il discorso della montagna. Utopia o programma?* (Brescia: Paideia, 2003), 31–33.

23. See Arturo Bellocq Montano, "What is Catholic Social Teaching in the Mission of the Church?" in *Handbook of Catholic Social Teaching: A Guide for Christians in the World Today*, ed. Martin Schlag (Washington, D. C.: The Catholic University of America Press, 2017), nn. 19–46.

24. See my chapter "Catholic Social Teaching on the Economy: Pope Benedict XVI's Legacy," in *Free Markets with Solidarity and Sustainability: Facing the Challenge*, ed. Martin Schlag and Juan Andrés Mercado, 178–96 (Washington, D. C.: The Catholic University of America Press, 2016).

25. For this useful distinction, see Lothar Roos, "Tugendethik und Ordnungsethik: Papst Franziskus und die Soziallehre der Kirche," *Die Neue Ordnung* 70, no. 6 (2016): 424–34.

26. For all these quotations, see Leo XIII, Encyclical Letter *Rerum Novarum* (May 15, 1891), 1–3.

27. See ibid., 4.
28. See Francis, *Address at the Conferral of the Charlemagne Prize*, May 6, 2016.
29. Ibid.
30. Ibid.
31. I analyze some institutions, including private property, markets, finance, etc., and some issues surrounding the ethics of these institutions, in the following sections. My goal is to point out at the beginning of my considerations the strengths but also the gaps in Francis's teaching to date.
32. Here the CSDC references John Paul II, Encyclical Letter *Centesimus Annus* (May 1, 1991), 6.
33. Here the CSDC quotes Leo XIII, *Rerum Novarum*, 8.
34. CSDC, 176–77 . Here the CSDC quotes John Paul II, Encyclical Letter *Laborem Exercens* (September 14, 1981), 14.
35. See Jos 13:1–7, 18–19.
36. See Mt 16:24–26; 19:16–30; Lk 12:33; Mk 10:17–21; Mt 6:24; Mt 6:19; Mk 10:23; Acts 4:32–35; Col 3:5; 1 Cor 6:10.
37. Cf. 1 Cor 7:30.
38. See Lk 16:9. Matthew S. Kempshall, in *The Common Good in Late Medieval Political Thought* (Oxford: Clarendon Press, 1999), 21–23, points to the convergence between Stoic and Augustinian thought. However, it should not be forgotten that Augustine was, of course, primarily inspired by the Bible.
39. Cf. Augustine, "Sermon 50," in *Sermons II (20–50) on the Old Testament*, trans. Edmund Hill, vol. 3.2, *The Works of Saint Augustine: A Translation for the 21st Century*, ed. John E. Rotelle (Brooklyn, N.Y.: New City Press, 1990), 345–46, n. 4.
40. Cf. Augustine, "Tractate 6," in *St. Augustine: Tractates on the Gospel of John 1–10*, trans. John W. Rettig, *The Fathers of the Church* 78 (Washington, D. C.: The Catholic University of America Press, 1988), 152, n. 25.2.
41. The *Decretum Gratiani* incorporated the reduced Augustinian teaching, stating that private property did not belong to natural but to civil law. See *Decretum Gratiani*, vol. 1, *Corpus iuris canonici*, ed. Emil Ludwig Richter and Emil Friedberg (Graz: Akademische Druckund Verlagsanstalt, 1955), Parts I, D.; VIII.
42. This idea is expressed by the concept of "the universal destination of goods," cf. CSDC, 171–84.
43. This notion expresses the contrast between communism, in which all property belongs to the State or the Communist Party, and thus to someone, and the patristic idea that things do not belong to anyone, and thus to all. Cf. Arthur Fridolin Utz, *Kommentar zu Thomas von Aquin, Summa Theologiae II-II, qq 57–79, Recht und Gerechtigkeit, Band 18 der deutsch-lateinischen Ausgabe der Summa Theologiae, übersetzt von den Dominikanern und Benediktinern Deutschlands und Österreichs* (Heidelberg: Gemeinschaftsverlag F. H. Kerle, 1953), 508. Cf. also Thomas Aquinas, *Summa Theologiae*, ed. Thomas Gilby, O. P., 61 vols. (Cambridge:

Blackfriars, 1964–80) II-II, q. 66, a. 1, where he distinguishes power over the nature of things, which belongs to God alone, and power over the use of things, which belongs to man.

44. Pope Francis quoted this phrase in his Apostolic Exhortation *Evangelii Gaudium* (November 24, 2013), 57. It is taken from John Chrysostom, "De Lazaro," in *Patrologiae cursus completus: Series graeca*, vol. 48, ed. J. P. Migne (Paris: Imprimerie Catholique, 1862), II, 6, p. 992.

45. Thus Thomas rendered two of Aristotle's arguments, adding one of his own on order: *Summa Theologiae*, II-II, q. 66, a. 2; Thomas Aquinas, *In Libros Politicorum Aristotelis Expositio*, ed. Raimondo Spiazzi (Roma: Marietti, 1966), Book 4, lectio 4; cf. also Odd Langholm, *Economics in the Medieval Schools: Wealth, Exchange, Value, Money & Usury According to the Paris Theological Tradition, 1200–1350* (Leiden: E. J. Brill, 1992), 210–16.

46. Cf. *Summa Theologiae*, II-II, q. 57, a. 3c and I-II, q. 94, a. 5 ad 3.

47. Cf. John Duns Scotus, *Ordinatio IV*, in *Opera Omnia*, vol. 13, ed. Commissio Scotistica (Civitas Vaticana: Typis Vaticanis, 2011), d. 15, q. 2, a. 1, n. 1, p. 79.

48. Cf. Scotus, ibid., d. 15, q. 2, a. 1, n. 2, p. 79. Scotus had already brought forth the same argument in *Ordinatio III*, d. 37, q. unica, in ibid., vol. 19.

49. Cf. Scotus, *Ordinatio IV*, d. 15, q. 2, a. 1, n. 1, p. 79.

50. See Alejandro A. Chafuen, *Faith and Liberty: The Economic Thought of the Late Scholastics* (Lanham: Lexington Books, 2003), 31–50.

51. Cf. John Locke, "The Second Treatise of Government," in *Two Treatises of Government and A Letter Concerning Toleration*, ed. Ian Shapiro (New Haven: Yale University Press, 2003), especially chapters V and VII, 111–21, 133–41. In the context of Locke's labor theory of property, the so-called "Lockean Proviso" is a certain corrective. Locke presupposed that the original acquisition of property through the mingling of work with natural resources occurred in circumstances in which there was an abundance of land, water, and other resources. Thus the acquisition of property by one person left ample possibility that property could also be acquired by others. See ibid., chapter V, paragraph 33.

52. Leo XIII speaks of private property in several passages of the encyclical, see 4, 8, 15, 22, 38 and 47. This last paragraph is especially clear: "The right to possess private property is derived from nature, not from man; and the State has the right to control its use in the interests of the public good alone, but by no means to absorb it altogether."

53. See Francis, *Evangelii Gaudium*, 189: "Solidarity is a spontaneous reaction by those who recognize that the social function of property and the universal destination of goods are realities which come before private property. The private ownership of goods is justified by the need to protect and increase them, so that they can better serve the common good."

54. John Paul II, *Centesimus Annus*, 35.

55. See Hans Kvalbein, "Poor/poverty," in *New Dictionary of Biblical Theology*, ed. T. Desmond Alexander and Brian S. Rosner (Leicester: Inter-Varsity

Press, 2003), 687–91; S. A. Panimolle, ed., *Ricchezza – Povertà nella Bibbia* [Wealth – Poverty in the Bible], vol. 59, *Dizionario di spiritualità biblico-patristica* (Roma: Borla, 2011); J. David Pleins, "Poor, Poverty (OT)," in *The Anchor Bible Dictionary*, vol. 5, ed. David Noel Freedman (New York: Doubleday, 1992), 402–14; Thomas D. Hanks, "Poor, Poverty (NT)," in ibid., 414–24.

56. See the book of Job; Ps 37, 51, 72, etc.

57. Pleins, "Poor, Poverty (OT)," 411–13; Kvalbein, "Poor/poverty," 688.

58. Cf. Frédéric Manns, "Ricchezza e povertà nel giudaismo intertestamentario," in Panimolle, ed., *Ricchezza – Povertà nella Bibbia*, 73–97.

59. Cf. Prv 6:11; 14:23; 21:5; 24:34.

60. Mt 19:24; Mk 10:25; Lk 18:25.

61. Mt 13:44–46.

62. Cf. Mt 25:31–45.

63. Some examples are: the calling of the rich man Levi in Matthew (Mt 9:9–13); dining with the rich Pharisee (Lk 7:36–50); as a guest of Lazarus, His anointment with precious balm (Jn 12:1–8).

64. Zacchaeus is full of joy (Lk 19:1–10); in contrast, the rich man who is not detached from his wealth goes away very sad (Mt 19:16–22).

65. "Tell the rich in the present age not to be proud and not to rely on so uncertain a thing as wealth but rather on God, who richly provides us with all things for our enjoyment. Tell them to do good, to be rich in good works, to be generous, ready to share, thus accumulating as treasure a good foundation for the future, so as to win the life that is true life." (1 Tim 6:17–19).

66. "Come now, you rich, weep and wail over your impending miseries. Your wealth has rotted away, your clothes have become moth-eaten, your gold and silver have corroded, and that corrosion will be a testimony against you; it will devour your flesh like a fire. You have stored up treasure for the last days. Behold, the wages you withheld from the workers who harvested your fields are crying aloud, and the cries of the harvesters have reached the ears of the Lord of hosts. You have lived on earth in luxury and pleasure; you have fattened your hearts for the day of slaughter. You have condemned; you have murdered the righteous one; he offers you no resistance." (Jas 5:1–6).

67. Cf. Kvalbein, "Poor/poverty," 687; Fernando Rivas Rebaque, *Defensor pauperum: Los pobres en Basilio de Cesarea: homilías VI, VII, VIII y XIVB* [Defender of the poor: The poor in Basil of Cesarea. Homilies VI, VII, VIII, and XIVB] (Madrid: BAC, 2005).

68. Cf. Paul Veyne, *A History of Private Life: From Pagan Rome to Byzantium*, vol. 1 (Cambridge, Mass.: Harvard University Press, 1987). Reprint 2012 as *The Roman Empire*.

69. See Augustine, "Of the Works of Monks," trans. H. Browne. In *Nicene and Post-Nicene Fathers, First Series*, vol. 3, ed. Philip Schaff. Buffalo, N.Y.: Christian Literature Publishing Co., 1887. New Advent website, ed. Kevin

Knight, *http://www.newadvent.org/fathers/1314.htm*.

70. See the analysis and a selection of texts in Maria Grazia Mara, ed., *Ricchezza e povertà nel cristianesimo primitivo* [Wealth and poverty in early Christianity] (Roma: Città Nuova, 1991).

71. See for instance Basil, "Homily VI (on avarice)," in Mara, *Ricchezza*, n.5, 169.

72. The first Church Father to deal with the question of wealth in a positive sense was Clement of Alexandria. Clement of Alexandria, *Who is the Rich Man That is Being Saved?*, ed. Percy Mordaunt Barnard, in *Early Christian Classics* 66 (London: Society for Promoting Christian Knowledge, 1901).

73. For a good overview of what the concept of commercial society means in the Anglo-Saxon context, see Christopher J. Berry, *The Idea of Commercial Society in the Scottish Enlightenment* (Edinburgh: Edinburgh University Press, 2013).

74. E.g. Thomas Aquinas, *Summa Theologiae*, II-II, q. 77, a. 4c. For more detail see Langholm, *Economics in the Medieval Schools*, 221–36, 331–37; Joel Kaye, *Economy and Nature in the Fourteenth Century: Money, Market Exchange, and the Emergence of Scientific Thought* (Cambridge: Cambridge University Press, 1998), 132.

75. Pope Benedict XVI's only social encyclical *Caritas in Veritate* is subtitled "On Integral Human Development in Charity and Truth." Even though it was published in 2009, it was meant to commemorate the fortieth anniversary of Pope Paul VI's 1967 encyclical on development, *Populorum Progressio*.

76. Francis, *Evangelii Gaudium*, 192.

77. This is a heading of one of the sections in Paul VI's encyclical *Populorum Progressio*.

78. See Francis, *Evangelii Gaudium*, 93–97.

79. John Paul II, *Centesimus Annus*, 34.

80. Odd Langholm, *The Merchant in the Confessional: Trade and Price in the Pre-Reformation Penitential Handbooks* (Boston: Brill, 2003), 244–55.

81. Cf. Diana Wood, *Medieval Economic Thought* (Cambridge: Cambridge University Press, 2002), 138–43; Langholm, *Economics in the Medieval Schools*, 408; Giacomo Todeschini, *Franciscan Wealth: From Voluntary Poverty to Market Society*, trans. Donatella Melucci (St. Bonaventure: Franciscan Institute Publications, 2009).

82. See for example Sir 26:20–27:2: "A merchant can hardly remain upright, nor a shopkeeper free from sin; For the sake of profit many sin, and the struggle for wealth blinds the eyes. Like a peg driven between fitted stones, between buying and selling sin is wedged in."

83. See Augustine, "Ennarationes in Psalmos," in *Corpus Christianorum, Series Latina*, vol. 39, (Turnholt: Brepols, 1956), Ps. 70, 17, p. 954; quoted, for example, by Thomas Aquinas in *Summa Theologiae*, II-II, q. 77, a. 4 *sed contra*.

84. For a description of this position, see Wood, *Medieval Economic Thought*,

110–20; Martin Schlag, "The Encyclical *Caritas in Veritate*, Christian Tradition and the Modern World," in *Free Markets and the Culture of Common Good*, ed. Martin Schlag and Juan Andrés Mercado (Heidelberg: Springer, 2012), 93–109.

85. Already in the twelfth century there were dissenting opinions to this condemnation, see Hugh of St. Victor, *Didascalicon: I doni della promessa divina. L'essenza dell'amore. Discorso in lode del divino amore* (Milano: Rusconi, 1987), book II, ch. 23, 111, where he exalts trade as productive of peace. This is probably due to Hugh's profound learning in ancient philosophy and in the liberal arts. He actually counts commerce as one of the seven technical sciences (book II, ch. 20), which he aligns with the seven liberal arts. Commerce is paired with rhetoric because, says Hugh, one needs eloquence in trade (book II, ch. 23).

86. John Paul II, *Centesimus Annus*, 42.

87. Benedict XVI, *Caritas in Veritate*, 35.

88. Benedict XVI, *Address in Westminster Hall*.

89. Cf. Benedict XVI, *Caritas in Veritate*, 75.

90. Ibid., 36.

91. For further reading turn to my chapter "Catholic Social Teaching on the Economy: Pope Benedict XVI's Legacy," in *Free Markets with Solidarity and Sustainability*.

92. Benedict XVI, *Caritas in Veritate*, 65.

93. See Thomas Aquinas, *Super Evangelium S. Matthaei Lectura*, ed. Raphael Cai (Turin: Marietti, 1951), comment on Mt 17:24–27, n. 1483, p. 226.

94. Mary L. Hirschfeld, "Reflection on the Financial Crisis: Aquinas on the Proper Role of Finance," *Journal of the Society of Christian Ethics* 35, no. 1 (2015): 63–82, 64.

95. Thomas Aquinas, *Summa Theologiae* II-II, q. 77, a 4c.

96. This was already expressed in a striking way by the Sephardic Jew Joseph de la Vega, who in 1688, only about seventy-five years after the birth of the first stock exchange in Amsterdam, characterized finance in the following words: "This enigmatic business is at once the fairest and most deceitful in Europe, the noblest and the most infamous in the world, the finest and the most vulgar on earth.... One can become rich without risk." Joseph de la Vega, *Confusion de Confusiones: Portions Descriptive of the Amsterdam Stock Exchange*, trans. Hermann Kellenbenz (Eastford, Conn.: Martino Fine Books, 2013), 3.

97. Francis, *Address to Representatives of the Confederation of Italian Cooperatives*, February 28, 2015.

98. Francis, *Evangelii Gaudium*, 58.

99. Francis, *In-Flight Press Conference of His Holiness Pope Francis from Paraguay to Rome*, July 13, 2015.

100. Instead of deploring this fact or rejecting financial capitalism, the Nobel Prize winner in economics Robert J. Shiller studies how finance could

become "democratic." By this he means a transparent system that benefits society as a whole on the basis of widespread information. See Robert J. Shiller, *Finance and the Good Society* (Princeton: Princeton University Press, 2013), 1–15.

101. Cf. Yakov Amihud, Haim Mendelson, and Lasse Heje Pedersen, *Market Liquidity: Asset Pricing, Risk, and Crises* (Cambridge: Cambridge University Press, 2012).

102. See for instance Joseph Stiglitz, "Financial Innovation: Against the Motion that Financial Innovation Boosts Economic Growth," *The Economist*, February 23–March 3, 2010: "Over the long sweep of history, financial innovation has been important in promoting growth"; and Thorsten Beck, "The Role of Finance in Economic Development: Benefits, Risks, and Politics," in *The Oxford Handbook of Capitalism*, ed. Dennis C. Mueller (Oxford: Oxford University Press, 2012), 161–203, 174: "There is strong historical, theoretical, and empirical evidence for a positive role of financial deepening in the economic development process."

103. See Luigi Zingales, "Does Finance Benefit Society?" (Working Paper, The National Bureau of Economic Research, 2015), http://www.nber.org/papers/w20894, 2.

104. I particularly refer to Abhijit V. Banerjee and Esther Duflo, *Poor Economics: A Radical Rethinking of the Way to Fight Global Poverty* (New York: Public Affairs, 2011), especially 157–81. Their empirical studies show, among other things, that development is enhanced by microcredit (they also show the limitations of microcredit). The authors concur with many others that finding ways to finance medium-sized enterprises is "the next big challenge for finance in developing countries," ibid., 181. See also Niall Ferguson, *The Ascent of Money: A Financial History of the World* (New York: Penguin Press, 2008), 13.

105. See Beck, "The Role of Finance," 174–82.

106. Zingales, "Does Finance Benefit Society?", 2. In table 1 of this Working Paper, Zingales reports that in 2013 and 2014, financial institutions have been forced to pay $139 billion in fines. Something must have seriously gone wrong!

107. Three out of the four parts of Thomas Piketty's book *Capital in the Twenty-First Century* (Cambridge, Mass.: Harvard University Press, 2014) analyze this development. I do not wish to imply an endorsement of Piketty's proposals for certain fiscal policies.

108. Dennis C. Mueller, Introduction, "The Good, the Bad, and the Ugly," in *The Oxford Handbook of Capitalism*, ed. Dennis C. Mueller (Oxford: Oxford University Press, 2012), 7.

109. See Zingales, "Does Finance Benefit Society?," 3.

110. Ibid., 5.

111. Ibid., 6.

112. See Amadeo de Fuenmayor, Valentín Gómez-Iglesias, and José Luis Illanes,

The Canonical Path of Opus Dei: The History and Defense of a Charism, trans. William H. Stetson (Princeton, N. J.: Scepter Publishers, 1994), 212–13, especially footnote 92.

113. Cf. Thomas Aquinas, *Summa Theologiae*, II-II, q. 77, a. 4 ad 3; also q. 187, a. 2. In his rule for monastic life, Benedict allows the monks to sell goods for their own livelihood but at a price below the market average in order to give all glory to God. Cf. Benedict, *The Rule of Saint Benedict*, trans. Leonard Doyle (Collegeville, Minn.: The Liturgical Press, 2001), n. 57, 124–25.

114. Thomas Aquinas, *Summa Theologiae*, II-II, q. 118, a. 1 c.

115. Gregory the Great, *Moralia in Iob Libri XXIII-XXXV*, in *Corpus Christianorum*, vol. 143 B, ed. Marci Adriaen (Turnhout: Brepols, 1985), XXXI, xlv, 15–18.

116. Eccl 10:15: *initium omnis peccati est superbia* (the beginning of every sin is pride); 1 Tim 6:10: *radix enim omnium malorum est cupiditas* (the root of all evil is greed). The Scholastic teachers reflected on these texts using the Latin Vulgate.

117. See Fabian Wittreck, *Geld als Instrument der Gerechtigkeit. Die Geldlehre des Hl. Thomas von Aquin in ihrem interkulturellen Kontext* (Paderborn: Schöningh, 2002).

118. An excellent overview is found in Juan Belda Plans, *La Escuela de Salamanca* [The School of Salamanca] (Madrid: BAC, 2000).

119. These Renaissance authors were, among others: Poggio Bracciolini, "De avaricia," in *Prosatori Latini del Quattrocento*, ed. Eugenio Garin (Milano: Riccardo Ricciardi Editore, 1952), 249–301; Leon Battista Alberti, *I Libri della Famiglia*, ed. Ruggiero Romano and Alberto Tenenti (Torino: Einaudi, 1969); Benedetto Cotrugli, *Il libro dell'arte di mercatura*, ed. Ugo Tucci (Venezia: Arsenale Editrice, 1990); Matteo Palmieri, *Vita civile*, ed. Gino Belloni (Firenze: Sansoni, 1982). For a general description, see Marco Pellegrini, *Religione e Umanesimo nel primo Rinascimento da Petrarca ad Alberti* [Religion and humanism in the early Rennaissance: From Petrarch to Alberti] (Firenze: Casa editrice Le Lettere, 2012); Langholm, *The Merchant in the Confessional*, 269–71.

120. Prologue to Book VI of *De iustitia et iure* (Madrid: Instituto de Estudios Políticos, 1968), 505. De Soto's stance on financial practices remained negative: they were full of "malice, plague, and poison," ibid., lib. VI, q. VIII, a 1, p. 581.

121. The long and complex history of usury has been well described by John T. Noonan, Jr., *The Scholastic Analysis of Usury* (Cambridge, Mass.: Harvard University Press, 1957); Gabriel Le Bras, "Usure," in *Dictionnaire de Théologie Catholique*, vol. 15.2, eds. A. Vacant, E. Mangenot, and E. Amann (Paris: Letouzey & Ané, 1950), 2316–72.

122. The Second (1139) and the Third (1179) Lateran Councils prohibited usury and declared that this condemnation was revealed by the Bible. The *Decretum Gratiani* (ca. 1159) dedicated a special section to it, repeating

the prohibition. Also Urban III, Letter *Consuluit nos* (between 1185 and 1187), in Heinrich Denzinger, *Enchiridion Symbolorum: A Compendium of Creeds, Definitions and Declarations of the Catholic Church,* ed. Peter Hünermann (San Francisco: Ignatius Press, 2012), 764, was very influential because it applied Lk 6:35 to usury. See Noonan, *Scholastic Analysis,* 18–20.

123. Particularly important was the Franciscan Peter John Olivi (1248–1298), who introduced this distinction, see his *Usure, compere e vendite: la scienza economica del XIII secolo* [Usury, buying, and selling: the economic science of the 13th century], eds. Amleto Spicciani, Paolo Vian, and Giancarlo Andenna (Novara: Europía, 1998). This book contains Olivi's *Tractatus de emptione et venditione, de usuris et de restitutionibus,* written in the thirteenth century, 73–170. See also the edition by Sylvain Piron, *Traité des contrats* (Paris: Les Belles Lettres, 2012), and an English translation, *A Treatise on Contracts,* trans. Ryan Thornton and Michael Cusato, OFM (St. Bonaventure, N. Y.: Franciscan Institute Publications, 2016).

124. The text is available in Denzinger, *Enchiridion Symbolorum,* 2546–50. Islamic finance today still functions on these principles in order to comply with the prohibition on *riba.*

125. Benedict XVI, *Caritas in Veritate,* 65.

126. Francis, Encyclical Letter *Laudato Si'* (May 24, 2015), 109.

127. Vatican Council II, Dogmatic Constitution *Lumen Gentium* (November 21, 1964), 30–38.

128. Benedict XVI, *Caritas in Veritate,* 36.

129. See Francis Cardinal George, *The Difference God Makes: A Catholic Vision of Faith, Communion, and Culture* (New York: The Crossroad Publishing Company, 2009), 23–27.

130. I have developed these ideas in my book *Cómo poner a dieta al caníbal: Ética para salir de la crisis económica* (Madrid: Rialp, 2015).

2

Pope Francis's Spiritual and Cultural Context

NOWADAYS IT DOES NOT CAUSE us any surprise if a priest talks about the social teaching of the Church, calling it by its proper name. In the 1970s, however, when Fr. Jorge Mario Bergoglio used this expression, it revealed a certain theological position: it was similar to a profession of faith, that a body of teaching by this name was still up-to-date, valid, and useful. After the Second Vatican Council the term "social teaching of the Church" had fallen into disrepute as something pre-conciliar, something that had somehow sided with the mighty whose power it had served to justify. What many theologians demanded then was that the Church take a prophetic stance, denouncing injustice and siding with the underprivileged, and this stance was first formulated as political theology and later as a theology of liberation. Something, however, went wrong with "liberation theology" in Latin America. The Marxist elements in it incited violence and armed conflict, and the poor remained poor. The struggle divided the Church, but Jorge Mario Bergoglio, as a Jesuit priest and later Archbishop of Buenos Aires, in his wish to serve the poor, stayed above this division, avoiding both welfare statism and armed violence. He endorsed the "theology of the people," developed by theologians Lucio Gera and Juan Carlos Scannone, and other thinkers like Alberto Methol Ferré. It is a variant of liberation theology that differs from mainstream liberationism on important points, as I will show further on. Figuratively speaking, the theology of the people weaves a new cloth with the same thread used by liberation theology.[1] In this sense it is important to note that Fr. Bergoglio, both as archbishop and as pope, has frequently referred to the social teaching of the Church, especially to the *Compendium of the Social Doctrine of the Church*. When he is asked about some of his outspoken criticisms of the contemporary economic system, he usually answers that everything he says is to be found in the social teaching of the Church, and that he has added nothing new.[2]

Pope Francis's statements on the economy have attracted media headlines. However, even though important, they are not really as original or innovative as they have been portrayed in some quarters if we consider past papal pronouncements on the subject. Other popes before him were also critical of capitalism. John Paul II is usually cited for his conspicuous endorsement of capitalism;[3] however, in 1993 he stated that "Catholic social teaching is not a surrogate for capitalist ideology. ...(which is) responsible for grave social injustices."[4] In 2007 Benedict XVI referred to both Marxism and capitalism as ideologies containing false promises.[5] John Allen has summed it up: "It's not the content of the social gospel but his verve in applying it that defines the Francis era."[6]

This verve certainly consists mainly in a call to action; however, it also raises theological and theoretical questions, which are the object of the following reflections, in which I will first analyze Francis's hermeneutical[7] paradigm shift. Then I will draw attention to the Pope's twofold spiritual and cultural inheritance: his Jesuit spirituality and his Latin American background. It is noteworthy that Francis's writing style is quite different from that of his predecessors. This change is conspicuous, and has been commented on.[8]

Change of Hermeneutics

John Paul II and Benedict XVI were confronted with major doctrinal difficulties in the wake of the Second Vatican Council, and there was a need for a re-orientation in the Church's teaching. It is not unusual in Church history to have a situation of confusion and polarization after major decisions and landmark dogmatic definitions at councils. Suffice it to mention the Christological struggles after the First Council of Nicaea and the rift in Christianity after the Council of Trent. The "naval battle in the darkness of the storm," an image evoked by St. Basil to describe the Church of the fourth century, was also employed by Pope Benedict XVI in his analysis of the situation of the Church after the Second Vatican Council.[9] The loss of priestly and religious vocations, hair-raising liturgical experiments, and ambiguities and falsehoods taught from Catholic university chairs and pulpits, certainly required doctrinal and disciplinary clarifications. This, among other achievements, was the ecclesial mission of John Paul II and of Benedict XVI. As a result of their common efforts, the Church now has the Catechism of the Catholic Church, the 1983 Code of Canon Law, and the analogous codification of canons for the oriental Churches. The papal encyclicals, the frequent trips and numerous speeches of John Paul II, as well as the teaching and liturgical impulses of Benedict XVI, have blazed the trail of the Church after the council with a clarity that is plainly visible to anyone prepared to look.

Both John Paul II and Benedict XVI applied what the latter defined as the "hermeneutics of reform." It means "renewal in the continuity of the one subject-Church," and implies the "combination of continuity and discontinuity at different levels."[10] It means continuity in the perennial principles of faith and Catholic morality, and discontinuity in their application when required by the historical circumstances. Thus the "hermeneutics of reform" is neither the hermeneutics of discontinuity and rupture (which accepts no connection with pre-existing realities) nor the hermeneutics of continuity (which denies historical discontinuity of any kind), but a combination of both. Such a hermeneutics of reform is frequently needed in the case of the Church's social doctrine. Economic, political, cultural, and social circumstances change quickly, and the Church may have difficulty keeping pace with proclaiming the criteria and directives of action that result from the application of its principles to this kaleidoscopic reality. The Pastoral Constitution of the Second Vatican Council *Gaudium et Spes* explained the necessary approach, according to which some formulations of the social teaching of the Church are of a transitory nature. Therefore, "interpreters must bear in mind ... the changeable circumstances which the subject matter, by its very nature, involves."[11] Thus the Catholic social tradition is a tradition of principles whose applications vary, not a tradition which exalts and ossifies these applications.

Succeeding to the clarifying work of John Paul II and Benedict XVI, Pope Francis seems to be more concerned with pastoral issues than with doctrine or teaching. Of course, there will always be the need for doctrinal clarity and vigilance: pastoral activity is impossible without leading souls to truth. However, Francis is not so much concerned with doctrinal questions; rather, he has returned to the originally intended pastoral approach of the Second Vatican Council, an approach which was desired by John XXIII, and was summarized by Pope Paul VI during its concluding session in the following way: "The old story of the Samaritan has been the model of the spirituality of the council. A feeling of boundless sympathy has permeated the whole of it." Adopting a "deliberately optimistic" stance, the council, so Paul VI said, had proposed "our own new type of humanism": a Christian humanism honoring and serving humanity without divorcing man from God. To the contrary, "a knowledge of God is a prerequisite for a knowledge of man as he really is, in all his fullness." This is the council's anthropological turn: "our humanism becomes Christianity, our Christianity becomes centered on God; in such sort that we may say, to put it differently: a knowledge of man is a prerequisite for a knowledge of God."[12] Pope Francis also frequently refers to Christian humanism in his statements.[13]

We can say that Pope Francis uses a "pastoral hermeneutics" or a "hermeneutics of evangelization."[14] In other words, after the confusion and polarization of the post-conciliar period, Francis seems to say that we can now finally get to work on what the Second Vatican Council was actually all about. It is not so much about doctrinal and dogmatic decisions but about going out to bring the faith to the men and women of our time. A pope is free to choose his own style and his own priorities, his own hermeneutics. Nowhere is it decreed that encyclicals must always be of a doctrinal or pedagogical character. Therefore we, as interpreters of his texts, must adapt to this change. We would get his teaching wrong if we understood it in the same way as we do academic texts or educational material. Pope Francis wants to move hearts, not to make theories. In his social encyclical on ecology *Laudato Si'*, for instance, Francis repeats one of his favorite sentences: "Realities are more important than ideas";[15] and in *Evangelii Gaudium* he expresses his fear that the document might be used for academic discussions rather than as a stimulus for action.[16]

Austen Ivereigh quotes the pope's former spokesperson Fr. Lombardi by way of explaining that we need to apply a "new hermeneutics" in order to understand the pope correctly: we need to seek the general meaning rather than getting lost in dissecting particular terms. Ivereigh adds, "This missionary, pastoral approach, whose object is to speak to the heart of the other, lies deep in Jorge Bergoglio's Jesuit soul and clashes directly with a monarchical view of the papacy in which the task of papal communication is clarity, consistency, and dignity." As an example of this style, Pope Francis gave two interviews to the Italian journalist Eugenio Scalfari, the former editor of the Italian newspaper *La Repubblica*. They were not recorded or transcribed, but the 90-year old Scalfari wrote them down from memory. Of course he got a number of things wrong, and the Vatican had to clarify; the interviews were removed from the Vatican's website. Scalfari had offered to show the Pope the interview before publication but the Pope had declined, saying he trusted Scalfari. It is apparent that for Francis his personal relationship with this journalist was more important than doctrinal correctness or his reputation. Francis wanted to reach out to Scalfari beyond the borders of the Church.[17] This is an attitude dear to Francis that shows up in one of the pope's first written documents, a letter to the Argentine Bishops' Conference, in which he characteristically declared that he preferred a Church with some bumps and bruises because she reaches out to people, to a Church that is sick from the illness of self-referentiality, closed in on herself, without the joy of serving the holy, faithful people of God.[18]

In order to understand his statements on the economy and his social teaching correctly, it is important to keep in mind this pastoral approach and change in hermeneutics. Take for instance this well-known paragraph from one of the Pope's first writings:

> Just as the commandment "Thou shalt not kill" sets a clear limit in order to safeguard the value of human life, today we also have to say "thou shalt not" to an economy of exclusion and inequality. Such an economy kills. How can it be that it is not a news item when an elderly homeless person dies of exposure, but it is news when the stock market loses two points? This is a case of exclusion. Can we continue to stand by when food is thrown away while people are starving?[19]

With these words and other passages in his pronouncements, Pope Francis expresses that he is not against the economy as such, but against "an economy [that] kills." He intends to provoke the comfortable. His words on the economy are a prophetic cry against the anesthesia of well-being that paralyzes us. We shake our heads and deplore the plight of our brethren but do nothing about it, sometimes because we are genuinely overwhelmed, more often because we refuse to leave our comfort zone. His words on the economy are not meant as economic theory, and therefore do not present any alternative economic system, but rather are a part of his evangelization. We cannot spread the Christian faith without spreading love for those who suffer and without struggling to improve their situation. He wants to provoke a conversion that responds to the question of what each Christian is going to do about the misery in the world.

Pope Francis does not criticize the markets "in the sense of the free exchange of goods and services and ordinary human economic activity, which [has] indeed generated wealth since the beginning of time; and even less [is] he proposing a collectivist or any other alternative 'system'. He [is] unmasking an idolatrous mind-set that [has] surrendered human sovereignty to a hidden deity, a *deus ex machina*, which [demands] to be left alone to function unimpeded."[20] Francis speaks from the point of view of the poor and their needs that cannot wait. Food, clothing, shelter, and emergency health care cannot wait for the steady growth of prosperity. This would be a paralyzing ideology: "By imagining that one day poverty would be magically solved by the market, [such an ideology] was an attitude that justified inaction in the here and now. Anyone who knew poor people, rather than read about them in econometric theory, understood immediately what Francis meant: waiting for the market to generalize prosperity was a different experience for the poor than for the wealthy."[21]

Pope Francis writes from his own Latin American experience, especially from the immense suffering of the poor and middle class in Argentina during the last few decades. Because of corruption, extractive institutions, incompetence, crony capitalism, etc., the poor are still waiting for relief. Some countries, especially in the Anglo-Saxon world, have been able to create inclusive political and economic institutions that have blessed the greatest part of the population with prosperity and stability. Alleviating the suffering of the poor will likely require a combination of humanitarian aid in times of need and the creation or defense of inclusive institutions.

The existence of strong institutions in the United States (and elsewhere in the West) does not mean that the Pope's message is irrelevant for the U.S. Inclusive institutions guarantee a level playing field for all, they impede those who would rig the rules, they act as a bulwark against corruption and the destruction of the checks and balances that promote political decision-making for the common good and not for the individual interests of powerful lobbies. Such institutions create an inclusive economy that is open to all working people, including the poor, thus creating widespread and sustainable prosperity. But aren't these very institutions in danger also in the U.S.? Whenever egotism and shortsighted selfishness cause us to ignore the necessity to serve those in need and the common good, we are unintentionally destroying the system which benefits us so powerfully. National interest rightly understood leads us to share and help other nations to develop, because a world in which all are better off is also better for us.

Cultural Transfer

The cultural transfer of achievements, ideas, and texts from one cultural setting to another or from one moral and narrative tradition to another is only possible through adaptive transformation. Simple literal translation is insufficient, and can even be damaging. People will either completely misunderstand or at the very least fail to grasp the full meaning of what is being said because the cultural context is missing. This need has long been recognized in the Church under the name of "inculturation." As cardinal of Buenos Aires, Bergoglio was keenly aware of the need for inculturation of the faith. Mariano Fazio reports that one of the Pope's favorite quotes is from John Paul II: "A faith that does not affect a person's culture is a

faith 'not fully embraced, not entirely thought out, not faithfully lived.'"[22] Inculturation, explained Bergoglio, means finding
the right balance between proclaiming the Gospel message
to a particular nation with the authenticity and strength that
characterizes the Word of God, and at the same time with all
the authenticity and strength of the cultural reality of that
nation.[23] As pope he underscores the same idea: "It is imperative to evangelize cultures in order to inculturate the Gospel."[24]

Something very similar is also true when it comes to trans-
ferring Francis's statements about the economy into cultures
that are different from that of the Holy Father's. This transfer
requires the hermeneutical effort of explanatory transformation, whereby a concept from one culture is explained in terms
that another culture can understand and accept. The difficulty of course is to get it right, neither diluting the urgency
nor exaggerating the provocative character of the message.
The danger for any attempt at interpretation is the "circular
trap": instead of really understanding and letting oneself be
challenged by something new, people who are caught in the
circular trap merely reinforce their own prejudices or precon-
ceived conceptions by projecting them into the text they are
reading. In the end, they find only themselves in the text, not
the other. Understanding Francis's message on the economy
is for this reason a challenge, which I would like to tackle
by first describing the sources and influences which inspired
his teaching, and the context in which his convictions were
originated and formulated. This is important because when he
went to Rome as pope he consciously decided not to change
his style.[25] Many of his statements as pope basically repeat
the same ideas he developed as an archbishop in Argentina.

I would like to single out two social realities which I think
have strongly influenced the Argentine Jesuit Fr. Jorge Mario
Bergoglio, now Pope Francis: first, his Jesuit spirituality,
particularly the development and renewal of the Society of
Jesus under the Superior General Fr. Pedro Arrupe; and second, the life of the Catholic Church in Latin America and its

socioeconomic context and theology, especially in his beloved country Argentina. The aim here is not to treat each of these topics at length, but only insofar as they are necessary to understand Pope Francis and his message on the economy.

Francis the Jesuit: The Renewal of the Society of Jesus under Fr. Pedro Arrupe and the Social Dimension of Faith

"I feel a Jesuit in my spirituality. . . . I have not changed spirituality, no. Francis, Franciscan, no. I feel a Jesuit and I think as a Jesuit."[26] These words show how deeply Francis is rooted in the tradition of his religious family, the Society of Jesus, and how strongly its spirituality influences him also as pope.

Jorge Mario's dream when becoming a Jesuit priest was missionary work in Japan. However, his superiors said it was not possible because of his poor health. This was a heavy blow, and Fr. Jorge Mario asked God for guidance. In Chile, where he was sent for his formation, he discovered his calling to serve the poor: it was the immediate contact with the misery he saw around the house he lived in that was the trigger. This contact with the poor made him more humane and more spiritual at the same time.[27] Later, though still a young man, when he had been entrusted with responsibility in the Society of Jesus as its provincial in Argentina, the superior general Fr. Pedro Arrupe (1907–91, in office 1965–83) was to be of decisive influence on Fr. Bergoglio.

There are interesting parallels in the characters and lives of Arrupe and Bergoglio. Fr. Arrupe came to Rome from far away and, after 27 years in Japan, did not know Rome and kept himself clear of the culture and mentality of the Roman Curia. Something similar can be said of Cardinal Bergoglio. Both were and are filled with a strong missionary spirit, both lived or live in strict poverty and austerity, and wish this style of life to be the basis of the Church's mission. Fr. Arrupe was and Pope Francis now is a devout priest, centered in the Eucharist.

Just as Francis has, so Fr. Arrupe in his time began a new relationship with the media, whom he treated as partners in the
task of evangelization.[28] What was distinctly different was the
"detonating trigger" in their lives—Fr. Bergoglio's was seeing
intense poverty, but Fr. Arrupe's was quite literal: he was celebrating mass in Hiroshima when the atomic bomb exploded
in the city. He was knocked down by the blast, but survived.
As soon as he was back on his feet, he organized help in the
city, operating on survivors in makeshift operating rooms with
inadequate instruments (he was a medical doctor). Later, a
few months before the end of the Second Vatican Council, Fr.
Arrupe was elected superior general of the Jesuits, and began
to thoroughly transform the order founded by St. Ignatius of
Loyola.[29] He wanted to modernize it, place it into the context
of modern life, and evangelize it. He renewed the order in such
a way that one speaks of the "third Jesuit order," the first being
the original founded by St. Ignatius of Loyola that thrived until
1773, when it was unjustly suppressed for political reasons; the
second, the Society of Jesus as *restored* in 1814; and the third,
the *renewed* order, which began after 1965 when Fr. Arrupe
was elected superior general.[30]

From 1967 onward, the order re-ordered its priorities
and redesigned the formation of young Jesuits, projects in
which Fr. Bergoglio took an active involvement. Contact with
the poor and suffering was put at the center of the novices'
education. The most pressing topics during that period, topics
which implicated both injustice and suffering, were nuclear
arms proliferation, the refugee crises, the defense of justice,
and the preferential option for the poor. Many Jesuits under-
went a doctrinal crisis at this time, and the order was accused
of collusion with Marxism, recourse to violence, a desire to
democratize the Church, rejecting Paul VI's encyclical on the
sanctity of conjugal life *Humanae Vitae*, disobedience to the
pope, horizontalism (i.e., the desire to reduce the Church's
mission to a mere social service), and religious syncretism.[31]
The list is quite daunting and troubling. Fr. Arrupe was aware

of these difficulties, but wished to introduce a new style of government based on trust, transparency, and simplicity.

In this environment, Fr. Arrupe convened the 32nd General Congregation of the Jesuits in 1974. It was characterized by a major shift toward social justice, the core expression of which was the congregation's Fourth Decree. This decree embodied the fundamental orientation of the renewed Society of Jesus, and its overall message was that faith in God was impossible without a tireless struggle against all forms of injustice in the world.[32] All of the Society's apostolates had to be re-thought and connected with the struggle for social justice. The congregation deplored the fact that a large portion of the order's apostolates were identified with the rich and powerful and founded on the security offered by well-being, science, and power. In the face of so much hunger and poverty in the world, the Jesuits decreed severe austerity for themselves, reducing their consumption and reflecting on their own lifestyle regarding food, drink, houses, trips, holidays, etc. The members of the order had to have direct experience of misery in order to be able to perceive the cries of the poor.

Pope Francis constantly denounces injustice, exclusion, and exploitation. His program of evangelization is intimately connected with the poor.[33] His message reflects the spirit of the Fourth Decree, as may be seen in the decree's essential core: "The mission of the Society of Jesus today is the service of faith, of which the promotion of justice is an absolute requirement. For reconciliation with God demands the reconciliation of people with one another."[34] Or another passage in the same document: "Our consecration to God is really a prophetic rejection of those idols which the world is always tempted to adore, wealth, pleasure, prestige, power."[35] Such a firm commitment to the poor is not new to the Catholic tradition of Anglo-Saxon countries. Bishops like Cardinal James Gibbons of Baltimore, who was an important contributor to the first social encyclical *Rerum Novarum*, continuously struggled to keep the Church on the side "of the poor people," and of the workers and laborers especially.[36]

Charity (love of neighbor) and love of God are intrinsically and inseparably linked. However, both have their specific manifestations, and one must not absorb the other. Love of God is shown in the liturgy, fidelity to the doctrines of the faith, prayer, and personal piety, but all this would be false "salvific individualism" if we were to separate it from love for those in need. On the other hand, love of neighbor is not enough in order to truly love God, and love of God is the Gospel's paramount commandment: charity is a necessary but not sufficient condition for us to love God.[37] These theological distinctions are not only theoretical, as we can see in their sociological repercussions in our own time. Despite appeals to unity among Catholics, lines of political division seep into the Church, splitting the faithful into "conservative" and "social justice" Catholics. This division is a curse for intellectual discourse, and is based on an error that must be avoided in Catholic social thought. This division has its source in a dichotomy that has emerged as a consequence of the false absolutes propounded by both sides.

Unfortunately this division also happened within the Jesuit order. Fr. Arrupe's renewal of the Society of Jesus to emphasize social justice created a split in the order. Had the order paid more heed to Pope Paul VI's Apostolic Exhortation *Evangelii Nuntiandi* and the Holy See's authoritative comments on the Fourth Decree, it might well have avoided a lot of self-inflicted damage. In *Evangelii Nuntiandi*, the pope made clear that spiritual and sacramental life take priority over any other aim in the church. At the same time, he appealed to Christian conscience by reminding the faithful that salvation is linked to social justice, human advancement, development, and liberation—while simultaneously affirming that our salvation is more important than any terrestrial goal.[38] The Holy See explicitly directed similar guidance to Fr. Arrupe.[39] As things developed, however, one group wanted to continue the traditional mission of Jesuit education in schools and universities, but the other wanted to join forces with liberation theology and intervene in politics, even if this entailed the use of violence. Fr. Bergoglio clearly and actively opposed the use of violence, and was never a liberation theologian. He struggled to find a way to serve the poor without getting involved in party politics, and strove to maintain unity among the Jesuits in his role as provincial superior in Argentina. However, in this he failed—when the military dictatorship took power in Argentina in the 1970s, the Jesuits in the country were split into two factions, as occurred elsewhere in the order.[40] However, as has already been mentioned, Fr. Bergoglio had developed, together with friends, his own theological position, the "theology of the people," which had become an alternative to liberation theology. We now present some of the important currents of theological thought mentioned here because they are essential for our topic.

Liberation Theology

Liberation theology was a consequence of a specific form of reception and interpretation of the Second Vatican Council's Pastoral Constitution *Gaudium et Spes* (GS) in Latin America. In his analysis of the document's reception ten years after publication, Joseph Ratzinger (the future Benedict XVI) noted that in Europe, especially the Netherlands, GS had initiated a phase of reconciliation with modernity and with the Enlightenment that ushered in "the certainty of attaining perfect unity with the present world" and "a transport of adaptation."[41] In Latin America the development was different: "The period of optimistic agreement with the modern spirit, with its progress and with its offer of development for underdeveloped countries, came almost abruptly to an end. . . . Latin America can find no promise of help for its problems in enlightened progress."[42] It finds in it instead the cause of its misery:

> The problem of Latin America was and is, in fact, not reconciliation with the spirit of the modern era, identification with the ideology of Western Europe and the United States.... The spirit of liberalism and capitalism fostered by the Anglo-Saxon powers had become an even more painful slavery, for these only apparently liberated countries, which, as a result, could certainly not find their identity in this spirit or regard it as their "return home." By a kind of inner necessity, therefore, the optimism of the countersyllabus gave way to a new cry that was far more intense and more dramatic than the former one.[43]

The moral imperative that emphasized the option of preferential love for the poor already existed before the council, but it burst dramatically into Catholicism in the 1960s and quickly became a breeding ground for every form of ideology.

Liberation theology was developed by Gustavo Gutiérrez, Leonardo Boff, Clodovis Boff, Jon Sobrino, and others. Gutiérrez did not invent the term "theology of liberation" but wrote the first monographic book on the subject and contributed to its diffusion.[44] He has stated that the text emerged from a talk given in July 1968,[45] shortly before the second general assembly of CELAM (the Latin American bishops' conference) in Medellín, in which Gutiérrez participated as an advisor. Even though Gutiérrez's thought and with him the whole theological movement have undergone major changes resulting from the evolution of historical circumstances, in particular the collapse of the so-called "real socialism" in the Soviet Union and disillusionment with Marxism, the basic tenets and the overall thrust of their model have not changed.

Liberation theology affirms that without a prior preferential commitment to the poor (in the broadest sense of "poor," including the underprivileged and the endangered), we are far from the Kingdom of God.[46] This implies that the first and overarching condition for the possibility of engaging in theology is that the theologian participate in liberating action. This is done through raising the political consciousness ("conscientization") of oppressed Christians and non-Christians who "discover the causes of their oppression, organize themselves into movements, and act in a coordinated fashion."[47] The Boff brothers have written that "before we can do theology we have to 'do' liberation."[48] Liberating practice comes before liberation theology because the latter is the critical reflection on the practice of liberation in light of the Word of God.[49] Thus, being or becoming a theologian requires a class conversion. No one who is not engaged in actively improving the human condition of the poor in this world can know Christ. Therefore, in liberation theology, hope and the praxis of improving the human condition on earth logically precede the comprehension of Christ. In Sobrino's formulation, hope and praxis are hermeneutical settings for knowing Christ.[50]

In such a view, the preferential option for the poor is not just an aspect of love for those in need but presents itself as the universal precondition for any reflection on faith. Class conversion is seen as a hermeneutical requirement for a correct understanding of revelation. Conversion means identifying with Christ, and further, a commitment to the process of liberating the poor and exploited through an analysis of the present situation and a plan of action for transforming the world.[51] Obviously, liberation theologians are aware of the hermeneutical circle implied in such an approach: the revelation of Christ requires us to be among the poor, but we only understand the revelation correctly if we are already there.[52] These theologians are not concerned about this circularity because the preference for the poor is an option; that is, a defining personal decision that stands at the beginning of the three steps or three "mediations" necessary to liberation theology. "Mediation" is a term taken from hermeneutical philosophy meaning that the process of understanding consists in integrating new situations "into meaningful wholes through a personal commitment to some kind of vision of how things ought to be."[53] The three mediations constitute the formal method of liberation theology; they are inseparable moments in *one* theological process, and follow the three-part structure of "seeing – judging – acting." This is important because Francis's "theology of the people" applies the same analytical structure, which John XXIII had already proposed in his encyclical *Mater et Magistra*.[54]

The first mediation in liberation theology is socioeconomic analysis ("seeing"), which asks not just *how* the poor are, but *why* they have come to be poor. In other words, the aim is to discover the causes of poverty. In order to do so, liberation theology adopts a dialectical explanation positing that poverty and oppression are based on exploitation and exclusion. According to liberation theology, this can only be overcome by an alternative social system created by a revolution of the poor themselves, who thus become active protagonists of change. In this analysis, Marxism is used freely as an instrument, though not as a normative ideology. Marx is a "companion on the way" but not the guide, who is Jesus Christ alone.[55] This position is shared by all theologians of liberation who, like the former Prefect of the Congregation for the Doctrine of the Faith, Cardinal Gerhard Müller, reject totalitarianism and atheist Marxism but still endorse elements of the Marxist analysis of modern capitalist and industrial economies. In his own theology of liberation, Müller adopts three of these elements: the theory–practice distinction, the idea that the human being is the subject and creator of social progress, and the "dependence theory."[56] In any case, the theology of liberation is opposed to capitalism and favors socialism.[57]

The second step ("judging") is the reading of reality through the eyes of revealed faith.[58] It implies a retrieval of the prophetic dimension of the Christian faith. This theological mediation of socioeconomic and historical structures presupposes a certain concept of salvation and of history. Gutiérrez and others point out that Christ's salvation transforms history and brings it to its fulfillment. There are not two histories, one profane and another salvific, pitched against each other or independent of each other. Everything takes place in the horizon of salvation.[59]

In the third step ("acting"), liberation theology seeks to be a "militant, committed, and liberating theology."[60] Theology must not limit itself to thinking about the world but rather should strive to transform reality, a reality that in the case of Latin America, say liberation theologians, cannot be separated from the hegemony exercised over it by the big centers of political and economic power.[61] Theology must fight for liberation from the oppression inflicted on Latin American countries by American capitalism, multinational corporations, debt, etc. As part of the theology of liberation, Gutiérrez advocates for a "permanent cultural revolution."[62] Accordingly, the construction of a just society must pass through some kind of phase of conflict and violence. "Cheap reconciliation" would be nothing but an ideology justifying deeply entrenched disorder and injustice.[63] The Latin American bishops have repeatedly renounced and rejected violence; this is not so clear among theologians of liberation.[64]

Even though some theologians of liberation have criticized Catholic social teaching,[65] in general they do not reject it, but rather refer to it as something on a different level with a different objective. Liberation theology moves outside the bounds of traditional Catholic social thought. Jon Sobrino has expressed it in radical fashion: the massive, unjust and lethal misery in the world is the only setting from which it is relevant to speak about God and Christ. The world of the poor is what makes us ponder, what enables us to think, and teaches us to reflect.[66]

Certainly, the challenge of having charity and empathy for the poor presented by liberation theology must resonate with every Christian: "Those committed to integral liberation will keep in their hearts the *little utopia* of at least one meal for everyone every day, the *great utopia* of a society free from exploitation and organized around the participation of all, and finally the *absolute utopia* of communion with God in a totally redeemed creation."[67] Once again, the problem is not the prophetic denunciation, vision, and aims, but the concrete path to attaining them. What are the right means to achieve these goals? The answer to this question affects the theological level, but even more so, the philosophical and economic ones. The evangelical Protestant theologian Helen Rhee has observed that while Catholic theologians opted for liberation theology and its understanding of the preferential option for the poor, "the poor themselves opted for the prosperity gospel (and Pentecostalism) in Latin America and elsewhere."[68] The streams of immigrants not heading for socialist countries that have implemented the dependence theory also confirm that liberation theology is not the solution for poverty but possibly one of its causes. Acknowledging this fact would open the door to improved assistance to the poor, especially in the Latin American context. This acknowledgment would improve the scope of investigation into the real causes of poverty (lack of opportunity, the absence of health services and education, exclusion, etc.) and improve strategies to overcome them. Actually, this is what the adherents of the "theology of the people," including Pope Francis, have in mind in their form of commitment to the poor. They have striven to remain faithful to the Magisterium of the Church, and they were able to do so because the popes have been keenly aware of and have consistently denounced the suffering and exclusion of masses of people in Latin America and elsewhere. Because of this awareness, the option for the poor entered the texts and formulations of Catholic social teaching.[69]

The first pontifical, magisterial use of an expression similar to "the preferential option for the poor" is to be found in the document of the Congregation for the Doctrine of the Faith *Libertatis Nuntius*,[70] which was aimed at critically purifying liberation theology. It assigns love for the poor the "highest priority" in the Church, which "wants to be the Church of the poor."[71] Then there was a quick succession of relevant documents,[72] notably *Libertatis Conscientia*.[73] From that point onward, John Paul II used the expression "option or love of preference for the poor" in many of his documents. He defined this attitude as "an option or a special form of primacy in the exercise of Christian charity."[74] John Paul II spoke in terms of love without "the conversional and hermeneutical emphases" given to the option for the poor by liberation theologians.[75] In this sense, John Paul II positioned the preferential option for the poor among the other elements of Catholic social teaching, not as its overarching and paramount feature.[76] This official formulation of "the preferential option for the poor" was the one received into the *Compendium of the Social Doctrine of the Church*, where it is situated as a subtitle in the chapter on the universal destination of goods.[77] The urgency with which John Paul II formulated his writings on the Church's necessary commitment to the poor leaves no doubt about the priority he assigned to love for the poor and suffering, the oppressed and downtrodden, to those whose human rights have been denied.[78] Pope Benedict XVI continued along the same lines, even though he did not use the expression "option for the poor" in his writings, thus avoiding any possible reference to liberation theology.[79] Not so Pope Francis.

The Theology of the People and Francis

Pope Francis has never called himself a theologian of liberation but rather a "son of the theology of the people."[80] It is true that liberation theology itself has to some extent shifted away from its first forms as described above toward the contents and methodology of the theology of the people, as developed by Lucio Gera, Juan Carlos Scannone, and others like Alberto Methol Ferré.[81] This shift puts the emphasis on culture instead of the socioeconomic structures.[82] However, it is also true that the liberationists of the first phase have not changed their message substantially and that the texts of their books have remained unaltered in recent editions. That is why I prefer not to simply identify the theology of the people with liberation theology.[83] There are certainly many points in common but there are also differences.

The theology of the people shares with liberation theology the three mediations characteristic of the latter, the three-part analysis of "seeing – judging – acting." However, the point of departure for the theology of people is not the poor but "the people," in which the poor figure preeminently. The "people" are the faithful, humble, and simple persons who possess an evangelical instinct,[84] or in the words of Pope Francis "*el santo pueblo fiel de Dios*" (the holy faithful people of God). This evangelical instinct is "a vaccine against the prevailing ideologies and political violence."[85] The people are the subject of a *specific* history (not of history in general) and of a *specific* culture. Culture is understood in the broad sense as common life in society, its ultimate meaning, its symbols and customs, its institutions and political structures. Culture and people are interrelated concepts in the theology of the people: a culture is made up of its ethos and values, and when one becomes aware of these one feels part of a people. Awareness of a common culture and a common moral heritage and commitment constitute a people. Inevitably there also is a political dimension: belonging to a people or nation means sharing in the same culture by means of particular political decisions. Culture is a political and ethical reality because it is rooted in the human need to live together in society. Thus the theology of the people is not apolitical; on the contrary, its message awakens the Christian sense of responsibility for public affairs. However, in contrast to liberation theology, the theology of the people includes everyone in the notion of "people," also the rich, unless the rich person rejects the common good by oppressing others—such persons are "anti-people." There are therefore different degrees of belonging to a people, according to each person's contribution to the common good. The poor have a preferential position among the people because they are more aware of their lack of power and thus of their need for community. "In a preferential way we call the multitude of the poor a people."[86] Thus, the preferential option for the poor in this theological framework is mediated through the notion of the "people."[87]

The theology of the people's methodological modification of the judging and acting steps of liberation theology boils down to a rejection of Marxism. Marxism presumes to derive from a scientific analysis of society, but Scannone insists on the need for discernment: there are different ways in which science can analyze society, and social science certainly possesses internal criteria for evaluating the reliability of its claims; however, as Scannone argues, in the perspective of faith, theology is able to view things more comprehensively. It includes God's wisdom and eternal law, and thus is a superior method that is able to purify the more limited methods of social analysis. Scannone thus underscores the priority of theology: the criteria of truth and the best tools for real comprehension stem from theology. This is an important point because it justifies a theological purification of those assumptions about human nature implied by the social sciences that appear to be incompatible with revelation. Theology need not accept these assumptions at face value, and can offer corrective criticisms. Pope Francis too rejects Marxism[88] and, as has already been mentioned, has expressed his preference for a model of the "social (market) economy." In this preference, Pope Francis has been influenced by the work of CELAM (Consejo Episcopal Latinoamericano—the Latin American Bishops' Conference), of which he was a member for many years.

Relevant for our topic are the general assemblies of CELAM in Medellín (1968), Puebla (1979), Santo Domingo (1992), and Aparecida (2007). Again it is Juan Carlos Scannone who summarizes and characterizes the particular theological position of the Latin American hierarchy, distinguishing it from the original form of liberation theology described above. The hierarchy underscores the biblical and ecclesial dimension of liberation, insisting on the importance of evangelization and spirituality. Even though it is aware of the importance of sociopolitical factors and sometimes refers to socioeconomic data, it does not use the socioeconomic analysis as part of theological discourse, but instead bases its theological reflections on anthropological and ethical foundations. "Liberation" is an important topic in this method of theological reasoning, and has the real intention of liberating, but liberation and the option for the poor are not the universal precondition for any new mode of theology.[89]

In this sense, the bishops spoke at Medellín about an effective preference for the poorest section of society.[90] They called on Christians to listen attentively to the imperative of their consciences and to live in solidarity, and pledged to offer a personal example of a poor church. "Preference" expresses non-exclusivity: the poor are the first but not the only ones who may expect love from us.

The long document of the general assembly at Puebla contains a chapter entitled "Preferential Option for the Poor."[91] In it the bishops speak of the need for the whole Church to opt for the poor and achieve their complete liberation.[92] Those engaged in prophetic denunciation and who have committed themselves to the cause of the poor have been criticized and persecuted; nevertheless, the poor themselves are encouraged to choose the option for the poor and struggle for the integrity of their faith, which includes claiming their civic rights.[93] This document does not offer a constructive program or vision of the institutional features that can effectively help the poor, but this omission was repaired by documents emanating from subsequent gatherings in Santo Domingo,[94] and especially in Aparecida, where Bergoglio played a leading role, entrusted with drafting the concluding document. In a chapter dedicated entirely to the preferential option of the poor,[95] the bishops from the assembly at Aparecida refer to the option as one of "the distinguishing features of our Latin American and Caribbean church."[96] They assign it a central function in pastoral care.[97] There are, however, no hints at class struggle; to the contrary, the Aparecida document includes the world of business and finance in its positive concern for the poor: "The preferential option for the poor demands that we devote special attention to those Catholic professional people who are responsible for the finances of nations, those who promote employment, and politicians who must create conditions for the economic development of countries, so as to give them ethical guidelines consistent with their faith."[98]

The gathering in Aparecida took place only a few years before Francis's election as pope, and we can see its influence in what he says about business and in his way of saying it. We will return to Francis's substantial pronouncements on business later on, and for now just hint at this way of speaking. Pope Francis employs the three-part analysis typical of liberation theology. In most of his teachings, he begins with an analysis of socioeconomic realities,[99] but he also usually states that he does not possess a monopoly on the correct interpretation of reality or the proposal of useful solutions.[100] Further discussion is invited, and there is often an appeal to specialists to find the right solution. As has already been described, Francis's affirmative vision is a social (market) economy "that invests in persons by creating jobs and providing training."[101] Pope Francis wants the poor to be included in the market economy instead of them receiving government handouts, as we shall see in greater detail later on.

The strong links Francis has with his native culture and its people require us to discuss the Latin American context.

Francis the South American: The Latin American Experience

Pope Francis is the first Latin American pope. He can only be understood as a Latin American pope and in the context of Latin America. What does this mean?

The Cultural and Socioeconomic Dimensions of Latin America

For someone like me, who is not from Latin America, understanding what it means that the pope is Latin American requires the effort of placing himself into the traditions and histories of the Latin American culture, which is different from the Anglo-Saxon culture. These differences have brought about semantic variations in everyday spoken language which cannot be bridged by literal translation, as well as differences in the ideas held by average citizens. The words seem to be the same but they mean something different in the cultural horizon of an Anglo-Saxon North American than in that of a Latin American. The concepts behind the words are not the same. I will give some examples, but I first wish to clarify that I am not claiming that everyone living in Latin America, or all Latin Americans living in the United States, or anyone from an Anglo-Saxon culture anywhere in the world understands these concepts in the way I will discuss below. That would be quite impossible in a pluralist society, especially among intellectuals, who are a class of people characterized by agreeing on hardly anything.

Despite the tendency of those from a Latin American culture to understand things differently than those from an Anglo-Saxon culture, it is true that professional economists all over the world, whether they are from the United States or one of the countries of Latin America, see and express things using the same or similar concepts. It suffices to look through the publications of the Economic Commission for Latin America and the Caribbean[102] to have tangible proof of this. This leading economic observatory, based in Latin American and staffed with Latin American economists, explains the economic situation of Latin America using the same conceptual tools employed by economists the world over. My remarks are not economic, however, but cultural, and they aim at identifying the intellectual sources of Pope Francis's message on the economy. The point I want to make here is that there is such a thing as a common cultural horizon based on a shared language, derived also from collective experiences and values, which we call a cultural tradition, and that our arguments tend to be most fruitful when they are held *inside* a single cultural tradition. When the arguments go back and forth *between* traditions, an intermediary is necessary to bridge the semantic gap. This is what I try to do, and I choose examples from the economic realm.

Capitalism

In the English-speaking Western world, especially in the United States, capitalism generally has positive connotations. The universe of meanings, nuances, and ideological uses and abuses of terminology related to capitalism is large, but in broad strokes "capitalism" usually describes the economic system that shaped and continues to shape the free American economy. Capitalism is not a single institution but is instead a free market economy embodied by a set of institutional arrangements: "Private ownership of the means of production, competitive product and factor markets, large banks and financial markets, contracts, property rights and judicial institutions to enforce them, and large corporations."[103] There have been important differences over time and in different places in the way these institutional features have been configured and combined. Capitalism is not a static order, but rather an evolving system that has often re-invented and re-invigorated itself during and as a result of crises. Thoughtful and even critical advocates of this system generally share this optimistic view of its resilience: "Capitalism is an adaptive system that mutates and evolves in response to a changing environment. When capitalism is seriously threatened by a systemic crisis, a new version emerges that is better suited to the changing environment and replaces the previously dominant form."[104]

The cultural and economic traditions of capitalism in Anglo-Saxon countries were strongly influenced by Adam Smith, whose ideas mirrored the shared values of the commercial society of his time. His well-known book *The Wealth of Nations* was so successful because it faithfully interpreted the feelings of its readers and expressed the intellectual currents of the Scottish Enlightenment dominant at the time. The values of industry, diligence, thrift, parsimony, prudence, etc., were already part of the culture, and Smith reinforced them: "Wherever capital predominates, industry prevails; wherever revenue, idleness….Capitals are increased by parsimony, and diminished by prodigality and misconduct….Parsimony, and not industry, is the immediate cause of the increase of capital."[105] Without parsimony, according to Smith, whatever industry acquires would be squandered. For Smith, capitalism is not only an economic system but a moral and political order based on natural liberty that creates prosperity for all, particularly for the lower classes of society. We find the same conviction in those who, with considerable emotion, present capitalism as a kind of sacred order in American society. For these people, it is not only about making money, but about an idea of ordered liberty, personal happiness, equal opportunity, and merit. American capitalism is and should be an economy of the people, by the people, and for the people.[106]

In the European and Latin American tradition, capitalism is often seen in a quite different and not at all positive light. German Cardinal Gerhard Ludwig Müller, who before becoming Prefect of the Congregation for the Doctrine of the Faith worked every year among the poorest of the poor in Peru during the summer months, characterizes capitalism in Latin America as a system aimed at the unfettered acquisition of personal wealth, the pursuit of which is taken as the ultimate criterion of human action. Such capitalism produces oppression and exploitation. Capitalism, says Müller, is a combination of money, other material means, and power in the hands of oligarchs or international centers of political and economic power.[107] There is not much space for a positive understanding of capitalism in those words, which not only express an understanding of capitalism that is devoid of the vocation to moral order we encounter in Adam Smith's vision, but see it as inherently immoral. Capitalism is presented as the enemy of the poor, not as the system that can create prosperity for all.

Such a view, on the one hand, has roots in Marxism. It is an essential element of Marx's socioeconomic analysis that capitalism is based on the extraction of surplus value from the labor of workers. In the Marxist view, capitalism can only be exploitive, and therefore calling someone a capitalist is certainly not a compliment. On the other hand, we also discover a strong skepticism toward capitalism in the tradition of Catholic social thought. Neither the encyclical *Rerum Novarum* nor *Quadragesimo Anno* clearly endorses capitalism; rather, they warn about its limitations, advocating workers' rights and other social concerns. This is particularly true of *Quadragesimo Anno*, in which Pius XI deplored the enormous social evils that had poisoned the world's economies after the Great Depression. He was convinced that "strict and watchful moral restraint enforced vigorously by governmental authority could have banished" them. The encyclical explicitly condemns communism and socialism, not capitalism; however, it also implicitly condemns a form of business that is solely concerned with increasing wealth by any means whatsoever, stating that seeking one's own selfish interests before everything else has led to the gravest of crimes being committed against others with any qualm of conscience.[108] In Pius XI's view, such a harmful economic order was founded on enlightened rationalism: "For since the seeds of a new form of economy were bursting forth just when the principles of rationalism had been implanted and rooted in many minds, there quickly developed a body of economic teaching far removed from the true moral law, and, as a result, completely free rein was given to human passions."[109] Pope Pius XI did not name the "new form of economy" he was criticizing; however, from his reference to the rationalism of the Enlightenment we can conjecture that he is referring to what in economic theory is called capitalism in its negative form, as evidenced by the skeptical treatment of this kind of capitalism in Catholic social thought. At that time the pope was heavily influenced by authors like Heinrich Pesch, Oswald von Nell-Breuning, and Gustav Gundlach, who were critical of both socialism and capitalism, proposing instead solidarism as an alternative form of socioeconomic order.[110]

Cardinal Reinhard Marx, who is a supporter of the German model of the "social market economy" or Ordoliberalism, and thus of the principle of regulated free markets, avoids using the expression "capitalism" in a positive way. He summarizes the Church's critical attitude toward capitalism by stating: "I know of no historical example anywhere in the world where a free market economy without any state intervention and regulation has been beneficial to the poor. Doubtlessly, it was the market economy that has laid the foundation for our welfare society but it has not created general welfare on its own."[111] Cardinal Marx maintains that there is no invisible market mechanism that could guarantee general welfare. He argues that political measures, not the market itself, have allowed the working class to participate in the economic success of free market systems, and that because of modern forms of usury, predatory consumer credit, immoral real estate mortgage practices, and similar abuses it has taken the Church longer to accept economic liberalism as a viable form of economic organization than it took her to come to terms with political liberalism.[112]

Before Reinhard Marx, Joseph Ratzinger had been equally clear in his criticism of what he, I argue mistakenly, took to be Adam Smith's economic proposal: "Following the tradition inaugurated by Adam Smith, this position [that an economy should be governed by economic laws alone] holds that the market is incompatible with ethics because voluntary 'moral' actions contradict market rules and drive the moralizing entrepreneur out of the game. For a long time then business ethics rang like hollow metal because the economy was held to work on efficiency and not on morality."[113]

In Catholic cultures like Latin America, it is thus not surprising that the word "capitalism" is not understood in the same positive way as it is in the United States. Other forms of economic order, which seem to be more in line with the statements of the Magisterium, tend to be better received in these Catholic cultures. Pope Francis's teachings are a clear example of this. In the only speech so far in which he has explicitly attacked capitalism by name, he attacks a form of economic organization that is idolatrously aimed at profit alone. That he associates capitalism with exploitation is clear in the following:

> One cannot say often enough, that capitalism continues to produce the discarded people it then tries to heal. The principal ethical dilemma of this capitalism is the creation of discarded people, then trying to hide them or make sure they are no longer seen. A serious form of poverty of a civilization is when it is no longer able to see its poor, who are first discarded and then hidden.[114]

Francis gives examples of what he is furious about: airlines that plant trees to compensate for the environmental damage caused by aircraft, and casinos that pay to care for the gambling addicts they have created. "And the day that the weapons industry finances hospitals to care for the children mutilated by their bombs, the system will have reached its pinnacle."[115] Of course he is right! Philanthropy alone cannot atone for crimes and injustices committed during the process of wealth creation. Business itself must create true value that benefits the entrepreneur, his employees, and the community he lives and works in. However, the model the Pope praises in the speech mentioned above, the "economy of communion," has not been widely adopted, even though it contains wonderful insights. This model represents a kind of "parallel structure" in comparison to the prevailing corporate models, the value of which is analogous to small, intense religious communities who "withdraw from the world" to live the Gospel in a more complete way. While these kinds of exemplary communities can raise their members to holiness and serve as a light to others, they are by their nature the exception to the rule. I think that most evangelization starts rather with an affirmation of what exists, which can hopefully then be purified. Most Christians must stay in the existing economy, obviously without being blind to what is sinful and needs to be improved. I believe that the same method—affirming what exists followed by attempts at purification—should be applied to liberalism, and particularly to "neoliberalism."

Liberalism

For some authors in the Anglo-Saxon tradition, the word "liberalism" refers to a set of beliefs that are the basis of our Western culture: a belief in fundamental moral equality between persons as the foundation of the legal system; a belief that enforcing moral convictions by means of law is a contradiction in terms; a belief in the defense of natural liberty through the assertion of natural rights as the only birthright of citizens; and a belief that only representative government is worthy of a society based on equality. Larry Siedentop argues that "in its basic assumptions, liberal thought is the offspring of Christianity."[116] In his view, liberalism establishes a high moral ideal and must not be confused with egotism or withdrawal into the private sphere. The temptation in Western culture, according to Siedentop, is reducing liberalism to a crude form of utilitarianism by excluding the concept of reciprocity, a concept which "gives liberalism its lasting moral value."[117] The importance of moral convictions in liberalism can also be seen in F.A. Hayek, L. udwig von Mises, and other representatives of Western liberalism.[118] However, it is worth pointing out that liberalism in most countries, especially in Europe and Latin America, was consistently and sometimes continues to be anti-clerical and especially anti-Catholic. Not infrequently this opposition involved violence and persecution. If liberalism stood up for religious freedom and toleration it often did so because of its indifference to religion and opposition to faith based on dogmas. Because of its anti-religious bent, liberalism saw the Catholic Church as an enemy, and consequently the Church rejected it up to the Second Vatican Council, which brought about a "new definition of the relationship between the faith of the Church and certain essential elements of modern thought."[119]

We must remember that it was and is a mistake to simply transport European ideas into Latin America without paying heed to its different trajectory of social development.[120] Daron Acemoglu and James A. Robinson, for instance, describe the historical facts in Guatemala after the Liberals took power in 1870. "Liberalism" in Guatemala meant something different than it did in Europe. In Guatemala, the Liberals for the most part belonged to the old families who maintained the extractive economic and political institutions they had created for their own benefit. Liberalism just meant re-organizing these institutions toward a new aim: the exploitation of coffee. Land privatization did not mean free, equal, and fair access to land ownership but confiscation of communal lands owned by indigenous peoples. The land passed into the hands of the existing elites, who used it to form large estates. In order to secure cheap labor the Guatemalan "liberal" state re-introduced forced labor.[121] If we compare the notion of Western liberalism as explained by Siedentop, we immediately see that Latin American liberalism was quite different, practically its opposite. It did not create inclusive institutions but extractive ones instead.

Historical developments in Argentina were similar to those in Guatemala, a fact which is especially relevant for the cultural horizon of Pope Francis. After becoming independent in 1816, Argentina was ruled by traditionally Catholic "warlords." They were replaced in power by the Liberals of Buenos Aires, who were generally Freemasons, and who installed a new constitutional system with a central government, a liberal free market, and a capitalist economy that brought great wealth to Argentina, opening the country's economy to the world, especially to Britain and France. Argentina became attractive to immigrants, mainly from Italy and Spain, until the Great Depression in 1929 that pushed Argentina into a crisis. In the liberal Argentine system the Catholic Church was not only tolerated but had the status of the state religion, even though the motive was one of political convenience: the

Liberals wished to use the church for their own purposes. This accommodation came apart in the early 1920s, but before then the social encyclical *Rerum Novarum* had found great resonance in Argentina. "The Church was the major source of protests against the liberal economy and politics of the day, drawing on the social teaching of the popes and new nationalist thinking in Argentina, both of which would influence the Peronist government in the 1940s and 1950s."[122] The opposition movement blamed liberal capitalism for the ills of society after the Great Depression. The Church in which Pope Francis grew up was "antiliberal in the Argentine sense of that word. Liberal was associated with the free-market, cosmopolitan, rationalist, authoritarian outlook of the Argentine belle époque."[123] This opposition drew on its Spanish Catholic heritage to demand that the liberal government apply Catholic social teaching in its economic and social policies.[124]

This historical situation explains why the word liberalism (sometimes referred to as "neo-liberalism") is practically a curse word for many Latin American Catholics: it means unfettered free markets that are abused to exploit the poor. Austin Ivereigh has written about a book, published following John Paul II's visit to Cuba, in which Bergoglio took the position that the Church:

> had no difficulty with capital accumulation that increases productivity – what he [Bergoglio] calls "capitalism as pure economic system" – but rather with "the spirit that has driven capitalism, utilizing capital to oppress and subject people, ignoring the human dignity of workers and the social purpose of the economy, distorting the values of social justice and the common good." Although neoliberalism respected religious values, he went on, it did so by relegating them to the private sphere, adding that "no one can accept the precepts of neoliberalism and consider himself Christian." The core Christian concept was that of solidarity – knowing how to share what God

has abundantly given. The opposite was neoliberalism, which "brings about unemployment, coldly marginalizing those who are superfluous," empties economic growth of human content, is "concerned only for numbers that add up," and "corrupts democratic values, by alienating from these the values of equality and social justice.[125]

In the Latin American cultural horizon, neoliberalism is often associated with borrow-and-spend policies—it was seen to have eviscerated the State after Marxist ideologies had deified it. The only way out, said Cardinal Bergoglio, was to build from below.[126] Bergoglio is not alone in this way of seeing things. For instance, Francisco Ivern, S.J., the former Vice-Rector of the Pontifical Catholic University of Rio de Janeiro, associates neoliberalism, on a practical level, with exaggerated economic domination by multinational corporations, abuse of private property, and unequal distribution of wealth. On a theoretical level, he sees it as tied to individualism, utilitarian pragmatism, unfettered competition, unrestrained consumerism and hedonism, and a lack of sensitivity to the needs and suffering of the poor. These are considered to be the "unvalues" of liberalism that permeate the life of the economic, political, and social institutions of society.[127]

Following the terminological distinction in Acemoglu and Robinson between "inclusive" and "extractive" institutions, the decisive difference between a positive and a negative experience with capitalism and liberalism seems to be whether a society is supported by inclusive institutions or extractive ones. Inclusive institutions guarantee property rights, create positive economic incentives, encourage human initiative, and unleash creativity. Fair and free competition plays an important role in this process: it lowers interest rates and channels profits not toward elites but in a diffused way throughout society, thus redistributing wealth non-coercively. These broadly distributed rights and benefits lead to equal and easy access to finance and loans.[128] Such inclusive, market-based economic institutions create a level playing field with equal opportunities. They pave the way for improved technology and education. Diffused educational and technological progress, supported by innovation and the availability of patent rights, presupposes inclusive institutions. Without this progress, a society stagnates and cannot afford broad access to education. However, before there can be inclusive *economic* institutions there must be inclusive *political* ones. Political institutions are inclusive when, on the one hand, they centralize power sufficiently to enforce legal rules, but on the other hand limit power effectively through the rule of law and a system of checks and balances in which no single power center can dominate over the others. If one of these elements is missing, political institutions become extractive, and, in consequence, the economic institutions become extractive too. Extractive economic institutions "are designed to extract incomes and wealth from one subset of society to benefit a different subset."[129] They hinder the creation of wealth and its spread throughout society, reserving it for an elite that lives off the efforts of the rest of the population.[130] Many people in Latin America have experienced extractive institutions in which political power and economic wealth are tied together in a zero-sum game. There is no growth and what little income there is, is siphoned off to the cronies of the powerful.

In the United States there is also a growing complaint of similar phenomena even though on a smaller scale. However, the experience of inclusive institutions is still preponderant in the U.S. This difference in experience can be discussed under the term "free markets."

Free Markets

In Catholic social teaching there is no doubt that free, ethically oriented markets embedded in a culture of work and under the rule of law and political vigilance are "the most efficient instrument for utilizing resources and effectively responding to needs."[131] It shares this conviction with the experience accumulated over time by secular market economies all over the world. On the other hand, Catholic social teaching is also aware of the limits of markets. Acemoglu and Robinson express an idea that we could find in an encyclical:

> [T]he presence of markets is not by itself a guarantee of inclusive institutions. Markets can be dominated by a few firms, charging exorbitant prices and blocking the entry of more efficient rivals and new technologies. Markets, left to their own devices, can cease to be inclusive, becoming increasingly dominated by the economically and politically powerful. Inclusive economic institutions require not just markets, but inclusive markets that create a level playing field and economic opportunities for the majority of the people.[132]

Latin America in general and Argentina specifically seem to have thus far experienced extractive institutions rather than inclusive ones. Therefore, their experience of free markets, deregulation, and privatization is different and even contrary to that of other cultures and countries. In some Latin American (and also former Soviet bloc) countries, "privatization" has simply meant converting state monopolies into private ones, not infrequently involving the old party or crony-capitalist networks that favor relatives and friends over others who might merit opportunities because of their competence and diligence. The result has been that countries with extractive institutions remain poor and are prevented from embarking on a path to economic growth.

Unfortunately, the blame for this situation is not infrequently placed primarily on the United States. Certainly it is true that commercial relationships between Latin America and the U.S. are "asymmetrical." Latin American countries are still mainly suppliers of commodities and agricultural products. The United States possesses a high level of technology and many productive industries whose products fetch high prices. With these advantages, the U.S. and other rich developed countries subsidize their agricultural production and adopt dumping policies in the developing countries for this production. This creates debt in Latin America.[133]

In Latin America, Europe, and other parts of the world, there is a deep resentment against American global hegemony. Defending the American point of view can earn you criticism for lacking intellectual independence and selling out, choosing the winning and powerful side. These pressures against taking an unpopular opinion are made worse by the fact that in countries with little tradition of political liberty, people are not used to speaking out openly and stating their opinions. In these countries, people tend to explain political developments by reference to hidden networks and secret groups manipulating political power behind the scenes—if something is wrong, the reaction is to seek its cause in some conspiracy or network of powerful corporations. I do not deny that American corporations have infringed on human rights and committed crimes in Latin America.[134] However, it is too easy to blame "*los extranjeros*" for all of these societies' economic ills. The problems of Latin America are not the market and globalization but the absence of inclusive institutions, and that is essentially a homemade problem.

Again, the personal experience of Pope Francis in his beloved country of Argentina can explain some of his formulations on the economy. Bergoglio and the whole of Argentine society lived through the broken promises of the first Peronist president in decades, Carlos Menem, who presided over the terrible economic crisis beginning in 2001. Menem followed a radically neoliberal economic and foreign policy, and unfortunately the worst connotations of the word "neoliberal" were confirmed. The government failed to build a social security net, the number of poor increased among the middle class, and unemployment soared. The government was hoping for a trickle-down of wealth to lower levels of society, but instead the rich became richer and the poor stayed poor. The worst development, however, was the corruption and crony capitalism, sometimes involving foreign companies, which became apparent when the whole system collapsed. There was insufficient institutional separation between the State, the market, and the judiciary to guarantee necessary checks and balances. New millionaires were created during the time of Menem, but the public deficit was staggering, doubling in only a decade. In 2001, Argentina endured the largest sovereign default in world history. Argentina once had Latin America's biggest middle class, but its members suffered the most: many lost their jobs and incomes and much of their savings. Parish soup kitchens sprang up everywhere, and the number of people needing them from middle-class families tripled.[135]

This is what Pope Francis has in mind when he calls on us to say "no" to an economy of exclusion and inequity that kills,[136] when he attacks trickle-down theories,[137] when he tongue-lashes "ideologies which defend the absolute autonomy of the marketplace and financial speculation,"[138] and when he expresses his profound concerns about consumerism and deeply rooted corruption.[139]

Latin American societies have attempted to rectify the problems they face, largely by turning to political movements of "the left." Methol Ferré points out that in Latin America the "left" is divided into two branches: the communist parties and the national popular movements. The latter do not share with the communist parties the notion of the proletariat as the vanguard of social change. Similarly to the theology of the people, their vision is an industrialized society in which the social classes join forces: the peasants with the farmers, the proletariat with the middle class and the entrepreneurs, and so on. This idea is reminiscent of the corporativist ideas propounded in Catholic social teaching before the Second World War, particularly in the encyclical *Quadragesimo Anno*. These popular movements are the most important sociopolitical phenomena in Latin America. They are made up of great masses of Catholics, and they include the labor and trade unions. Except for the party that came out of Fidel Castro's revolution in Cuba, which started as a popular movement but had no other powerful ally against the United States except the Soviet Union, there has been no important communist party in Latin America.[140]

The pope is neither left nor right in the political sense. In Argentina, Bergoglio was convinced that he had to remain above partisan divisions for pastoral reasons. This even led him to a decision not to vote, not without certain qualms of conscience as to whether he was acting against a duty of citizenship. The last time he voted was in 1960, and since then he has taken the position that he must be the father of all and must not get involved in party squabbles.[141] This did not prevent him from being very outspoken and intensely involved in Argentine politics, and now as pope he has continued to address politics, but on a global level. He has a natural affinity with the popular movements as expressions of the values of the ordinary people. He abhors "enlightened" avant-garde elites that do everything *for* the people in a centralized, homogenizing, and uniform way but never *with* the people from the periphery, and never respecting the people's diversity. No wonder Pope Francis has spoken with ardor to the Latin American grassroots movements, in which he senses "fraternity, determination, commitment, a thirst for justice."[142] He is "pleased to see the Church opening her doors to all of you, embracing you, accompanying you and establishing in each diocese, in every justice and peace commission, a genuine, ongoing and serious cooperation with popular movements." His support is for "so many farm workers without land, so many families without a home, so many laborers without rights, so many persons whose dignity is not respected." He advocates on behalf of these people for the three "L's": labor, lodging, and land.

Pope Francis does not claim to be a theologian nor an intellectual;[143] he is a pastor from Latin America with a keen sensitivity to social problems and injustice. In his writings as Pope he has rarely used the words capitalism or (neo-) liberalism or similar words. Even though he does not usually mention these terms explicitly, however, his statements on the economy have not exactly been friendly toward the concepts they represent. In order to understand his views, we must consider that words mean different things in the different historical and cultural contexts of Latin America and the Anglo-Saxon world. When he speaks about the economy, Pope Francis is not necessarily thinking about the American economic system but instead about the cultural horizon of his own experience. However, the underlying values are valid in both systems. Human dignity, liberty and equality, justice, and rule of law are aims shared by both worlds. Who would not agree that labor, lodging, and land are basic requisites for the pursuit of happiness? Opinions diverge when it comes to the question of how to achieve these aims. As I will try to show, Francis leaves us ample freedom in searching for the best path to overcome the social evils he denounces. In order to understand this, however, we need to transfer the intentions of his language into a different cultural context.

Actually, Pope Francis undertook some of this work himself during his trip to the United States, where he recognized that part of the great effort to reduce poverty "is the creation and distribution of wealth. The right use of natural resources, the proper application of technology and the harnessing of the spirit of enterprise are essential elements of an economy which seeks to be modern, inclusive and sustainable."[144] In order to escape from extreme poverty, men and women must be "dignified agents of their own destiny."[145] This language is in tune with the American cultural context, and this approach enabled him to then also address some of the social topics relevant to American society: problems related to immigration, the instability of families, the right to life, racial questions, violence, drug trafficking, and war.[146]

Despite the challenges of "translation," those of us in highly developed countries need not, in striving to be faithful to the

Pontiff's teaching, avoid economic concepts that are familiar to us but prone to misunderstanding elsewhere, particularly in Latin America. We are free to speak any way we wish. However, if we want to be understood in a Catholic sense and across the cultural divide, it seems advisable to temper certain terms, as John Paul II did in *Centesimus Annus* where he endorsed not capitalism but *good* capitalism, rejecting its corrupted form. He carefully described the system he found morally acceptable—a free economy, in which human creativity can make privately owned means of production fruitful for all in an open and inclusive market through virtuous and principled entrepreneurship—as opposed to a system of mere rent-seeking. The same effort is necessary when we speak of liberalism, free markets, individualism, competition, etc. For the sake of clarity in communication, the expressions "ordered liberalism" or "liberalism of rules" should be contrasted with forms of "exploitative liberalism" or "libertarianism"; "ethical and legal free markets" with "unfettered," "deified," or "wild" markets; "responsible" or "relational" individualism with "egoistic" or "selfish" individualism; and "unbridled competition" with "fair competition." Even though his formulations are not as intellectually fine-tuned as those of his predecessors, Pope Francis does make certain distinctions. For instance, while he denounces theories that "defend the absolute autonomy of the marketplace and financial speculation" and "the interests of a deified market, which become the only rule,"[147] he also has a positive view of the market as an economic space of exchange that can provide benefits to many people. I am not explaining away Francis's moral challenge for our Western capitalist economies; his words are not only relevant for Latin America but also deliver a powerfully prophetic message to American society, which is at present beset by many grave social problems.[148]

After describing the historical panorama of Catholic social thought in chapter 1, and analyzing the general cultural and theological contexts and sources of influence on Pope Francis in this chapter, we can now turn to our central topic: the pope's specific teachings on the economy and business.

Notes to Chapter Two

1. See Evangelina Himitian, *Francesco: Il Papa della gente* [Francis: The pope of the people] (Milano: BUR, 2013), 177–80.
2. For his time as Archbishop, see for example Sergio Rubin and Francesca Ambrogetti, *El Jesuita. La historia de Francisco, el Papa argentino* (Barcelona: Vergara, 2013), 83; also Jorge Mario Bergoglio-Papa Francesco, *Interviste e conversazioni con i giornalisti: Due anni di Pontificato* (Vatican City: Libreria Editrice Vaticana, 2015), 119, 215.
3. Cf. *Centesimus Annus*, 42.
4. John Paul II, *Discorso ai Rappresentanti del Mondo Accademico e della Cultura nell'Ateneo della Capitale*, September 9, 1993.
5. Benedict XVI, *Inaugural Address at the Fifth General Conference of the Bishops of Latin America and the Caribbean*, May 13, 2007.
6. See John L. Allen, *The Francis Miracle: Inside the Transformation of the Pope and the Church* (Des Moines: Time Books, 2015), 140.
7. Hermeneutics is the art of interpretation or the capacity to understand the meaning of things in their essential context. It is different from and more than mere explanation of the efficient causes of facts as they exist.
8. See for example R. R. Reno, "Thy Will be Done," *First Things*, August-September 2015, 6.
9. Benedict XVI quoted this passage from St. Basil in his *Christmas Address to the Roman Curia*, December 22, 2005.
10. Ibid.
11. *Gaudium et Spes*, part 1, n. 1.
12. Pope Paul VI, *Address During the Last General Meeting of the Second Vatican Council*. December 7, 1965.
13. See e.g., Francis, *Laudato Si'*, 141, 181; and his *Address to the Participants in the Fifth Convention of the Italian Church*, November 10, 2015.
14. See the interesting considerations in Mariano Delgado and Michael Sievernich, "Zur Rezeption und Interpretation des Konzils der Metaphern," in *Die großen Metaphern des Zweiten Vatikanischen Konzils: Ihre Bedeutung für heute*, ed. Mariano Delgado and Michael Sievernich (Freiburg: Herder, 2013), 15–32, particularly 29–31. See also Clemens Sedmak, *A Church of the Poor: Pope Francis and the Transformation of Orthodoxy* (Maryknoll: Orbis Books, 2016), 161. Sedmak correctly reads Francis as having changed "epistemic practices," that is, methods of finding truth.
15. Francis, *Laudato Si'*, 110, 201.

16. Francis, *Evangelii Gaudium*, 201: "I fear that these words too may give rise to commentary or discussion with no real practical effect. That being said, I trust in the openness and readiness of all Christians, and I ask you to seek, as a community, creative ways of accepting this renewed call."

17. Austen Ivereigh, *The Great Reformer*, 383.

18. Francis, *Carta a Los Participantes en la 105 Asamblea Plenaria de la Conferencia Episcopal Argentina*, March 25, 2013.

19. Francis, *Evangelii Gaudium*, 53.

20. Ivereigh, *The Great Reformer*, 213. I have put the sentence into the present tense. Ivereigh is writing about his reactions to *Evangelii Gaudium*.

21. Ibid., 214.

22. John Paul II, *Christifideles Laici*, 59.

23. See Mariano Fazio, *El Papa Francisco: Claves de su pensamiento* (Madrid: Rialp, 2013), 58–60. The quotation from John Paul II is from *Christifideles Laici*, 59.

24. Francis, *Evangelii Gaudium*, 69.

25. Bergoglio-Papa Francesco, *Interviste e conversazioni*, 179 quotes Francis from an interview published in *Il Messagero*, June 29, 2014: "As regards my style I have not changed from how I was in Buenos Aires" (my translation).

26. Francis, *Press Conference During the Return Flight from Rio de Janeiro*, July 28, 2013.

27. Himitian, *Francesco*, 47–49.

28. See Gianni La Bella, introduction to *Pedro Arrupe: Un uomo per gli altri* [Pedro Arrupe: A man for others], ed. Gianni La Bella (Bologna: Il Mulino, 2007), 7–48, especially 9, 15–19.

29. Himitian, *Francesco*, 58–60; Gianni La Bella, introduction to *Pedro Arrupe*, 7–48.

30. See La Bella, introduction to *Pedro Arrupe*, 13–23.

31. See ibid., 24–26.

32. On the new expression of the mission of the Society of Jesus as presented in the Fourth Decree, see Urbano Valero, *El proyecto de renovación de la Compañía de Jesús (1965–2007)* [The project of the renewal of the Society of Jesus (1965–2007)] (Bilbao: Mensajero – Sal Terrae, 2011), 175–88.

33. See e.g., *Evangelii Gaudium*, 48: "We have to state, without mincing words, that there is an inseparable bond between our faith and the poor. May we never abandon them."

34. *Decree 4 of the 32nd General Congregation of the Society of Jesus, December 2–March 7, 1975*, in *Documents of the 31st and 32nd General Congregations of the Society of Jesus*, ed. John Padberg, S.J. (St. Louis: Institute of Jesuit Sources, 1997). http://onlineministries.creighton.edu/CollaborativeMinistry/our-mission-today.html.

35. Ibid. One of Francis's favorite rallying cries is: "No to the new idolatry of money!" See e.g., *Evangelii Gaudium*, 55.

36. Gibbons unwaveringly defended the rights of workers against exploitation and inhuman working conditions, and supported their petitions for just

wages, insurance, and a reduction of daily working hours. At the same time he opposed attempts to nationalize industries like the railroads and the telegraph companies. He felt that public ownership of such companies would concentrate too much power in the hands of the government, and thus undermine the constitutional system of checks and balances. See e.g., John Tracy Ellis, *The Life of James Cardinal Gibbons, Archbishop of Baltimore, 1834–1921* (Westminster: Christian Classics, 1987), 486–546.

37. This was the subject of an important theological debate between Karl Rahner, who postulated the identity of charity and love of God, and Hans Urs von Balthasar, who upheld the priority of the categorical acts of love of God. See Karl Rahner, "Über die Einheit von Nächsten- und Gottesliebe," in *Sämtliche Werke*, vol. 12, ed. Johann Friedrich Herbart (Freiburg: Herder, 2005), 76–91; Hans Urs Von Balthasar, *The Moment of Christian Witness*. San Francisco: Ignatius Press, 1969. Reprint 1994.

38. See Paul VI, Apostolic Exhortation *Evangelii Nuntiandi* (December 8, 1975), 25–38, especially 28, 35.

39. Among other things, the Holy See reminded the Jesuits that their task as a religious and not a secular institute was to counsel and advise, not to replace the laity in the promotion of justice. It is the duty of the lay faithful to be active in politics and the shaping of society. Even though sometimes too passionate and even biased, for a critical appraisal of the Society of Jesus and Fr. Arrupe, see Ricardo de la Cierva, *Jesuitas, Iglesia y Marxismo 1965–1985: La teología de la liberación desenmascarada* [Jesuits, Church, and Marxism 1965–1985: Liberation theology unmasked] (Madrid: Plaza & Janes, 1986), 419–94. A more balanced view is given by Valero, *El proyecto*. The Holy See's reaction to the Fourth Decree of the 32nd General Congregation can be found in *El Proyecto* at 461–62.

40. See Himitian, *Francesco*, 57–79.

41. Joseph Ratzinger, *Principles of Catholic Theology: Building Stones for a Fundamental Theology* (San Francisco: Ignatius Press, 1987), 383.

42. Ibid., 384.

43. Ibid., 385. Ratzinger calls *Gaudium et Spes* a "countersyllabus," alluding to the list of condemnations of modern errors published by Pius IX in 1864 called the "syllabus," which *Gaudium et Spes* derogates.

44. Gustavo Gutiérrez, *Teología de la Liberación* (Salamanca: Ediciones Sígueme, 2009). This is the eighteenth Spanish edition (first edition 1971). An important preface was added to the fourteenth Spanish edition (1990). Throughout this chapter I quote from the books in their original language; the translations into English are mine where the books are not quoted with an English title.

45. See ibid., 17.

46. See ibid., 37.

47. Leonardo Boff and Clodovis Boff, *Introducing Liberation Theology* (Maryknoll, N.Y.: Orbis Books, 2015) (28th printing, originally published 1986), 5.

48. Ibid., 22.

49. See Gutiérrez, *Teología*, 32.
50. See Jon Sobrino, *Jesucristo liberador: Lectura histórico-teológica de Jesús de Nazaret* (Madrid: Trotta, 1991), 35.
51. See Gutiérrez, *Teología*, 245.
52. See Sobrino, *Jesucristo liberador,* 46–47; Gutiérrez, *Teología,* 126.
53. For a very useful introduction to hermeneutics in philosophy, the humanities, theology, law, and science, see Jens Zimmermann, *Hermeneutics: A Very Short Introduction* (Oxford: Oxford University Press, 2015). The quoted passage is on p. 69. This approach overcomes the separation of concepts into facts and values characteristic of a scientistic stance.
54. See John XXIII, Encyclical *Mater et Magistra* (May 15, 1961), 236.
55. See Boff and Boff, *Introducing Liberation Theology*, 24–28.
56. This is a Latin American theory based on Marxism that blames the lack of development of poor nations on their dependence on powerful nations, which in turn work to maintain their position of dominance over the poor countries and to reduce the "periphery" to suppliers of raw materials.
57. See Gustavo Gutiérrez and Gerhard Ludwig Müller, *Dalla parte dei poveri: Teologia della liberazione, teologia della chiesa* (Padova: Messaggero di Sant'Antonio; Bologna: EMI, 2013), 88, 102–03; Boff and Boff, *Introducing Liberation Theology,* 16–17. Of course, the terms "capitalism" and "socialism" are highly ambiguous in their details. Most liberation theologians nowadays opt for a form of the social market economy. However, they have not removed their explicit support for Marxist analysis from their books even in the most recent editions.
58. Boff and Boff, *Introducing Liberation Theology,* 32–39; Gutiérrez and Müller, *Dalla parte*, 94–97.
59. See Gutiérrez, *Teología*, 194–203. For a critique see José Luis Illanes, "Teología de la liberación: Análisis de su método," [Liberation theology: an analysis of its method] *Scripta Theologica* 17, no. 3 (1985): 743–88, especially 760–82.
60. Boff and Boff, *Introducing Liberation Theology*, 39.
61. See Gutiérrez and Müller, *Dalla parte*, 101; Gutiérrez, *Teología*, 70–72.
62. Gutiérrez, *Teología*, 87.
63. Ibid., 99.
64. Take for instance Boff and Boff in *Introducing Liberation Theology*. Nowhere in the book is there a clear, explicit rejection of violence. To the contrary, there are passages where the use of "physical force" against oppression is justified as a necessary last resort (40), others in which the use of violence is reported neutrally as a matter of fact, and in which parishioners are legitimized in their choice to engage in violence because of the encouragement of their pastors, see 14, 27, 40, 67.
65. See e.g., Gutiérrez, *Teología*, 122.
66. See Sobrino, *Jesucristo*, 52–56. This statement (and others) by Sobrino have been criticized by the Congregation for the Doctrine of the Faith on the grounds that he uses an incorrect methodology. Congregation for

the Doctrine of the Faith, *Notification on the Works of Father Jon Sobrino, SJ*, November 26, 2006; Congregation for the Doctrine of the Faith, *Explanatory Note on the Notification on the Works of Father Jon Sobrino, SJ*, November 26, 2006. The only correct epistemological setting for any theological interpretation is the ecclesial faith. The Church in its entirety, that is, the lay faithful together with the hierarchy who exercise the charism of the Magisterium, is the "pillar and foundation of truth" (1 Tim 3:15).

67. Boff and Boff, *Introducing Liberation Theology*, 94–95.

68. Helen Rhee, *Loving the Poor, Saving the Rich: Wealth, Poverty, and Early Christian Formation* (Grand Rapids: Baker Academic, 2012), 217.

69. I have published an expanded version of the next few pages in the chapter "The Preferential Option for the Poor," in *The Development of Catholic Social Teaching*, ed. Gerard Bradley and Christian Brugger (Notre Dame: Notre Dame University Press, forthcoming).

70. Published in 1984 by the Congregation for the Doctrine of the Faith under the English title *Instruction on Certain Aspects of the "Theology of Liberation,"* August 6, 1984.

71. Ibid., XI. 2 and 5.

72. See the *Relatio finalis* of the Extraordinary Synod of Bishops, December 8, 1985, http://romana.org/art/1_2.6_1.

73. See Congregation for the Doctrine of the Faith, *Libertatis Conscientia: Instruction on Christian Freedom and Liberation*, March 22, 1986, 68.

74. John Paul II, Encyclical Letter *Sollicitudo Rei Socialis* (December 30, 1987), 42; John Paul II, *Centesimus Annus*, 11. He also used a similar expression in documents whose main topic that was not directly social in nature; for example, the Encyclical Letter *Redemptoris Mater* (March 25, 1987), 37; the Apostolic Exhortation *Ecclesia in America* (January 22, 1999), 18, 58; the Apostolic Letter *Tertio Millennio Adveniente* (November 10, 1994), 51; the Apostolic Letter *Novo Millennio Ineunte* (January 6, 2001), 49–50 ; and the Apostolic Exhortation *Vita Consecrata* (March 25, 1996), 82, 90.

75. See Rohan M. Curnow, "Which Preferential Option for the Poor? A History of the Doctrine's Bifurcation," *Modern Theology* 31, no. 1 (2015): 27–59, 44. See also Dennis P. McCann, "Option for the Poor: Rethinking a Catholic Tradition," in *The Preferential Option for the Poor*, ed. Richard John Neuhaus (Grand Rapids: Eerdmans, 1988), 35–52.

76. Gustavo Gutiérrez does not make these distinctions, but simply affirms that the popes have accepted the preferential option for the poor, see Gutiérrez, *Teología*, 28–29.

77. CSDC, 182. There is another mention of the preferential option of the poor at 449.

78. See John Paul II, *Novo Millenio Ineunte*, 49–50.

79. See Benedict XVI, *Message for the World Day of Peace 2009*, December 8, 2008, 15; *Homily for the Celebration of First Vespers of the First Sunday of Advent for Unborn Life*, November 27, 2010; Apostolic Exhortation *Africae Munus* (November 19, 2011), 26–27.

80. See Juan Carlos Scannone, *Quando il popolo diventa teologo: Protagonisti e percorsi della teología del pueblo* (Bologna: EMI, 2016), 45. Scannone is careful to note that Bergoglio is not a "theologian" of the people but in his pastoral work he has been inspired by the theology of the people, in particular by the preferential option for the poor, see 47, 54.

81. See Alberto Methol Ferré and Alver Metalli, *Il Papa e il Filosofo* [The Pope and the philosopher] (Siena: Cantagalli, 2014).

82. See Scannone, *Quando il popolo*, 26–27.

83. I am aware of the fact that one of its founders considers the theology of the people to be part of the movement of liberation theology, see Scannone, *Quando il popolo*, 5.

84. See Juan Carlos Scannone, *Teologia de la Liberación y Doctrina Social de la Iglesia* [Liberation theology and the social doctrine of the Church] (Buenos Aires: Guadalupe-Cristiandad, 1987), 61.

85. See Austen Ivereigh, *The Great Reformer*, 116.

86. Lucio Gera, "Pueblo, religión del pueblo e iglesia," in *Escritos Teológico-Pastorales de Lucio Gera*, vol. 1, *Del Preconcilio a la Conferencia de Puebla (1956–1981)*, ed. Virginia Raquel Azcuy, Carlos M. Galli, and Marcelo González (Buenos Aires: Agape Libros – Facultad de Teología UCA, 2006), 717–44, 731.

87. See Scannone, *Teologia*, 61–66; Lucio Gera, "Cultura y dependencia a luz de la reflexión teológica," in *Escritos Teológico-Pastorales*, 605–59; Gera, "Pueblo," 729.

88. "The Marxist ideology is wrong. However, during my life I have known many Marxists who were good persons, that is why I don't feel offended" (for being called a Marxist), in Bergoglio-Papa Francesco, *Interviste e conversazioni*, 119 (my translation).

89. See Scannone, *Teología*, 55.

90. See the chapter, "Pobreza de la Iglesia," nn. 9–15, in Consejo Episcopal latinoamericano, *II Conferencia General del Episcopado Latinoamericano: Documentos finales de Medellín*, 1968, http://www.celam.org/doc_conferencias/Documento_Conclusivo_Medellin.pdf. See also Gutiérrez, *Teología*, 28.

91. See Chapter I, "Opción preferencial por los pobres," nn. 1134–65, in Consejo Episcopal latinoamericano, "La evangelización en el presente y en el futuro del América Latina," in *Documento de Puebla: III Conferencia General del Episcopado Latinoamericano*, 1979, http://www.celam.org/doc_conferencias/Documento_Conclusivo_Puebla.pdf.

92. Ibid., n. 1134.

93. Ibid., n. 1137–38.

94. See Consejo Episcopal latinoamericano, *Documento de Santo Domingo: IV Conferencia General del Episcopado Latinoamericano*, 1992, http://www.celam.org/doc_conferencias/Documento_Conclusivo_Santo_Domingo.pdf.

95. See Consejo Episcopal latinoamericano, *Document of Aparecida: V General Conference of the Latin American Episcopate*, 2007, nn. 391–98, http://www.celam.org/aparecida/Ingles.pdf.

96. Ibid., n. 391.

97. Ibid., n. 396.

98. Ibid., n. 395.

99. See *Evangelii Gaudium*, 52–75; *Laudato Si'*, 17–59.

100. Francis, *Evangelii Gaudium*, 184: "Furthermore, neither the Pope nor the Church have a monopoly on the interpretation of social realities or the proposal of solutions to contemporary problems." See also *Laudato Si'*, 60–61.

101. Francis, *Address at the Conferral of the Charlemagne Prize*, May 6, 2016.

102. In Spanish the acronym for this UN commission is CEPAL. Its publications can be found on its website, Economic Commission for Latin America and the Caribbean, "Publications," http://www.cepal.org/en/publications.

103. Dennis C. Mueller, "The Good, the Bad, and the Ugly," 1–14, 3.

104. Anatole Kaletsky, *Capitalism 4.0: The Birth of a New Economy* (London: Bloomsbury, 2011), 2–3.

105. Adam Smith, *An Inquiry into the Nature and Causes of the Wealth of Nations*, vol. 1, ed. R.H. Campbell and A.S. Skinner (Indianapolis: Liberty Fund, 1979), II, iii, 1–16, p. 337.

106. Cf. Luigi Zingales, *A Capitalism for the People: Recapturing the Lost Genius of American Prosperity* (New York: Basic Books, 2012), 2; Rodney Stark, *The Victory of Reason: How Christianity Led to Freedom, Capitalism, and Western Success* (New York: Random House, 2005), 56; Michael Novak, *The Spirit of Democratic Capitalism* (New York: Touchstone, 1982).

107. Cf. Gutiérrez and Müller, *Dalla parte*, 35.

108. Cf. Pius XI, Encyclical Letter *Quadragesimo Anno* (May 15, 1931), 134.

109. Ibid., 133.

110. See especially Heinrich Pesch, *Liberalismus, Sozialismus und christliche Gesellschaftsordnung*, vol. 2 of *Die sociale Frage beleuchtet durch die "Stimmen aus Maria-Laach"* (Freiburg: Herder, 1899).

111. Reinhard Marx, *Das Kapital: Ein Plädoyer für den Menschen* (München: Pattloch, 2008), 81. The translation is mine.

112. Ibid., 82–83.

113. Joseph Ratzinger, "Market Economy and Ethics," in *Church and Economy in Dialogue: A Symposium in Rome*, ed. Lothar Roos (Cologne: Bachem, 1986), 13–16, 13.

114. Francis, *Address to Participants in the Meeting "Economy of Communion," sponsored by the Focolare Movement*, February 4, 2017.

115. Ibid.

116. Larry Siedentop, *Inventing the Individual: The Origins of Western Liberalism* (London: Penguin Books, 2015), 332.

117. Ibid., 363.

118. See for instance Friedrich August von Hayek's analysis of the origins of the rule of law, one of the mainstays of liberalism, Friedrich August Hayek, *The Constitution of Liberty: The Definitive Edition, The Collected Works of F.A. Hayek* 17, ed. Ronald Hamowy (Chicago: The University of Chicago Press, 2011), 232–60.

119. See Benedict XVI, *Christmas Address*, 2005.

120. This is what Methol Ferré and Metalli affirm convincingly in *Il Papa*, 76.

121. See Daron Acemoglu and James A. Robinson, *Why Nations Fail: The Origins of Power, Prosperity, and Poverty* (New York: Crown Business, 2012), 348.

122. Ivereigh, *The Great Reformer*, 21.

123. Ibid.

124. See ibid., 21–30.

125. Ibid., 238. The book by Bergoglio, which Ivereigh is quoting here, is Grupo de reflexión 'Centesimus Annus,' *Diálogos entre Juan Pablo II y Fidel Castro* [Dialogues between John Paul II and Fidel Castro] (Buenos Aires: Editorial de la Ciencia y Cultura, 1998). According to Ivereigh, *The Great Reformer*, endnote 18 on page 400, Jorge Mario Bergoglio is described on the cover as the coordinator of the Grupo de reflexión.

126. Ivereigh, *The Great Reformer*, 268–73

127. See Francisco Ivern, "L'analisi marxista," in *Pedro Arrupe*, 797–807, particularly 802–06.

128. See Acemoglu and Robinson, *Why Nations Fail*, 7–36.

129. Ibid., 76.

130. Ibid., 76–82.

131. John Paul II, *Centesimus Annus*, 34.

132. Acemoglu and Robinson, *Why Nations Fail*, 323.

133. Methol Ferré and Metalli reflect this conviction, cf. *Il Papa*, 128.

134. See John Gerard Ruggie, *Just Business: Multinational Corporations and Human Rights* (New York: W.W. Norton, 2013), 1–36 for some of the facts.

135. See Ivereigh, *The Great Reformer*, 218–67.

136. See Francis, *Evangelii Gaudium*, 53.

137. Ibid., 54.

138. Ibid., 56.

139. Ibid., 60.

140. See Methol Ferré and Metalli, *Il Papa*, 45–51.

141. See Himitian, *Francesco*, 80.

142. All of the quotations in this paragraph come from Francis, *Address at the Second World Meeting of Popular Movements*, July 9, 2015.

143. Cf. Francis, *In-Flight Press Conference from Korea to Rome*, August 18, 2014, where he said "I am no theologian."

144. Francis, *Address to the Joint Session of the United States Congress*, September 24, 2015.

145. Francis, *Address to the Members of the General Assembly of the United Nations Organization*, September 25, 2015.

146. For instance: "The innocent victim of abortion, children who die of hunger or from bombings, immigrants who drown in the search for a better tomorrow, the elderly or the sick who are considered a burden, the victims of terrorism, wars, violence and drug trafficking, the environment devastated by man's predatory relationship with nature – at stake in all of this is the gift of God, of which we are noble stewards but not masters." Francis, *Address to the Bishops of the United States of America*, September 23, 2015.
147. See Francis, *Evangelii Gaudium*, 56.
148. Suffice it to mention abortion and other violations of innocent life, but also the problem of poverty, often linked to race, and with it low life expectancies, child mortality, obesity, teen pregnancy, divorce, single parenthood, crime, and high incarceration rates. Drug use, school dropout rates, ecological depredations, and other issues, are also of great concern.

3

Pope Francis's Message on Business
and the Economy

WHAT IS A POPE'S TEACHING competence in economic matters? Of course the pope, any pope, does not teach economics or develop economic theories. The Church has a religious mission, not a scientific or political one. In her recent Magisterium, the Church has underscored the fact that she does not offer technical solutions but strives to attune society to the requirements of human dignity.[1] The Church reserves the right to lift her voice on particular political and economic questions "when the fundamental rights of a person or the salvation of souls require it."[2] Speaking about the social problems in Latin America, Benedict XVI formulated this conviction in his precise language:

> If the Church were to start transforming herself into a directly political subject, she would do less, not more, for the poor and for justice, because she would lose her independence and her moral authority, identifying herself with a single political path and with debatable partisan positions. The Church is the advocate of justice and of the poor, precisely because she does not identify with politicians nor with partisan interests.[3]

The Distinctiveness of Pope Francis

It is not clear that Pope Francis has been moving along the same lines with the same conviction as Benedict XVI in this regard. On the one hand, he has stated repeatedly that it is not his task to analyze or propose concrete solutions for specific social or economic problems[4] and further that "neither the Pope nor the Church have a monopoly on the interpretation of social realities or the proposal of solutions to contemporary problems."[5] Pope Francis thus leaves enough room for economics in its empirical dimension to objectively gather and analyze data. The facts are the facts, mostly very complex facts; their interpretation is another matter. In his ecological encyclical *Laudato Si'*, Francis makes it clear that a variety of such interpretations and proposals are possible. In discussing climate change and other ecological topics, he is aware that "different approaches and lines of thought have emerged regarding this situation."[6] He continues: "On many concrete questions, the Church has no reason to offer a definite opinion; she knows that honest debate must be encouraged among experts, while respecting divergent views."[7] On genetically modified organisms, for instance, he calls for "a broad, responsible scientific and social debate" that is "capable of considering all the available information and of calling things by their name."[8]

On the other hand, however, following his pastoral hermeneutics, Francis is keenly interested in the socioeconomic context of evangelization and the need to denounce blatant injustice. He therefore intentionally delves into specific questions, more than his predecessors did.

In *Evangelii Gaudium*, Pope Francis affirms that the pastors of the Church "cannot help but be concrete – without presuming to enter into details – lest the great social principles remain mere generalities which challenge no one."[9] He wants them "to draw practical conclusions" and to "have greater impact" on current controversies.[10] In an audacious formulation, he posits the right of pastors "to offer opinions on all that affects people's lives, since the task of evangelization implies and demands the integral promotion of each human being. It is no longer possible to claim that religion should be restricted to the private sphere and that it exists only to prepare souls for heaven."[11] This statement goes beyond what *Gaudium et Spes*, n. 76 ("the fundamental rights of a person or the salvation of souls"), provided for, as becomes apparent in the immediately following lines: "We know that God wants his children to be happy in this world too, even though they are called to fulfillment in eternity, for he has created all things 'for our enjoyment' (1 Tim 6:17), the enjoyment of everyone. It follows that Christian conversion demands reviewing especially those areas and aspects of life 'related to the social order and the pursuit of the common good.'"[12]

In order to avoid a clericalism that the Second Vatican Council wanted to overcome, these words should be applied to the Church in its entirety, both ministers and the ordinary faithful in the midst of the world. Pastors have the task of formulating the principles of the Church's social teaching (together with lay experts), while the laity have the task of applying them in freedom in their mission of sanctifying work in a pluralist secular sphere. The Second Vatican Council reminded the laity of their calling to holiness and of their responsibility to shape earthly affairs in light of the Gospel. The sacred ministers and the religious orders have a different mission in the Church. They counsel the laity and give them spiritual support but must not interfere in the laity's field of competence. Pope Francis does not intend to revoke these prescriptions, as becomes apparent when he quotes Paul VI: "It is up to the Christian communities to analyze with objectivity the situation which is proper to their own country."[13] He has also spoken against the clericalization of lay Christians, which in many cases is a consequence of a sinful complicity between priests and laypeople. The priest clericalizes, but the layperson asks for and accepts it in order to mimic the clergy in their protected ecclesiastical sphere. This leads to a lack of maturity among laypeople and to an absence of Christian witness in the world. Laypeople reduce their own prophetic vocation to that of a representative of the hierarchy.[14]

Starting from the Peripheries

We can see what Pope Francis has in mind by looking at his own words and actions, for instance in Bolivia. Pope Francis spoke to the recyclers of paper, old clothes, and used metal; to the small craftsman, the street vendor, the trucker; to down-trodden workers; to the native farmwife; and to the fisherman barely hanging on against the domination of large corporations. He spoke to those who live in shantytowns and hamlets, to the victims of discrimination and the marginalized. He encouraged the students, the young activists, and the "missionaries who come to a neighborhood with their hearts full of hopes and dreams, but without any real solution for their problems,"[15] and called on them to change a global economic system that "has imposed the mentality of profit at any price, with no concern for social exclusion or the destruction of nature."[16] He wants "change, real change, structural change."[17]

Even though he has met people who work in business, Pope Francis does not expect this radical cultural change to originate at the center, that is, starting from the businesspeople, economic leaders, and the rich, but from the "periphery," from the people. This is very much in the spirit of the "theology of the people." Besides, Jorge Mario Bergoglio, since his youth, has had to work very hard to make a living. The culture of work has shaped his character profoundly, and he shares the "American dream" of immigrants who, like his ancestors, left Europe in order to work their way up. He therefore naturally considers work to be at the core of the social teaching of the Church. One would misinterpret his strong words against a business that only seeks profit if one were to conclude that they necessarily mean he is in favor of big government. Government, says Bergoglio, should foster a culture of work, not of necessarily temporary social assistance. He consequently criticizes policies that only reduce working hours or only increase social entitlements. The first right step is to create sources of work (*"fuentes de trabajo"*). "The key to the social question is work. The working man is at the center."[18] Just handing out government aid would be as debasing as excluding the poor through market mechanisms resulting from what Francis call the "idolatry of money." Francis demands bread and work for everybody: "Moreover there is no worse material poverty, I am keen to stress, than the poverty which prevents people from earning their bread and deprives them of the dignity of work."[19] As archbishop, every year on August 7, the feast day of St. Cayetan, patron saint of work, he celebrated Mass in the saint's shrine in Buenos Aires. St. Cayetan is very popular in Argentina, with millions of faithful seeking his intercession so that they can find bread and work.

Business is a Noble Vocation When it Serves the Common Good

Certainly, the decisive question, which the pope does not attempt to answer, is how to effectively achieve the creation of work and foster the creation of wealth and prosperity for all. As a priest and member of a religious order, Francis has the advantage of being able to observe—and to criticize—social and economic developments with great objectivity (some might say from a detached vantage point). One sometimes gets the impression that he is speaking from the outside to a system in which he does not participate, whose logic and laws he does not fully understand or even like. He himself is quite outspoken about this: "I am considerably allergic to all things economic, because my father was an accountant and when he couldn't finish his work at the factory, he brought the work home, on Saturday and Sunday; old books with gothic titles. My father worked... and I would just watch him.... I am quite allergic."[20]

Nevertheless, Pope Francis is not anti-business, as he has made explicit on several occasions, for instance in his ecological encyclical: "Business is a noble vocation, directed to producing wealth and improving our world. It can be a fruitful source of prosperity for the areas in which it operates, especially if it sees the creation of jobs as an essential part of its service to the common good."[21] What he has in mind as a positive role model is the entrepreneur who serves others and the community in which he or she lives. He actually considers this to be a path to holiness:

> I have known rich people, and here [in Rome] I am promoting the cause of beatification of a rich Argentine businessman, Enrique Shaw, who was rich but holy. Somebody can have money; God has given it to him so that he manages it well. And this man administered it well, not in a patronizing way but in a way which made those grow who were in need of this support. What I always attack is the feeling of security in wealth: don't place your assurance on money.[22]

Pope Francis is against rent-seeking forms of wealth creation, and in favor of principled business and entrepreneurship.[23] He said so explicitly talking to workers, entrepreneurs, managers, and also unemployed people in a factory in Genoa:

> "The entrepreneur is a fundamental figure in any good economy: there is no good economy without good entrepreneurs…, without your creativity, without your creation of work and of products…. True entrepreneurs know their workers because they work side to side with them. Let us not forget that an entrepreneur is first of all a worker. If he or she has no experience of the dignity of work, he cannot be a good entrepreneur. He shares the fatigue of the workers and also their joy at solving problems together, of creating something together. And when he has to fire someone it is always a painful decision which he would avoid if he could…. An illness of

business is the progressive transformation of entrepreneurs into speculators. An entrepreneur must absolutely not be confused with a speculator: they are two different types of person….: the speculator is a figure similar to what Jesus calls "mercenary" in the Gospel and opposes him to the Good Shepherd. The speculator does not love his firm, does not love the workers, but considers firm and workers as mere means to make profit. When the economy is made up of good entrepreneurs, businesses are friends of the people and also of the poor. When it falls into the hands of the speculators, all is ruined. With the speculators, the economy loses its face and it loses faces. It is an economy without a face…. Do not be afraid of entrepreneurs because there are so many good ones! No! Fear the speculators. However, paradoxically sometimes the political system seems to encourage the speculators of work and not those who invest and believe in work…, because it creates bureaucracy and controls on the basis of the hypothesis that all economic agents are speculators…."[24]

The pope appreciates business people because of the good they do. Therefore the impression one sometimes gets that the pope is not interested in business or considers it to be secondary is only true in the sense that his pastoral strategy starts with the existential peripheries. It was and is his conviction that in order to evangelize all, including the rich, you have to start with the poor. This attitude also characterized his ministry in Buenos Aires, where Bergoglio "showed no interest at all in the middle-class world of Catholics – not the world of business, or banking, or the arts or university."[25] As pope he has made clear where his preferences lie—visiting asylums for the homeless and giving priority to the suffering and poor—but he has also shown interest in businesspeople and questions of finance.

Looking at the Moral Message Behind Francis's Economic Views

When Pope Francis speaks or writes on economic topics one is not always sure whether, from a strictly economic point of view, his statements are adequately backed up by empirical data. Nevertheless, the moral message is quite clear to see. In what follows I try to show that the possible flaws in his economic theory do not obscure the moral message that is primarily intended. I am not an economist, so I am cautious in my economic judgments, leaving them to people more specialized than myself. My point in the following pages is the pope's moral message.

In his encyclical *Laudato Si'*, for instance, Francis affirms a "vocation to work" and repeats one of his favorite ideas: that assistance to the poor can only be "a provisional solution."[26] He states that "the broader objective should always be to allow them a dignified life through work."[27] The pope blames technological progress for replacing humans with machines, but there is a debate about whether this is really the case. Is there really enough empirical proof that technology replaces labor? Hasn't technological progress produced more jobs over time than it has eliminated through the process of "creative destruction"?[28] It is not the pope's competence (nor mine) to answer such questions, and the following sentence, which is taken from the paragraph of *Laudato Si'* quoted above, makes clear that the pope is arguing from a moral, not an economic perspective: "To stop investing in people, in order to gain greater short-term financial gain, is bad business for society."[29] This is the moral value Pope Francis aims at: social concern in business decisions.[30]

Other passages are unclear in an economic and political sense: "To ensure economic freedom from which all can effectively benefit, restraints occasionally have to be imposed on those possessing greater resources and financial power."[31] It would be more correct to say that such restraint should always be placed on the powerful, not only occasionally.

Furthermore, this restraint should be exercised by *general* laws, those, for instance, establishing antitrust regulations, rules of fair competition, and the imposition of taxes, in a fair and equitable way for all without singling out individuals. Otherwise, government intervention can easily become arbitrary and abusive.

The notion that "small is beautiful" seems to underlie what the pope writes, for example when he argues against "economies of scale" in order to favor "productive diversity and business creativity."[32] Economies of scale, however, usually favor the consumer because they lower prices, and are not necessarily opposed to diversity and creativity, which flourish in a regime of freedom that allows adaptation to changing needs and circumstances. Small- and medium-sized enterprises are very important, especially in developing economies, and they should be encouraged and facilitated by public measures.[33] However, there are some business ventures that require the pooling of capital, strong leadership, and disciplined cooperation that can only be provided by a large corporation. There can be little doubt that Pope Francis appreciates the need for big, organized corporations—none of the airplanes he uses for his trips could have been built without them. What he opposes is financial capitalism when it becomes detached from real production and industry.

As regards the relationship between business and politics, Pope Francis states that "politics must not be subject to the economy, nor should the economy be subject to the dictates of an efficiency-driven paradigm of technocracy."[34] This is true; however, this does not mean that politicians should interfere with economic mechanisms or replace the markets. Arguably many of the problems the pope criticizes (e.g., unemployment and financial crises) have been produced more or less unintentionally by government interference. Actually the pope says in the next line: politics and economics must enter into "a frank dialogue."[35] Francis denounces bailouts of banks with tax money and in general criticizes the present financial system.

In economic terms, one can rightly criticize the exponential expansion of the monetary and credit sector. However, immediately afterwards, the economist is challenged by the following sentence: "Production is not always rational, and is usually tied to economic variables which assign to products a value that does not necessarily correspond to their real worth,"[36] and "this frequently leads to an overproduction of some commodities, with unnecessary impact on the environment and with negative results on regional economies."[37]

It is true: overproduction or the lack of effective demand can occur. Artificial demand or "bubbles" are frequently the consequences of the greed of financiers, mortgage brokers, builders, real estate agents, and consumers. As human beings, our foresight, willpower, and information are limited, and the economic power of a given person may be unequal to others. Thus the perfect equilibrium of the free market suggested by the economic models is difficult to encounter in reality. However, often overproduction has occurred because of the unintended effects of government intervention, either because demand is created artificially and not sustainably, or because of government subsidies. Thus, the market is distorted. Moreover, the notion of "real worth" seems to allude to the existence of an objective value of goods that opens the vast debate on how to define it. Francis does not think about market transactions in a scientific way, but rather uses common sense. Is it just that the latest singing sensation should make so much money? That a music CD should sell for $18 when it cost a few cents to make? Economists talk about marginal benefit and the rationality of the market and the individual as determiner of economic value (well, it's worth $18 to me!). The down-to-earth person, and to these Francis is speaking, says, "Those are just theories, not worth the air you are taking up to expound them. It's just not worth that much, and the fact that you are willing to spend that on what could feed a whole family for a week shows that the market is very good at tricking you." The pope's *moral* message is quite clear: the economy should serve the common good, produce goods that are really good, and offer services that truly serve the human person.

The pope opposes the domination of financial capitalism and favors work, thrift, and entrepreneurship. He expresses this in another passage: "Once more, we need to reject a magical conception of the market, which would suggest that problems can be solved simply by an increase in the profits of companies or individuals."[38] In reality, free markets limit profits through competition, as Adam Smith showed long ago. Competition in free markets lowers prices for consumers, cutting company revenues and interest rates on capital. However, the pope is not attacking competition, but rather the belief that increasing profits is a panacea. This becomes apparent in the following line of *Laudato Si'*: those who are "obsessed with maximizing profits"[39] are unlikely to take other values into consideration. Of course, competition only exists when businesspeople pursue profit, and that is good. Being "obsessed with maximizing profits," however, means something negative. The obsession with profit maximization can be the cause of the elimination of competition through the creation of monopolies, trusts, and cartels. Adam Smith had no delusions:

> To widen the market and to narrow the competition, is always in the interest of the dealers. To widen the market may frequently be agreeable enough to the interest of the public; but to narrow the competition must always be against it, and can serve only to enable the dealers, by raising their profits above what they naturally would be, to levy, for their own benefit, an absurd tax upon the rest of their fellow-citizens. The proposal of any new law or regulation of commerce which comes from this order, ought always to be listened to with great precaution, and ought never to be adopted till after having been long and carefully examined, not only with the most scrupulous, but with the most suspicious attention. It comes from an order of men, whose interest is never exactly the same

with that of the public, who have generally an interest
to deceive and even to oppress the public, and who
accordingly have, upon many occasions, both deceived
and oppressed it.[40]

Ivereigh gives a practical example from the pope's life that
illustrates his words. There was a public tragedy in Buenos
Aires in 2005: a club burned down killing nearly 200 young
people. Afterwards it was discovered that the safety exits had
been chained and padlocked to prevent people from coming
in without paying, and that the number of people allowed in
exceeded capacity. There had been a web of corruption among
the police and high magistrates to cover up abuses in the club.
An obsession with maximizing profit, with gain, had been put
before people's safety.[41]

The consequence the pope draws from the obsession for
maximizing profit, however, is problematic from an economic
point of view: "That is why the time has come to accept de-
creased growth in some parts of the world, in order to provide
resources for other places to experience healthy growth."[42] This
may imply that the world economy is a zero-sum game, which
is incorrect: economic growth in one nation does not mean a
decrease in others. That was precisely the error of the mercan-
tilist doctrine. Obviously, the pope is not trying to resuscitate
mercantilism, nor is he blind to the deficiencies of centralized state planning.[43] He is arguing against wasting money
and resources on overproduction and overconsumption, for
a "sustainable use of natural resources," and for progress and
development with economic benefits in the medium term.[44]
These are valid moral aims.

The combination of an economically debatable yet morally
strong affirmation can also be found in the pope's criticism
of those who say: "Let us allow the invisible forces of the
market to regulate the economy, and consider their impact on
society and nature as collateral damage."[45] This is an obvious
allusion to Adam Smith's invisible hand. Smith's seminal book

on economic theory, *The Wealth of Nations*, has often been oversimplified and reduced to a set of slogans.[46] One of these oversimplifications is that Smith was a libertarian who taught that the market should be left to itself in a naïve belief that it would self-regulate by some mechanism called the "invisible hand." In reality, Smith was certainly not a libertarian—he posited a political and economic system characterized by natural liberty together with limited government, operating in the context of certain societal and political institutions, the rule of law, and individual virtue, all working together to create social harmony and balance, resulting in benefits for everyone.[47] Like Smith, Pope Francis advocates for an economy firmly limited by a strong ethical, legal, and cultural framework.

The pope is not trying to develop a rigorous economic theory. His words are more about practice than teaching and theory. He is a prophet raising his voice against injustice, exclusion, and unsustainable forms of economic organization, and in so doing he is upholding certain values. This becomes apparent when he makes the moral argument for a sustainable form of development at the service of the common good,[48] and against short-term thinking,[49] and when he warns against externalities,[50] making it clear that a "variety of proposals" are possible for implementing his vision. Francis wants a different cultural paradigm, a "bold cultural revolution,"[51] a "new lifestyle,"[52] that places the human person, including the poor, at the center, and sees material means as a mere instrument; this requires overcoming what the pope calls the "technocratic paradigm" that would exclude ethical considerations from the conduct of business and from the development of technological progress.[53] He makes an appeal for integral development[54] and a new kind of progress, "healthier, more human, more social, more integral."[55] In this sense, following Romano Guardini (whom he also quotes), the whole third chapter of *Laudato Si'* is a critique of power.[56] The renewal Francis wishes to inaugurate is based on Christian humanism: "We urgently need a humanism capable of bringing together the different fields of knowledge, including economics, in the service of a more integral and integrating vision."[57] Christian humanism is "a genuine and profound humanism to serve as the basis of a noble and generous society."[58]

These and other passages underscore the fact that Francis's message on the economy is moral and evangelical. He is a "Gospel radical" who when asked about specific economic situations and problems quickly employs the category of sin.[59] Asked whether the Argentine situation of exploding poverty was a question of flawed economic policies, Archbishop Bergoglio answered: "I would say that, deep down, it is a problem of sin."[60] Similarly, when asked in an interview about whether the capitalist system was irreversible in history, Francis said that he didn't really know how to answer the question. He did, however, reject the "idolatry" of money and deplore the throwaway culture of the opulent Western societies. His vision is moral: "Let us strive to build a society and an economy in which the human person and his good, not money, are at the center."[61]

Francis does not assign this task only to government, much less to bloated bureaucracies. He appeals to the responsibility of everybody in society: we are obliged to share food, clothing, health, and education with our sisters and brothers. Some will call me a communist priest, Archbishop Bergoglio said; however, "what I am saying is pure Gospel."[62] Jesus will judge us according to our deeds in society. Jesus "will also condemn us for the sin of blaming the government for poverty, when it is a responsibility we must all assume to the extent we can."[63]

Reading Pope Francis Positively

Some of Pope Francis's statements have been met with concern and confusion: Is the pope against capitalism? Is he criticizing the United States? Why is he considered to be a champion of the left? Is he a socialist? In this chapter I want to show what he positively stands for.

From what has been said so far, the following should have become clear: first, Pope Francis disavows any monopoly on the proper moral interpretation of social phenomena and thus leaves ample room for economists to analyze the objective empirical data; and second, the faithful are free to find their own ways to implement the aims Pope Francis is impressing on the Christian conscience. A number of these aims have already been mentioned: the common good as the overall criterion and guide for all economic activity; the need for integral human development; the necessity of a dignified life through work. Other aims that are dear to Pope Francis can be discovered by "flipping the omelet" from negative condemnation to positive recommendation. In other words, changing his "nos" into "yeses": every time the Holy Father criticizes certain practices as unacceptable and rejects them as immoral he expresses a value he wishes to protect. If he says "no" to "an economy that kills," he presupposes the value of human life, and therefore says "yes" to an economy that gives life and happiness. A "no" to an economy that excludes the poor means endorsing an economy that includes them. Condemning an economy without an ethical grounding and "creative" financial capitalism that has lost touch with the real economy is a call for businesses that put ethics at the heart of their mission and serve the real needs of their stakeholders. Condemning corruption implies healing society of this grave affliction and establishing the rule of law. In order to do something positive and worthwhile it is not sufficient to know only what is wrong, but it is necessary to single out the values it is worth struggling for. G.K. Chesterton, who was himself keenly interested in economic affairs, expressed this idea in a book with the provocative title *What's Wrong With the World*. He answered the question himself: "What is wrong is that we do not ask what is right."[64] We do not ask what things are *here for*, we are only interested in how efficient they are. In today's crises we need impractical people, thought Chesterton; we need theorists who tell us what the economy is here for because the economy is a means, and we should construct the means keeping in mind its end. These thoughts would resonate strongly with Francis. Understood in this way, the objectives the Holy Father proposes for the economy can serve to motivate us. They certainly pose a challenge to the laity in general, and particularly to those who work in business. Lofty goals can discourage if they are utopian; but they can also stimulate human genius to strive for creativity in order to overcome obstacles. The virtue of hope comes into play if the good to be achieved is a real good that is difficult but not impossible to attain.

The pope's moral message on the economy certainly requires intellectual humility. As pope he has waived his own interpretive monopoly. This should stimulate others, both on the right and the left, to do the same. There are already too many people who wish to instrumentalize the pope and Catholic teaching to support their own purposes. The pope himself has declared that he feels himself to be neither on the right nor the left.[65] More than a few Catholics and non-Catholics who praise the pope actually praise their own ideas, measuring the pope's ideas against theirs. They obey selectively, when it suits them, and on the points that fit with their personal agendas. In these cases, we are far from a humble and respectful acceptance of what the Holy Father proposes to the faithful. The same goes for those Catholics who fervently defend innocent unborn life and the family, but do not hesitate to sometimes bitterly criticize the social encyclicals. Pope Francis has something to say to all of us. He reminds the conservatives that poverty and inequality are problems, and that they require not only individual but also collective action, and the liberals that social justice is not enough—the Church is the bride of Christ, not a social institution or an NGO.

So how should we read Pope Francis's moral messages on the economy? What is his contribution to Catholic social teaching? As has already been stated, the pope understands his teachings to be firmly within the boundaries of traditional Catholic social teaching. Pope Francis has not revolutionized the social teaching of the Church; therefore, new, unheard-of content is hardly to be expected. His "strong moral messages" that I present beginning on page 127 below shock us *not* because the pope's message is somehow un-Catholic and crypto-Marxist, but because after the 1991 encyclical *Centesimus Annus* many of us thought that being Catholic meant holding a free-market ideology. This is a misinterpretation both of that encyclical itself and of John Paul II's intentions. Even though Francis refuses to write in "academic-speak" and instead prefers the outrageous metaphor and the unforgettable image, his message is quite as Catholic as anything else in the Catholic tradition, as I try to show beyond a shadow of a doubt. Francis has stressed some topics in a new and forceful way, and he has given an interesting new spin to others. In what follows, I try to point out his main interests relating to the economy and highlight what can be considered original and new. The frame for all of his social teaching is the "preferential option for the poor," firmly rooted in his "theology of the people." I therefore discuss the preferential option first, as it is the foundation and background for all that follows.

A Poor Church for the Poor: The Theology of Poverty

Pope Francis did not choose his name only out of devotion to one of the most popular saints in Christian history. His name is symbolic of a program that he is constantly explaining and unfolding in his speeches, and in a particular way in his gestures. From the first days of his pontificate, he has made it clear that he chose the name of the saint of Assisi because of his great love for poverty and the poor. In so doing, Francis was simply continuing his commitment to the poor, prominent among the "holy and faithful people of God." During his pontificate, this commitment has taken on certain characteristics and connotations on which we now reflect.

Before the millions of faithful gathered in Rome or in front of television screens at home during the simultaneous canonizations of John Paul II and John XXIII, Pope Francis praised the new saints as men who had been courageous enough to touch the wounds of Christ in the suffering of the people. He urges us to do the same:

> Jesus wants us to touch human misery, to touch the suffering flesh of others. He hopes that we will stop looking for those personal or communal niches which shelter us from the maelstrom of human misfortune and instead enter into the reality of other people's lives and know the power of tenderness. Whenever we do so, our lives become wonderfully complicated and we experience intensely what it is to be a people, to be part of a people.[66]

He explains what he means by the expression "to be part of a people." It means overcoming the fracture in our lives between our work, our calling to service, and our private lives: if "we separate our work from our private lives, everything turns grey and we will always be seeking recognition or asserting our needs. We stop being a people."[67] "To be part of a people" means recognizing God's image in each human person for whom Jesus spilled His blood on the Cross. Each person is thus worthy of my dedication: "Consequently, if I can help at least one person to have a better life, that already justifies the offering of my life. It is a wonderful thing to be God's faithful people."[68] For Pope Francis, being "part of a people" means that "clearly Jesus does not want us to be grandees who look down upon others, but men and women of the people."[69] Francis wants humble Christian witnesses to our hope, not aggressive attackers who accuse and condemn others. From these words we can take the positive exhortation to throw away the trappings of the past, to discard any futile concerns over sterile formalisms that remain external to others and do not change or warm their hearts. Francis does not want a Church caught up in self-referential introspection. However, at the same time, the pope's words must not be misunderstood as a rejection of any form of authority, of moral judgment, or of canon law. Otherwise, the Church as an institution would cease to exist. Belonging to the people also means respecting the institutional nature of the Mystical Body of Christ, with its structures, clear teachings, and rules.

Pope Francis's love for the poor is primarily *Christian* love, understood as both a theological and pastoral category. He himself has said: "Poverty for us Christians is not a sociological, philosophical or cultural category, no. It is theological. I might say this is the first category, because our God, the Son of God, abased Himself, He made Himself poor to walk along the road with us."[70] Here again we can plainly see the influence that the "theology of the people" exercises on Francis: the poor holy people of God are a source of religious experience for all, not passive receivers of our largesse. Francis is thus able to fully insert his love for the poor into the program of cultural transformation we call "the New Evangelization," in continuity with his predecessor Benedict XVI. Francis states:

> They (the poor) have much to teach us. Not only do they share in the *sensus fidei*, but in their difficulties they know the suffering Christ. We need to let ourselves be evangelized by them. The new evangelization is an invitation to acknowledge the saving power at work in their lives and to put them at the center of the Church's pilgrim way. We are called to find Christ in them, to lend our voice to their causes, but also to be their friends, to listen to them, to speak for them and to embrace the mysterious wisdom which God wishes to share with us through them.[71]

This is the reason, explains Pope Francis, why he wants a "poor Church for the poor." He does not advocate pauperism, nor does he reduce his vision to the mere remedy of social evils: the poor for Francis are teachers of what Christ wants the Church to know here and now.

In his actions and words, Francis expresses what Benedict XVI taught in his encyclicals, two of which explicitly name charity in their titles: *Deus Caritas Est* (2005) and *Caritas in Veritate* (2009). Charity is the central driving force, the most convincing argument, the aspect that draws people toward personal and cultural transformation. Charity is the heart of evangelization because only true and disinterested love is credible, only love opens minds and hearts to trust in God's and the Church's words. Christian faith by necessity turns into culture, and Christian culture begins with love for the poor. Christ Himself taught as much: "For if you love those who love you, what recompense will you have? Do not the tax collectors do the same? And if you greet your brothers only, what is unusual about that? Do not the pagans do the same?"[72] We do not need Christ in order to love the rich or to return favors. We need Christ who has loved us unto the Cross in order to love without expectation of reciprocity, in sacrifice and pain. We need Christ in order to love the poor. In Pope Francis's words:

> The Church has always been present in places *where culture is worked out. But the first step is always the priority for the poor.* Nevertheless we must also reach the frontiers of the intellect, of culture, of the loftiness of dialogue, of the dialogue that makes peace, the intellectual dialogue, the reasonable dialogue. The Gospel is for everyone! This reaching out to the poor does not mean we must become champions of poverty or, as it were, "spiritual tramps"! No, no this is not what it means! It means we must reach out to the flesh of Jesus that is suffering, but also suffering is the flesh of Jesus of those who do not know it with their study, with their intelligence, with their culture. We must go there![73]

These words can give peace of mind to people who perhaps feel overwhelmed by Francis's appeals and are not immediately involved in caring for beggars and poor people. A middle-class person who supports his or her family, trying to give them a dignified and happy life, good education and health, is busy all day with intense work and may not be able to dedicate time to other activities. He or she might easily feel confused by the pope's demands to go to the peripheries. It would certainly be contrary to God's will to neglect professional, religious, and family duties to serve the needy. However, all of us can make a personal examination of conscience about our degree of "benevolence," as the Fathers of the Church called the second social principle (after justice, the first). Benevolence means the will to act well. It presupposes the desire to do good and a big heart for the needs of others. This attitude of goodwill and social charity opens our eyes to what each of us can and should do in his or her particular circumstances. Maybe it's the "little bit more" that we can do without abandoning other duties but have put off out of laziness or tiredness.

In this context it may also be useful to recall a maxim of Catholic moral theology: "supererogatory" acts are not strictly obligatory in a moral sense. A supererogatory act is the *better* action that corresponds to every *good* action we take. Whatever good we do we could always have done something better. Instead of going to the movies with a friend, we could have given the money to the poor, or studied, or worked, or done community service with the time. A person who invites his friends to a meal could have given the amount spent on the meal to charity. The list could be extended infinitely, and if taken very seriously, the acting person ends up entangled in perplexities or burdened by scruples. What virtue requires is to *act well* according to the cardinal virtue of practical wisdom, which guides us as to what is good and reasonable, and not necessarily to the "better," supererogatory act. Of course, we are free to do this "better" act, but it is not binding in the sense of an obligation. The Holy Spirit with His gifts and inspirations indicates the moments and situations that do require a heroic action going beyond what is "reasonable" and "normal," as in the case of a call to martyrdom or other extreme self-sacrifice for others. These acts of heroism need not always result in a cruel martyrdom ending in death. They can also exist in a life of witness to moral truth through obedience to absolute moral norms and in sacrifice at the service of the poor, as was the case of St. Mother Teresa of Kolkata. These Christians are witnesses to the faith that is alive through charity. But Christians in ordinary circumstances are also called to a kind of martyrdom as a consequence of their faithfulness to Christ. Being faithful to one's vocation as a Christian means going against the tide, be it through loyalty in friendship, chastity before marriage, or struggling for peace in situations of conflict.[74] As has been shown, Pope Francis has strongly re-affirmed the Church's preferential option for the poor as a principle of Catholic social teaching. However, we can ask: What about the middle class? Why only talk about the poor? Actually, Pope Francis has admitted to having neglected the middle class in his messages.[75] These considerations on the preferential option for the poor and the role of the middle class pose the question of what poverty is and who is to be counted among the poor, which we will now address. We will see that poverty and "the poor" are much richer as theological concepts than how they are used in everyday common language.

Poverty Can Be Either Objective or Chosen

In its objective dimension, poverty is measured by external and objective criteria such as income. Of course, income is not the only criterion, and is certainly not sufficient by itself for defining human well-being, but it is easy to measure.[76] Regardless of how it is measured, objective poverty can be "relative" or "absolute." Relative objective poverty exists everywhere and at all times because there will always be some people who have more than others. Those who have less are considered to be "poor" compared to those who have more (the "rich"), although the "poor" in rich countries may be better off than the "rich" in poor countries. Nevertheless, the

sting of inequality hurts and is made worse by human insatiability. Even in societies where all have enough to eat, can
clothe themselves and their families, have a decent place to
live, receive education, etc., there will always be others who
have better food, more expensive clothing, bigger and more
comfortable homes, and higher levels of education. There is
no end to human desires; we are insatiable. And it's not bad to
aim higher in life—this desire is an engine of human progress.
The problem is our excessive desire to seek ever more things
without knowing when enough is enough. It is an error to
seek happiness in the possession of material goods.[77] In any
case, the battle against poverty should not be identified with
an attempt to remove all inequality (relative objective poverty)
because it will always be with us.[78]

Absolute objective poverty or misery, however, can and
must be abolished: it is the absence of material resources that
are necessary for a dignified human life. Pope Francis calls it
"destitution," which "is poverty without faith, without support,
without hope."[79] Of course, the measure of what we may deem
necessary for a dignified life varies and, in fact, has changed
enormously with improvements to our standard of living. The
standard of living many of us now enjoy is luxurious in comparison with the high mortality, poor hygiene, and insufficient
nutrition of past centuries. Even so, despite the relativity of
the measure of what is considered to be a decent standard of
living, there is no doubt that there exists a minimum without
which one survives only in misery: constant hunger, illness
without medical care, infant mortality, and other evils that
trap those who are affected in a situation from which they are
unable to break free. The existence of such poverty is a structure of sin that cries to heaven and demands the reaction of
human conscience. In fact, thanks to the wealth created by the
free globalized market, absolute objective poverty has fallen in
recent decades. Even though in official statistics such poverty
is mostly defined in quantitative terms (e.g., anyone who falls
below a certain amount of money per person per day), Pope

Francis uses a qualitative definition based on exclusion from the possibility of earning a living through work. Absolute objective poverty for Francis means being structurally trapped in a situation of misery and being excluded from the possibility of development, thus stripping people of the dignity of work and their ability to provide for themselves.[80] "For it is through free, creative, participatory and mutually supportive labor that human beings express and enhance the dignity of their lives."[81] Absolute poverty is a real evil and a terrible scourge for many families.

Chosen poverty is a different concept: this is a voluntary renunciation of material goods practiced by those who want to follow Christ through the virtue of poverty of spirit. By Christ's poverty we have become rich:[82] "Christ's poverty which enriches us is His taking flesh and bearing our weaknesses and sins as an expression of God's infinite mercy to us. Christ's poverty is the greatest treasure of all: Jesus's wealth is that of His boundless confidence in God the Father, His constant trust, His desire always and only to do the Father's will and give glory to Him."[83] This kind of spiritual poverty is a grace and a virtue, consisting in inner detachment from the goods one uses, in modesty and even austerity in personal material wants. Material goods are available, but the person who chooses to be poor renounces dominion over them.

As pastor, Pope Francis is concerned about both dimensions of poverty, but contrary to the general perception, I think his main interest is in chosen poverty. His strong emphasis on poverty addresses and challenges Christians primarily in wealthy countries, and therefore is a call to acquire or maintain the spirit of poverty as proclaimed by Christ in the Sermon on the Mount. It is a message that the Western world, so strongly affected by practical materialism, greatly needs. Practical materialism leads to forgetfulness of God and gives a sense of false security. It clogs the heart and makes it impermeable to God's subtle calling and grace. The pope is focusing the energies of the Church on this message. A "poor Church for the poor" is not a church devoid of all material means. If he really wanted that, Pope Francis would have to leave his humble room in the Casa Santa Marta, because it too is the property of the Church. He would have to cancel all trips because they cost a lot of money. This, however, would not be the "poor Church" he has in mind. Chosen poverty is not pauperism; it does not mean becoming "spiritual tramps," as the pope himself said.[84] A poor Church is a Church that puts all her material assets at the service of the Gospel, the liturgy, and charity for the poor. A poor Church uses material means honestly and according to canon law and good managerial practices in order to advance the Gospel and extend the kingdom of Jesus Christ in conformity with the principles of Catholic social teaching. Being a poor Church and remaining so is a constant challenge, requiring constant vigilance and adaptation to changing circumstances.

Pope Francis adds two special nuances to his call to chosen poverty: he links it with hope, and he connects objective and chosen poverty. Why do hope and chosen poverty go together? Because the spirit of poverty is an antidote to acedia, a kind of despair. In some parts of the Western world, particularly in Europe, what is lacking is the divine virtue of hope. Our civilization is in a state of collective acedia. Acedia is a sickness of the soul, a kind of boredom with the things of God, a spiritual fatigue, a paralysis in the struggle for the good because of the sacrifice involved. Acedia causes us to pursue happiness not in God and in His spiritual gifts but in sensual pleasures and the acquisition of money. Instead of drinking from the pure fountain of God's love, a person who falls into acedia begins to lick muddy water from a puddle, trying to quench his thirst for the living God by seeking His dim reflection in His Creation. Pope Francis has used incisive words to express this:

> Do not let yourselves be robbed of hope! Please, do not let yourselves be robbed of it! And who robs you of hope? The spirit of the world, wealth, the spirit of vanity, arrogance, pride. All these things steal hope from you. Where

do I find hope? In the poor Jesus, Jesus who made himself poor for us…It is impossible to talk about poverty,
about abstract poverty. That does not exist! Poverty is the
flesh of the poor Jesus in this hungry child, in the sick
person, in these unjust social structures. Go, look over
there at the flesh of Jesus. But do not let yourselves be
robbed of hope by well-being, by the spirit of well-being
which, in the end brings you to become a nothing in life!
The young must stake themselves on high ideals: this is
my advice. But where do I find hope? In the flesh of the
suffering Jesus and in true poverty. There is a connection
between the two.[85]

In this passage, Francis alludes to the connection between
chosen poverty as a personal and individual virtue and the
destitution of the needy. His message is rooted in his experience
of the renewal of the Jesuit order as described in Chapter 2:
Christian faith has a social dimension that changes the world
in which the Gospel is proclaimed through the Christian message of love and compassion. In an analogous way, spiritual
poverty, even though it is a subjective and personal virtue,
cannot be lived out properly in an individualistic sense, as
if it were a private virtue. In order to be truly poor in spirit
and exercise the virtue of poverty, we need to confront ourselves with objective poverty in a practical and operative way.
"A theoretical poverty is no use to us. Poverty is learned by
touching the flesh of the poor Christ, in the humble, in the
poor, in the sick and in children."[86] We acquire the beatitude
of poverty by apprenticeship with the "humble, the poor,
the sick and all those who are on the existential outskirts
of life."[87] Pope Francis does not mince words: "We cannot
become starched Christians, those over-educated Christians
who speak of theological matters as they calmly sip their
tea. No! We must become courageous Christians and go in
search of the people who are the very flesh of Christ, those
who are the flesh of Christ!"[88]

It is worth remembering, however, that these words not only reflect the pope's indignation about the unjust suffering of so many innocent brothers and sisters, but they also summon and challenge our faith in the truly supernatural character of the Church and its mission to spread the Gospel. It is not force and human resources, money and power, that achieve the task of sharing and spreading the faith. We must not confuse the Gospel of Christ with political and social efficiency. The Gospel is spread through fraternal love and solidarity from within and even below the life of society.[89]

Poverty for the Laity

We are trying to break through a wall in order to understand Pope Francis's message, a wall of prejudice and intellectual pride that makes us unreceptive to the inspirations the Holy Spirit wishes to communicate to us through the pope's words. However, the fact that it is necessary to break through a wall may have various explanations besides our own deficiencies. Pope Francis surely would be clearer and less in need of interpretation if he sought and accepted more advice from specialists. And there is also the fact that he speaks from the tradition of a religious order, which may make it difficult for the laity to bring his countercultural program into effect. A member of a religious order or congregation takes public vows of chastity, poverty, and obedience. A lay person does not, and cannot, live poverty in the same way as a religious who renounces possession of any earthly goods. If poverty were to be reduced to the model practiced by religious, then the laity would be excluded from this virtue and would have to settle for a lesser degree of holiness. However, this would contradict the universal call to holiness of all Christians enshrined in the documents of the Second Vatican Council. All Christians are called to holiness; there are no second-category Christians, and thus all are called to live out the virtues corresponding to the evangelical counsel of poverty.

As shown in Chapter 1, in the medieval Scholastic tradition there existed a kind of "pauperism" which condemned the pursuit of profit and economic gain as greed. The Renaissance humanists changed this by their vindication of civic republicanism, thus defining a new relationship between culture and faith. In a long historical process with many twists and turns we have reached the contemporary appreciation of the importance of the political and economic institutions of modernity. Certainly this development was not linear, and there were many failed attempts in this intellectual development. Nevertheless, some attempts, even though unfruitful at the time they were proposed, contributed precious intuitions; for example, Machiavelli's distinction between political and individual ethics and Mandeville's recognition of the potentially positive social effects of individually selfish acts. These ideas needed purification and cultural transformation in order to positively shape society. As for how a Christian layperson immersed in manifold worldly tasks, with a family to take care of, can live the spirit of poverty in his or her relationship to earthly goods, it was above all St. Josemaría who conceived not only of a poverty adapted to the laity, but a truly lay poverty. For him, virtues, not vows, were required in order to live poverty.[90] St. Thomas, the universal Doctor, knew no "virtue of poverty." For him, poverty was an evangelical counsel accepted by the members of religious orders in a public vow.[91] What St. Josemaría taught the laity were the virtues relating to money and the spirit of poverty, well-known also to Aristotle and St. Thomas: liberality and magnificence. Liberality (also generosity or largesse) is the virtue of spending money well: money ought to be spent for the right aim, in the correct amount, and at the right time. Liberality is the virtue which allows us to avoid waste and profligacy on the one hand, and greed on the other. Magnificence (the desire to accomplish great things) is that virtue that makes us devote large sums of money if needed to achieve great goals, especially those undertaken in the service of the common good. Today we would call it the courage to take economic risks for large projects.

The pagans also knew and practiced the virtues of liberality and magnificence. For Christians, two dimensions are added to these virtues. The first is the preferential love for the poor. It is a characteristic feature of the Bible and the Fathers of the Church that Christians should be actively concerned about the weak, the sick, and those on the fringes of human existence. A beautiful, unbroken line runs from the passages in the Acts of the Apostles describing the life of sharing and generosity among the first followers of the Risen Lord in Jerusalem[92] to the early Church Fathers, who established social centers in their dioceses that tended to the sick, the elderly, the poor, and strangers,[93] and then to the contemporary efforts of Christians to relieve suffering all over the world.

The second dimension in which Christian faith extends the virtues known to paganism is an attitude of inner detachment from everything except God, which Jesus demands of those who wish to follow Him. This is the meaning of the parable of the camel passing through the eye of the needle: it is believed that the "eye of the needle" referred to a small gate through which one could enter into the city of Jerusalem. In order to pass through this narrow gate, one had to remove unnecessary equipment. Only those with "very light baggage" reach heaven. St. Josemaría outlined some specific criteria for those who wish to become saints living in the world, while at the same time aspiring to a certain standard of well-being, which requires the use of material means: own your property in a spirit of responsibility and accountability; possess nothing superfluous; do not complain when something necessary is lacking, provided that you have made an effort to get it; be generous in supporting the Church, aware of the fact that being Christian costs something also in an economic sense; and be magnanimous in community service, tackling pressing social issues on your own and with friends without waiting for others to take the lead or the government to step in.

I now move to summarizing the pope's strong moral messages on the economy. Each of these could be the topic of a monograph. Here I limit myself to summarizing Pope Francis's messages simply, striving to explain and transfer their meaning into the Western cultural context.

Strong Moral Messages to Business

In keeping with the positive perspective offered in the previous section, I strive to summarize Pope Francis's teaching on the economy in seven strong moral messages.

1. An authentic faith is never completely personal and always involves a deep desire to change the world

Pope Francis repeats this idea frequently. He is not innovating with this point; he is simply taking up the prophetic, biblical tradition, and the renewal brought about by the Second Vatican Council. Both John Paul II and Benedict XVI said similar things before him. This is not surprising: it has always been the firm conviction of the Catholic Church that the Christian faith has a public and social dimension and cannot be confined to one's private life. Having received baptism, the Christian partakes in a triple vocation or mission: the priestly, prophetic, and pastoral.[94] We see this in the first Christian community as described in the Acts of the Apostles:

> They devoted themselves to the teaching of the apostles and to the communal life, to the breaking of the bread and to the prayers. Awe came upon everyone, and many wonders and signs were done through the apostles. All who believed were together and had all things in common; they would sell their property and possessions and divide them among all according to each one's need.[95]

And again in another well-known text:

> The community of believers was of one heart and mind, and no one claimed that any of his possessions was his own, but they had everything in common. With great power the apostles bore witness to the resurrection of the Lord Jesus, and great favor was accorded them all. There was no needy person among them, for those who owned property or houses would sell them, bring the proceeds of the sale, and put them at the feet of the apostles, and they were distributed to EACH according to need.[96]

In these passages we learn that the first proclamation of the faith is followed by the teaching of the Apostles (*didaché*), lived out in liturgy (*leitourgia*), and put into effect in active concern for the needy (*diakonia*). Only when each of these elements is present is there properly the Church as community (*koinonia*). This was the ecclesiological message of the Second Vatican Council: its four Constitutions mirror each one of these essential elements. *Dei Verbum* speaks about revelation and the interpretation and proclamation of the Word of God; *Sacrosanctum Concilium* refers to the liturgy; *Gaudium et Spes* concerns service to the needy; and *Lumen Gentium* describes the Church as the people of God gathered into a community. Certainly holiness is personal, but there is no holiness without love of neighbor, without outrage at injustice, and without concern for those who suffer hardship and trouble. To forget that would mean falling into an individualistic notion of salvation that strives exclusively for a false kind of personal excellence and individual piety. Thus the prophetic mission in particular is essential to the biblical faith: in the name of God, men and women rise to proclaim truth and justice in the face of untruth (or misinformation), injustice, and oppression; and in doing so they oppose political and economic abuses of power. This is the way Francis expresses it:

> An authentic faith—which is never comfortable or completely personal—always involves a deep desire to change

the world, to transmit values, to leave this earth somehow better than we found it. We love this magnificent planet on which God has put us, and we love the human family, which dwells here, with all its tragedies and struggles, its hopes and aspirations, its strengths and weaknesses. The earth is our common home and all of us are brothers and sisters. If indeed "the just ordering of society and of the state is a central responsibility of politics," the Church "cannot and must not remain on the sidelines in the fight for justice." All Christians, their pastors included, are called to show concern for the building of a better world. This is essential, for the Church's social thought is primarily positive: it offers proposals, it works for change and in this sense it constantly points to the hope born of the loving heart of Jesus Christ.[97]

2. "Let us free ourselves from the idolatry of money!"—Wealth must serve, not rule, and consumerism should be rejected

The service of mammon, or the idolatry of money, means exclusion from the Kingdom of God: "You cannot serve God and wealth."[98] Practical materialism and consumerism are great and constant threats to Christian life everywhere and in every time, but perhaps especially in our highly developed economies of today. St. Paul wrote that the "spirit of the world" blocks the gifts of the spirit of the Lord.[99] Pope Francis echoes him by warning: "The great danger in today's world, pervaded as it is by consumerism, is the desolation and anguish born of a complacent yet covetous heart, the feverish pursuit of frivolous pleasures, and a blunted conscience...God's voice is no longer heard, the quiet joy of his love is no longer felt, and the desire to do good fades."[100]

Freedom from the idolatry of money means placing spiritual values over material wealth, thus vanquishing practical materialism. Pope Francis expressed this in 2014 in his message to the World Economic Forum in Davos: "Without ignoring, naturally, the specific scientific and professional requirements of every context, I ask you to ensure that humanity is served by wealth and not ruled by it."[101] Money is the lifeblood of society and the economy, as San Bernardino wrote.[102] Without money, the exchange of goods would be very difficult. Pope Francis does not doubt this: "It takes money to do all these things! ... The Pope tells you: you must invest, and you must invest well!"[103] However, every human reality can be abused. This is unfortunately all too obvious where money and finance are concerned. Avarice and insatiability poison this lifeblood of the economy. It is the task of financial institutions to ensure that finance is a real public good: "Money must serve, not rule!"[104] The financial system needs to be cleansed of "poison"; that is, of the sinful elements that have caused it to deviate to some extent from its service to the real economy. This effort requires reflection, study, and persuasive arguments that there is a need for both ethical business practices and for integrating an ethical dimension into economic theory.

One of the abuses that Pope Francis has been addressing is taken from the repertoire of Scholastic moral teaching: the struggle against usury. As was discussed in Chapter 1, this is in no way a new topic in the tradition of Catholic social thought; however, we are not used to this kind of language anymore. The pope has given this teaching a new actuality, adding a new twist to the traditional topic of freedom from the idolatry of money: "I hope that these (anti-usury) institutions may intensify their commitment alongside the victims of usury, a dramatic social ill. When a family has nothing to eat, because it has to make payments to usurers, this is not Christian, it is not human! This dramatic scourge in our society harms the inviolable dignity of the human person."[105]

Along these lines, I think we need to reflect on the moral dimension of debt, credit, and monetary expansion, particularly the illegitimacy of consumer credit. I am not referring to an occasional high charge to a credit card, or the purchase of real estate or of a car through sustainable and realistic loans.

What I have in mind is a style of life where one habitually lives beyond his or her means, and the general atmosphere of consumerism that induces private debt.[106] I also consider excessive public debt to be a real evil that imposes the burdens of contemporary opportunistic and intemperate policies on future generations. The amount of public debt Western nations have accumulated is one of the major sources of rent-seeking. The rich who have capital enough to buy bonds receive interest from the taxes paid by the whole population.[107] Building a normative barrier against credit and monetary expansion, against unwise private debt, and against skyrocketing public debt would be to heed the Bible's warning that "the borrower is the slave of the lender."[108]

Related to this, another aspect of Catholic social teaching to which Francis has given a new accent is his critique of consumerism. This was a theme present in both John Paul II and Benedict XVI; however, Francis attacks consumerism with a new passion.[109] He defines it as the "self-centered culture of instant gratification,"[110] and identifies it as the root of many social and ecological evils. He holds that "the market tends to promote extreme consumerism in an effort to sell its products." As a result, "people can easily get caught up in a whirlwind of needless buying and spending. Compulsive consumerism is one example of how the techno-economic paradigm affects individuals."[111] In contrast, "Christian spirituality proposes a growth marked by moderation and the capacity to be happy with little."[112] The pope is not at all opposed to economic growth and consumption as such. Actually, his vision of an "ecology of daily life"[113] is based on the dreams of many to have a dignified life in a middle-class society. Consumerism, however, extends consumption beyond its reasonable and moral limits by encouraging us to buy new things simply to satisfy our acquisitive urge, causing us to replace gadgets, machines, and other items that still serve their purpose well only for the kick of possessing something new. Consumerism reduces investment, thrift, and savings, thus undermining the basis of a healthy capitalist economy. It is an evil that certainly stimulates production in the short run but in the long run gobbles up resources through waste and weakens the moral stamina of our society.

It is worth recalling the old adage falsely attributed to Alexis de Tocqueville but nevertheless wise:

> I sought for the greatness and genius of America in her commodious harbors and her ample rivers – and it was not there . . . in her fertile fields and boundless forests and it was not there . . . in her rich mines and her vast world commerce – and it was not there
>
> . . . in her democratic Congress and her matchless Constitution – and it was not there. Not until I went into the churches of America and heard her pulpits aflame with righteousness did I understand the secret of her genius and power. America is great because she is good, and if America ever ceases to be good, she will cease to be great.[114]

Consumerism is especially harmful to moral goodness when it reduces sexuality to mere pleasure to be consumed on a whim, without heeding family ties and the true purposes of sexuality. Immoral uses of our sexuality tend to destroy the family, the basic unit of cohesion in society, which is built on the stable foundation of fertile matrimony between a man and a woman. When applied in the context of human relationships, consumerism turns the other into an object to be used and enjoyed for as long as it suits one's fancy, and then discarded. Pope Francis has expressed this conviction with respect to the right to life, combining his economic concerns with the inviolability of the human person. He often repeats his warning against a "throw-away" culture:

> We know that human life is sacred and inviolable. Every civil right rests on the recognition of the first and

fundamental right, that of life, which is not subordinate
to any condition, be it quantitative, economic or, least of
all, ideological. "Just as the commandment 'Thou shalt
not kill' sets a clear limit in order to safeguard the value
of human life, today we also have to say 'thou shalt not' to
an economy of exclusion and inequality. Such an economy kills.... Human beings are themselves considered
consumer goods to be used and then discarded. We have
created a 'throw away' culture which is now spreading."
And in this way life, too, ends up being thrown away.[115]

3. The poor must be included in the market economy, giving them access to the creation of wealth

A lot has been said already about poverty and its importance
to the pope's teaching. Francis's vision of the economy is one
that is structured to include the poor, and fights poverty by
creating prosperity for all. "The need to resolve the structural
causes of poverty cannot be delayed, not only for the prag-
matic reason of its urgency for the good order of society, but
because society needs to be cured of a sickness which is weak-
ening and frustrating it, and which can only lead to new crises.
Welfare projects, which meet certain urgent needs, should be
considered merely temporary responses."[116]

In other words, Francis does not want more handouts but
rather the creation of work and employment. How this is techni-
cally to be done is not within the pope's competence, and Francis
does not address this question. He does not, however, seek the
solution only in government intervention or administrative
action but also and primarily in business and businesspeople. It
is noteworthy that he appeals to individuals both in the economy
and in politics, reminding them of their moral obligations,
rather than offering theories about how institutions should
operate.[117] He calls businesspeople "artisans of development
for the common good"[118] who have a "noble" "entrepreneurial
vocation in the true spirit of lay missionaries."[119] Francis scoffs

at offering assistance through small amounts of charitable giving, which is hardly more than a first step. Rather, "it is important to steer economic affairs in the direction of the Gospel, namely at the service of the individual and of the common good."[120] The first among his ethical challenges to the market is "to create good job opportunities."[121]

The consistent thrust of the pope's message on business is to center the economy on the common good.[122] Francis first defines the common good traditionally as "the sum of those conditions of social life which allow social groups and their individual members relatively thorough and ready access to their own fulfillment,"[123] but then gives it his own characteristic spin by insisting that it include the preferential option for the poor. He uses strong language: "The principle of the common good immediately becomes, logically and inevitably, a summons to solidarity and a preferential option for the poorest of our brothers and sisters,....it demands before all else an appreciation of the immense dignity of the poor in the light of our deepest convictions as believers. ...This option is in fact an ethical imperative essential for effectively attaining the common good."[124]

What is surprising in this formulation is that Francis does not use the concept of "social justice." Actually, even though he speaks a lot about justice, he has used the expression "social justice" only once in connection with his concern for the poor.[125] This is not a coincidence. "Social justice," in traditional Catholic social teaching, is the basis for an appeal to public authorities to intervene in order to conform human society to the needs of the common good.[126] Francis, in contrast, appeals to the people, to civil society as a whole, including the political and economic elites. This is his way of understanding the preferential option for the poor, in keeping with the theology of the people. It expresses solidarity as love of the common good, and the weak and underprivileged are those who are most in need of a society based on solidarity. Thus it is correct to link the three terms common good, solidarity, and the preferential option for the poor. The pope becomes quite lyrical in his defense of an economy at the service of the common good that includes the poor:

> Business is in the common interest. Although it is a privately owned and operated firm, for the simple fact that it pursues goals of general interest and importance, such as, for example, economic development, innovation and employment, it should be protected as a good in itself. The first to be called to this work of protection are the institutions, but also entrepreneurs, economists, banking and financial agencies and all subjects involved must not fail to act with competence, honesty and a sense of responsibility. Business and the economy need an ethic to function properly; not any ethics, but ethics which place the person and the community at the center.[127]

This leads us to the next of Francis's strong messages.

4. Justice and solidarity (charity) are necessary elements of a just economy

In order to be truly free, the market needs a legal framework, ethical norms and virtues, and a culture that promotes human dignity. Only an ethical market deserves to bear the name "free market" because true freedom requires a moral aim and sense in order for it to be exercised reasonably. A person in a desert without knowledge of where to go to find the next oasis is free in the sense of being unconstrained; however, one would hardly call wandering lost in the desert real freedom. Only when the path can be clearly seen are we free to walk on it or not. Ethical norms and virtues are this path in the desert. Ethics is not an optional add-on to business for those who have a weak conscience, like a sauce one can pour or not over the roast according to one's taste; it is an integral part of the economy. Among the virtues and norms that sustain our markets, justice and charity are those virtues that regulate our actions affecting other people, and are therefore foremost among all other virtues. Justice and charity transform mere power and force into true authority, which empowers others and enables transformative leadership. They preserve peace and harmony in our societies. The motives of our decisions must go beyond mere utility and pleasure. The business of business is not just *business*; only *just* business is business. Pope Francis puts it thus: "It is the duty of all men and women to build peace following the example of Jesus Christ, through these two paths: promoting and exercising justice with truth and love; everyone contributing, according to his means, to integral human development following the logic of solidarity."[128]

The mission of the Church and of Catholic social teaching is not the imposition of some foreign doctrine on others or on society as a whole. It is not Catholic indoctrination of people of other religions or moral traditions. In a long and sometimes painful process, the universal Church has learned, in part from the American tradition of religious liberty, that she cannot *impose* her teaching through the intervention of government or by legal coercion, but should instead freely *propose* to societies her message of faith and meaning. Her mission can be compared to a lighthouse on the shore or a control tower at the airport. In themselves, these buildings might be quite attractive, especially a lighthouse perched on a cliff or braving the onslaught of the waves, covered with the froth of the ocean. In nice weather, we can admire lighthouses for their beauty or simply ignore them as we might any other building. However, when it gets dark and the sea is stormy, the lighthouse shows us the way into the harbor and saves our lives. It helps us exercise our freedom for our own good. Only a madman would accuse the lighthouse or the airport control tower of limiting his freedom.

Catholic social teaching is an appeal to *see* how our actions affect others—especially the poor and marginalized—to *judge* with principles that encourage business to promote the full integral development for which it is responsible, and to *act* with a renewed energy to bring forth God's equity and justice in concrete places of business. Political, social, and economic injustice, wherever it appears, calls Christians to action, to compassion, and to solidarity. This is especially true for Christians with the privileges and responsibilities of leadership. Businesses should produce goods that are truly good, services that truly serve, and wealth that truly creates value. These three maxims show that businesses are multidimensional realities. They should not be reduced to a single objective such as maximization of profit. Rather, application of these three maxims can order business in such a way that its benefits (and burdens) are shared in common with multiple stakeholders. It is precisely in this ordering that business can participate in the common good.[129]

Pope Francis has given this traditional teaching of the Church an added color in *Laudato Si'* by his use of the concept of "integral ecology."[130] This is an understanding of the way we should protect the environment and exercise our stewardship over the natural resources of Creation that integrates the different aspects of life in society, aware of the fact that all these aspects and fields of action are interrelated. Francis calls for an "economic ecology"[131] and a "social ecology,"[132] implying that "every ecological approach needs to incorporate a social perspective."[133] The pope envisages a win-win situation in which the environment and society are not thought of as costs but rather as opportunities for sustainable business in the long run. The basis of an "integral ecology" is the commitment of all to the common good. It is important not to think in exclusive dichotomies, but to discover alternatives to our usual practices. There is always a solution. In India, for instance, some years ago hungry elephants were marauding the fields of poor farmers. In order to protect their crops the villagers resorted to killing the elephants until they discovered a simple remedy: threads drenched in chili peppers tied around the fields were enough to chase the elephants away. The smell of the peppers seems to be so unbearable to these giants of Creation that they come nowhere near it.[134] In a similar way, we can find modes in which business, the just demands of people and families, and the environment are not seen as opposed or mutually exclusive but rather can be integrated to create a beneficial system for all.

5. *"Inequality Is the Root of Social Ills"*[135]

Globalization has reduced poverty but increased inequality.[136] "Inequality is the root of social ills," Francis affirms. In this sentence, the original Spanish word "*inequidad*" expresses the Holy Father's concern better than the English translation "inequality": what he criticizes is *unjust* inequality, inequity, and unfairness that is the result of hardheartedness or exclusion.[137] Injustice always refers to morally wrong human acts, to sin and its consequences, not to natural situations or differences. God has created all people equal in dignity and rights; but he has also created us unequal and different in those natural qualities, talents, and strengths that individuals through their free will and effort develop to different degrees. In a certain sense, God Himself created inequality in the history of salvation: a specific people was chosen over and above others; from this people God chose Moses over and above others to be the mediator of the covenant on Mount Sinai; Christ was born in a specific village to one maiden and not anywhere or to anyone else, and the list goes on.

The prospect of reaping the fruits of one's own labor is highly motivating, and different degrees of effort will result in different outcomes, and consequently, *just* differences. The attempt to equalize the situation of everyone, regardless of differences, ends in totalitarianism. Even a society that managed to grant absolute equality of opportunity to all (which is impossible) would still be unable to guarantee equal outcomes in the use of this opportunity because the diligence, motivation, and skills of people differ. We can therefore rightly doubt that it is a problem when some live in great abundance and others do not as long as those who are relatively poor possess what they need for a dignified and happy life. Relative poverty will always be with us, and begrudging others their prosperity simply because they have more would be engaging in the capital sin of envy. In other words, the moral issue is not achieving equality in all things but rather fighting misery, because misery, not inequality, debases human dignity. Inequality is something we must accept and bear, and yes, harness to promote the cause of development.

However, inequality or divergent levels of prosperity can also be the result of wrongful acts or unjust structures. Whoever tips the scales in his own favor such that the playing field is no longer level for all, or whoever rigs the rules in order to exclude others creates unjust inequalities. Unfortunately, our world is full of such unjust inequalities. Pope Francis desires prosperity and integral and sustainable development for all.[138] This is achieved by reasonable opportunities for all under conditions of fair competition based on ethics, trust, and cooperation. Furthermore, the capacity to make use of existing opportunities needs to be justly distributed: access to education and health care, a culture of life, and solid families are essential elements of economic development.

Finally, when inequality exists to such an extent that some live in absolute poverty and misery while others next door live in overabundance, then the consciences of the rich or relatively well-off should compel them to act: refusing help in humanitarian emergencies or failing to strive toward including the poor into the networks of production and prosperity would be a manifestation of hardheartedness, which is a sinful consequence of avarice and a lack of justice and mercy.

6. A "Pure Market" Does Not Work

A "pure" market is not the same thing as a free market. The free market is not simply the most effective way to organize an economy, but the form of organization most in keeping with human dignity. Only in freedom can individuals develop their creative potential and express their preferences concerning consumption and the kind of occupation they should have; only in freedom can people associate in businesses they themselves found and own. Only a free market is an ethical market. But the reverse is also true: only an ethical market is a free market. The free market is not just an economic fact, but a cultural achievement. In order to be free, a market needs a legal framework, virtues, and a culture of creativity, work, and enterprise. Ethics is an integral part of the economy that structures it from within. Without a shared core of moral values there is no real trust, and without trust society lacks what is most important for a functioning economy: social capital.[139] Trust is a prerequisite for economic exchange, for credit, and for any form of economic cooperation. To establish trust within a society it is not enough for its members to be able to predict the behavior of others. Foreseeing that I will be cheated grants me reliable knowledge of the future and I adapt to this knowledge, but this does not create trust. It makes me cautious and withdrawn. In order for mutual trust to exist, both sides to an exchange must keep their promises and fulfill their duties; in a word, they must be morally reliable. Widespread trust in a society is a result of a long-standing record of such morally reliable behavior. The government also plays an important role in the creation of trust. The enforcement of just laws and the protection of private property and individual freedoms ensure the fulfillment of contracts and redress for tort, thus stimulating exchange. In addition to this, in all the major developed countries of the world, the State offers a social safety net to protect people who cannot work due to illness, age, or involuntary unemployment. With a well-designed safety net, more people dare to move freely into the heights of life and enterprise, without—maintaining the metaphor—fear of falling in case of an accident or catastrophe. However, it is not at all easy to find the right balance between providing a safety net and creating a social system that encourages individual effort. In Europe, and also in the United States, despite the best of intentions, we have created "handout" systems that often in- duce "learned helplessness" and rob us of the joy of deserved personal success.[140]

Pope Francis is against this kind of "handout" system, as has been stated above. So why does he lash out against "pure markets," and what are they? What makes Francis furious is when people are treated as mere soulless pawns that can be sacrificed callously to the idol of profit by large anonymous mechanisms. He expresses this anger in words that convey a forceful and just moral message: "As long as the problems of the poor are not radically resolved by rejecting the abso- lute autonomy of markets and financial speculation and by attacking the structural causes of inequality, no solution will be found for the world's problems or, for that matter, to any problems."[141] We have too often absolutized the market, to which God appears as an "unmanageable" threat;[142] the poor and the environment become nothing more than a nuisance to the "interests of a deified market."[143] Francis's solution is that by serving the poor we will be set free from this idolatry. Certainly this is nothing new in the tradition of Catholic social thought—it does not go beyond what Cardinal James Gibbons and others demanded in the last quarter of nine- teenth-century America.

The new spin that Pope Francis adds to the discussion on markets, I think, is his accent on relationality. With this expres- sion, we refer to the notion that the human person is essentially not only an individual substance but is also constituted by his or her being in relationship with others. "Relation," in the Aristotelian categories, is an accidental; that is, something that is non-essential and only exists in something else, like color or size. However, when applied to the human person, relation, relationship, is much more than this because we are created in the image of the triune God. We are persons because we exist in relationship to others. Sociability and relationship not only do not diminish our personhood—sharing with others and accommodating their needs are not merely limitations on our desires for personal growth—in fact, they constitute our nature as human beings. Being human means being part of a mesh of human relationships. This notion should cause us to rethink the way we conceive of society.[144] The Second Vatican Council formulated this idea in its Pastoral Constitution:

> Indeed, the Lord Jesus, when He prayed to the Father, "that all may be one...as we are one" *opened up vistas closed to human reason*, for He implied a certain likeness between the union of the divine Persons, and the unity of God's sons in truth and charity. This likeness reveals that man, who is the only creature on earth which God willed for itself, cannot fully find himself except through a sincere gift of himself.[145]

Pope Benedict XVI elaborated further: "The Trinity is absolute unity insofar as the three divine Persons are pure relationality. ...In particular, in the light of the revealed mystery of the Trinity, we understand that true openness does not mean loss of individual identity but profound interpenetration. ...The Christian revelation of the unity of the human race presupposes a metaphysical interpretation of the 'humanum' in which relationality is an essential element."[146]

Pope Francis frequently repeats the idea that "everything is related."[147] He underscores our relationship to one other, to God, and to the whole of creation, in which we are constituted as persons, and his vision culminates in a Trinitarian reading of the universe:

> The divine Persons are subsistent relations, and the world, created according to the divine model, is a web of relationships. Creatures tend towards God, and in turn it is proper to every living being to tend towards other things, so that throughout the universe we can find any number

of constant and secretly interwoven relationships. This leads us not only to marvel at the manifold connections existing among creatures, but also to discover a key to our own fulfillment. The human person grows more, matures more and is sanctified more to the extent that he or she enters into relationships, going out from themselves to live in communion with God, with others and with all creatures. In this way, they make their own that Trinitarian dynamism which God imprinted in them when they were created. Everything is interconnected, and this invites us to develop a spirituality of that global solidarity which flows from the mystery of the Trinity.[148]

The theological novelty in Benedict XVI's and Francis's formulations consists in their having brought the Second Vatican Council's opening to "vistas closed to human reason" to its logical conclusion. At the council the preparatory draft of *Gaudium et Spes* proposed to make the analogy between the Trinity and the relationship between human persons explicit. However, 148 Fathers rejected the formulation in the draft as "obscure," four as "untrue," two as "incomprehensible," and one even as "reckless."[149] The time was not yet ripe for relationality. This has changed, and Francis has taken it to its limit.

The risk of such a vision is that it is too grandiose and thus becomes vague and impractical, something that Francis fears. Applied to the economy, however, the idea of relationality has many concrete consequences. This is not the place to analyze this question in detail because Pope Francis has not done so.[150] However, as noted, his predecessor Benedict XVI made suggestions along these same lines that can help us understand what Francis is talking about. Francis explicitly refers to Benedict's teaching and builds on it.[151] Benedict XVI framed business as a space of human relationship, not only of material transactions. If there is a climate of mutual trust, the market is the "economic institution that permits encounter between persons, inasmuch as they are economic subjects."[152]

The economy, in such a vision, is not simply a mechanism of the *homo oeconomicus*, following the harsh logic of profit maximization at all costs, and is not a mechanical apparatus at all. It is a network of human relationships, certainly governed by self-interest rightly understood, and by justice in contracts, but open to the human dimension. This includes the possibility of generating honest, caring friendships, whereas the usual "friendships" in business are purely utilitarian: usually, business "friendships" last no longer than the mutual monetary gains to be had by the parties. Businesspeople who are open to authentic relationships will be capable of true friendship beyond their expectations of material advantage. Relationality enriches business with a human sense of fraternity that Benedict XVI called "gratuitousness," "gift," and "reciprocity."[153] He formulated his message as a challenge, not as a detailed directive for action, because the goals he sets out are difficult to attain: their implications for business are not immediately obvious, and quite to the contrary, they may seem difficult to put into practice. However, gratuitousness and gift do not imply giving things away for free—that would not really be possible in business. Giving a gift is not identical to giving a present. Benedict's "logic of gift" and "gratuitousness" express that the human person has no price but dignity, and must therefore be at the center of all economic activity as its foundation and aim. Our business relationships can be of a very different character: exploitative, domineering, unjust, hostile, etc.; or, to the contrary, empowering, helpful, just, friendly, etc. The way we enter into the market is a consequence of a choice we make in our interior life: Who do we want to be? What kind of person am I choosing to become through my business activities? If we decide to respect others in their dignity, even to love them as brothers and sisters, then we have made the "gift" Benedict XVI is talking about: we have gratuitously decided to renounce any powers of dominion over others but instead to serve them. This implies a long-term, sustainable vision of business, and rejects short-term greed which does not consider human costs. It also affects the way we conceive of competition.

Pope Francis regrets that "today everything comes under the laws of competition and the survival of the fittest, where the powerful feed upon the powerless."[154] Following his predecessor in this too, he proposes a new approach to competition as an essential element of the free economy. Fair competition always and everywhere lowers prices, thus making goods and services available to the poor. It also stimulates creativity and drives businesspeople to be faster than their competitors in offering new and better products. Initially, when a product is introduced, its price may be high because the inventor retains his or her patent, and therefore has a monopoly position, but as soon as competitors enter the market, prices decrease and the product is made widely available. What at the outset was a luxury only the rich could afford (this was true for cars, refrigerators, cell phones, computers, and many other products) ends up being part of the normal standard of life for the vast majority of people, thanks to competition. These goods now define Western culture in its technological dimension. Competition is certainly tough because ineffective businesses fail, and others will take their place in the market. It is hard for the entrepreneur and the investor to lose money and to have expended effort in vain; however, even as long ago as the fifteenth century, St. Bernardino of Siena (died 1444) said that in the interest of the common good inefficient businesses must be allowed to fail in order to ensure the best use of resources.[155]

On the other hand, moral boundaries apply to competition. There are two ways to be better than someone else: either by really being the best, or by cheating and ruining the competitor's reputation. Cheating hurts the consumer; denigrating others is destructive and unfair. The social teaching of the Church calls for a form of competition that is constructive of the common good, not destructive. It is up to each individual entrepreneur and manager to find ways of engaging in fair competition, but the government also has the important task of oversight for the purpose of enforcing the rules of fair play.

Even in the heat of competition, we should not forget that we are all brothers and sisters. Fraternity (we could also call it social charity, solidarity, or love) is the social principle which fosters a constructively competitive environment. In the Bible there are two pairs of brothers that exemplify the positive and negative forms of competition in a paradigmatic way: Jacob and Esau, and Cain and Abel. In the first case, Jacob wins the competition for the birthright: it is he and not his brother who receives the blessing of his father. Moreover, he achieves this cunningly, using all available means, but he does not forget that Esau is his brother. Jacob not only lets Esau live, but gives him great gifts and good pasture. In the other case, in contrast, one of the competitors, Cain, fails to live up to the demands of fraternity, and kills his brother Abel. That is an example of destructive, fratricidal competition. In business one can push a competitor out of the market by honestly offering better products and services, but a businessperson should never forget that his or her competitor is a brother or sister, not a thing or a commodity.

Even though we do not really want to return to organizational forms from the past and want to avoid adopting a romantic attitude like distributism and other dreamy movements of social reform,[156] the guilds and fraternities of the past might contain useful lessons for us today. Craftsmen in the same trade (tailors, carpenters, blacksmiths, and others) were united in a brotherhood. They remained competitors, but in the case of illness, death, or disability they helped one another. Thankfully, in the Western world many similar institutions have been created in modern times, often unwittingly applying the social wisdom of Christian fraternity. The same spirit has animated cooperatives, a form of organization which Pope Francis seems particularly fond of. He has great hope that cooperatives will assist with the development of the weakest sectors of society, especially unemployed young people. The pope told members of Italian cooperatives:

This great leap forward which we propose the cooperatives take, will give you the confirmation that all that you have already done is not only positive and vital, but also continues to be prophetic. For this reason you must continue to invent — this is the word: invent — new forms of cooperation, because the maxim, "when a tree has new branches, the roots are deep and the trunk is strong," also applies to cooperatives.[157]

7. Corruption Destroys the Free Economy

We come to the last point of our summary of the pope's strong moral messages on the economy, and we can be brief. The widespread phenomenon of corruption is a pressing moral concern brought up frequently by Pope Francis. Already as archbishop of Buenos Aires he spoke out against this social cancer, and as pope he has raised his voice on many occasions to denounce the global scourge of corruption.[158]

Corruption destroys the free market. In corrupt systems, personal effort is not rewarded because the crony with connections to politicians is given precedence over the person who has employed the country's scarce economic resources in a better and more responsible way. In a corrupt society, there is no fair competition under which consumers choose who best serves their material needs; material goods in these societies tend to be low-quality and restricted in quantity because the system of production is warped by politicians and local chieftains. Corruption squanders economic means in an unproductive way and thus impoverishes society. It weakens and undermines the common good. It can rightly be called the cancer of the economy. As cancer cells sap the vital energy of the human organism, corruption diverts the energies of the social body away from the common good, using them parasitically without any beneficial effect for others. An economy that is corrupt and unethical cannot be free in a Christian sense; it is in the hands of an oligarchy. Corruption can be forgiven only if what was taken is given back. This principle is a basic tenet of the rule of law, a basic ingredient of any market economy founded on inclusive institutions. And although Pope Francis has repeatedly denounced corruption as a sin, rather than a destructive economic principle, its indirect effect on the economy can be great.

The pope does not mince words: parents who feed their children with "unclean bread" earned through bribes and corruption starve their children of dignity, because dishonest work robs everyone of dignity.[159] The implications for social life are clear in the following passage of the document in which Francis proclaimed the Extraordinary Jubilee Year of Mercy:

> This festering wound [of corruption] is a grave sin that cries out to heaven for vengeance, because it threatens the very foundations of personal and social life. Corruption prevents us from looking to the future with hope, because its tyrannical greed shatters the plans of the weak and tramples upon the poorest of the poor. It is an evil that embeds itself into the actions of everyday life and spreads, causing great public scandal. ...If we want to drive it out from personal and social life, we need prudence, vigilance, loyalty, transparency, together with the courage to denounce any wrongdoing. If it is not combated openly, sooner or later everyone will become an accomplice to it, and it will end up destroying our very existence.[160]

Returning to the beginning of this chapter, and linking it to the next one, we reaffirm the centrality of poverty for grasping the pope's message on the economy and business. Chosen poverty, understood as inner detachment from material possessions and love for the poor, is the key to overcoming our crisis of materialism and maintaining the spiritual health of the West. A spirit of poverty is a prerequisite for the "awe-filled contemplation of creation"[161] that we need to face the challenges of the future.

Notes to Chapter Three

1. Benedict XVI, *Caritas in Veritate*, 9: "The Church does not have technical solutions to offer and does not claim 'to interfere in any way in the politics of States.' She does, however, have a mission of truth to accomplish, in every time and circumstance, for a society that is attuned to man, to his dignity, to his vocation."

2. Vatican Council II, *Gaudium et Spes*, 76.

3.. Benedict XVI, *Inaugural Address at the Fifth General Conference of the Bishops of Latin America and the Caribbean*, May 13, 2007.

4. See for example, Francis, *Evangelii Gaudium*, 51, 182, 184.

5. Ibid., 184.

6. See Francis, *Laudato Si'*, 60.

7. Ibid., 61.

8. Ibid., 135.

9. Francis, *Evangelii Gaudium*, 182.

10. Ibid., quoting CSDC, 9.

11. Ibid.

12. Ibid., quoting John Paul II, *Ecclesia in America*, 27.

13. Ibid., 184, quoting Paul VI, Apostolic Letter *Octogesima Adveniens* (May 14, 1971), 4.

14. See Francis, *Address to the Leadership of the Episcopal Conferences of Latin America*, July 28, 2013. See also Francis, *Letter to Cardinal Marc Ouellet, President of the Pontifical Commission for Latin America*, March 19, 2016; Juan Vicente Boo, *El Papa de la Alegría* [The Pope of Joy] (Barcelona: Espasa, 2016), 40–41.

15. Francis, *Address at the Second World Meeting of Popular Movements*.

16. Ibid.

17. Ibid.

18. Sergio Rubin and Francesca Ambrogetti, *Pope Francis*, 21. See also Mariano Fazio, *El Papa Francisco*, 21–23.

19. Francis, *Address to the Centesimus Annus Pro Pontifice Foundation*, May 25, 2013.

20. Francis, *In-Flight Press Conference of His Holiness Pope Francis from Paraguay to Rome*.

21. See Francis, *Laudato Si'*, 129.

22. Francis, "Interview for Televisa, March 6, 2015," in Jorge Mario Bergoglio-Papa Francesco, *Interviste e conversazioni*, 326.

23. "I urge you to follow his [Enrique Shaw's] example, and that Catholics ask for his intercession to be good business people." Francis, *Address to Participants in the International Conference of the Christian Union of the Business Executives (UNIAPAC)*, November 17, 2016.

24. Francis, *Pastoral Visit to Genoa: Encounter with representatives of the world of work*, May 27, 2017. (My translation.)

25. See Austen Ivereigh, *The Great Reformer*, 303, quoting a senior priest.

26. Francis, *Laudato Si'*, 128.

27. Ibid.

28. This expression is usually associated with the Austro-American economist Joseph A. Schumpeter, even though he was not the first one to use it. It refers to the cycles of growth and innovation that imply overcoming what is old or outmoded. See Joseph A. Schumpeter, *Capitalism, Socialism and Democracy* (New York: Harper, 2008), 81–87. The book was first published in 1942.

29. Francis, *Laudato Si'*, 128.

30. In his homiletic style he sometimes drives a point home by using a rhetorical ellipsis, leaving out words or ideas that need to be added by the reader. See e.g. ibid., 106 and 109.

31. Ibid., 129.

32. Ibid.

33. See CSDC, 291.

34. Francis, *Laudato Si'*, 189.

35. Ibid.

36. "*Valor real*" in the Spanish original of *Laudato Si'*, 189, and again at 190.

37. Francis, *Laudato Si'*, 189.

38. Ibid., 190.

39. Ibid.

40. Adam Smith, *The Wealth of Nations*, vol. 1, I.xi, 267.

41. Francis, *Laudato Si'*, 276.

42. Ibid., 193.

43. See ibid., 195.

44. See ibid., 191.

45. Francis, Laudato Si', 123. See also the other examples he gives.

46. See Kenneth E. Carpenter, *The Dissemination of* The Wealth of Nations *in French and in France 1776–1843* (New York: The Bibliographical Society of America, 2002).

47. See Athol Fitzgibbons, *Adam Smith's System of Liberty, Wealth, and Virtue: The Moral and Political Foundations of* The Wealth of Nations (Oxford: Clarendon Press, 1995); Knud Haakonssen, ed., *The Cambridge Companion to Adam Smith* (Cambridge: Cambridge University Press, 2006).

48. Francis, Laudato Si', 43–52.

49. See ibid., 36.

50. See ibid., 34–41.

51. Ibid., 114.

52. Ibid., 203.

53. See ibid., 108–10.

54. See ibid., 13.

55. Ibid., 112.

56. See especially ibid., 104, 108; also Romano Guardini, "Das Ende der Neuzeit: Ein Versuch zur Orientierung," in Romano Guardini, *Werke*, ed. Franz

Heinrich (Paderborn: Schöningh, 1989), 9–94; Romano Guardini, "Die Macht:Versuch einer Wegweisung," also in *Werke*, ibid.

57. Francis, *Laudato Si'*, 141.

58. Ibid., 181.

59. See for instance Francis, "Interview for Televisa, March 6, 2015," in Jorge Mario Bergoglio-Papa Francesco, *Interviste e conversazioni*, 326: "Wealth can become unjust if we don't pay a just wage. That is a mortal sin." He also said in this interview that failing to fund pensions and benefits is sin.

60. See Rubin and Ambrogetti, *Pope Francis*, 129.

61. Francis, "Interview given to Andrea Tornielli for La Stampa in 2015," in Jorge Mario Bergoglio-Papa Francesco, *Interviste e conversazione*, 255.

62. See Rubin and Ambrogetti, *Pope Francis*, 130.

63. Ibid, 130–131.

64. G.K. Chesterton, *What's Wrong With the World* (Leipzig: Tauchnitz, 1910), 13.

65. "Nowadays left and right is a simplification that does not make sense. Half a century ago, it made sense, now it doesn't" (my translation). Francis, "Interview for Televisa, March 6, 2015," in Jorge Mario Bergoglio-Papa Francesco, *Interviste e conversazione*, 326.

66. Francis, *Evangelii Gaudium*, 270.

67. Ibid., 273.

68. Ibid., 274.

69. Ibid., 271.

70. Francis, *Address at the Vigil of Pentecost with the Ecclesial Movements*, May 18, 2013. Words to the same effect can be found in *Evangelii Gaudium*, 198.

71. Francis, *Evangelii Gaudium*, 198.

72. Mt 5:46–47.

73. Francis, *Address to Participants in the Ecclesial Convention of the Diocese of Rome*, June 17, 2013, emphasis added.

74. See John Paul II, Encyclical Letter *Veritatis Splendor* (August 6, 1993), 93; John Paul II, *Address at the Fifteenth World Youth Day*, August 19, 2000.

75. See Francis, *In-Flight Press Conference of His Holiness Pope Francis from Paraguay to Rome*.

76. See Angus Deaton, *The Great Escape: Health, Wealth, and the Origins of Inequality* (Princeton and Oxford: Princeton University Press, 2013), 24. Amartya Sen has argued convincingly that income or possession of goods cannot be the sole measure of well-being. Instead, he proposes that the decisive factor is the capabilities we have to lead worthwhile lives. Amartya Sen, *The Idea of Justice* (London: Penguin Books, 2010), 226–33.

77. This is the focus of Robert Skidelsky and Edward Skidelsky, *How Much is Enough? Money and the Good Life* (London: Penguin Books, 2013).

78. For an economic analysis and an attempt at predicting the future of inequality, see Branko Milanovic, *Global Inequality: A New Approach for the Age of Globalization* (Cambridge, Mass.: The Belknap Press of Harvard University Press, 2016).

79. Francis, *Lenten Message*, December 26, 2013, 2.

80. See Francis, *Address to the Centesimus Annus Pro Pontifice Foundation*.

81. Francis, *Evangelii Gaudium*, 192.

82. Cf. 2 Cor 8:9.

83. Francis, *Lenten Message*, 1.

84. See Francis, *Address to Participants in the Ecclesial Convention of the Diocese of Rome*.

85. Francis, *Address to the Students of the Jesuit Schools of Italy and Albania*, June 7, 2013.

86. Francis, *Address to the Participants in the Plenary Assembly of the International Union of Superiors General*, May 8, 2013.

87. Ibid.

88. Francis, *Address at the Vigil of Pentecost with the Ecclesial Movements*.

89. See ibid. This is an idea that Francis repeats frequently.

90. See Josemaría Escrivá, *Conversations with Monsignor Escrivá de Balaguer* (Dublin: Ecclesia Press, 1972), 111.

91. The subject of poverty referred to as a "counsel" appears in the *Summa Theologiae* in the discussion of issues relating to the "state of perfection" (religious life). Cf. Thomas Aquinas, *Summa Theologiae* II-II, q. 186, a. 3.

92. Acts 2:42–45; 4:32–35.

93. See for example Gregory Nazianzen, "On St. Basil," in *Funeral Orations by Saint Gregory Nazianzen and Saint Ambrose*, trans. Leo P. McCauley et al., *The Fathers of the Church* 22, eds. Roy Joseph Deferrari et al. (Washington, D.C.: The Catholic University of America Press, 1953), n. 63.

94. See Vatican Council II, *Lumen Gentium*, 10–12.

95. Acts 2:42–45.

96. Acts 4:32–35.

97. Francis, *Evangelii Gaudium*, 183, quoting Benedict XVI, *Deus Caritas Est*, 28.

98. Mt 6:24.

99. See 1 Cor 2:12–14.

100. Francis, *Evangelii Gaudium*, 2.

101. Francis, *Message to the Executive Chairman of the World Economic Forum on the Occasion of the Annual Meeting at Davos-Klosters*, January 17, 2014.

102. See Bernardino of Siena, "Sermo 42" and "Sermo 43," in *Quadragesimale de Evangelio aeterno*, vol. 4, *S. Bernardini Senensis, Opera Omnia, Quadragesimale de Evangelio aeterno* (Quaracchi: Collegio S. Bonaventurae, 1956), 365–66 and 383. The reader should be aware that in these same passages, Bernardino expresses some deplorable anti-Semitic convictions. What I cite as his worthwhile contributions do not rely on this prejudiced rhetoric.

103. Francis, *Address to Representatives of the Confederation of Italian Cooperatives*.

104. Francis, *Evangelii Gaudium*, 58.

105. Francis, *General Audience*, January 29, 2014. The officially translated summary is available in English. The full text is available in Italian.

106. See the profound historical analysis of Brad S. Gregory, *The Unintended Reformation: How a Religious Revolution Secularized Society* (Cambridge, Mass.: Harvard University Press, 2012), particularly 235–97. Gregory posits an intrinsic link between capitalism and consumerism. I do not fully agree with this—good capitalism based on work and virtue tends to reduce consumption in favor of investment. In capitalism as it actually exists, though, I believe his judgment is correct.

107. At the dawn of the modern economy, Adam Smith already foresaw the growth of public debt, and David Hume warned: "Either the nation must destroy public credit or public credit will destroy the nation." See "Essay of Public Credit" 360–I, quoted in Christopher J. Berry, *The Idea of Commercial Society*, 183.

108. Prov 22:7.

109. See the impressive list of references in *Laudato Si'*, at 34, 50, 184, 203, 209, 210, 215, 219, 232.

110. Ibid., 162.

111. Ibid., 203.

112. Ibid., 222.

113. Ibid., 147–54.

114. The actual source of this quotation is unknown.

115. Francis, *Address to the Italian Pro-Life Movement*, April 11, 2014. The Pope quotes his own *Evangelii Gaudium*, 53.

116. Francis, *Evangelii Gaudium*, 202.

117. See for instance what he wrote in 2014: "The international business community can count on many men and women of great personal honesty and integrity, whose work is inspired and guided by high ideals of fairness, generosity and concern for the authentic development of the human family. I urge you to draw upon these great human and moral resources and to take up this challenge with determination and far-sightedness." Francis, *Message to the Executive Chairman of the World Economic Forum*.

118. Francis, *Speech to the Christian Union of Business Executives*, October 31, 2015.

119. Ibid.

120. Ibid.

121. Ibid.

122. See Francis, *Laudato Si'*, 156–58.

123. Ibid., 156, quoting *Gaudium et Spes*, 26.

124. Ibid., 158.

125. See Francis, *Evangelii Gaudium*, 201.

126. See e.g., Pius XI, *Quadragesimo Anno*, 110.

127. Francis, *Speech to the Christian Union of Business Executives*.

128. Francis, *Address to the Participants in a Conference Sponsored by the Pontifical Council for Justice and Peace Celebrating the 50th Anniversary of Pacem in Terris*, October 3, 2013.

129. See *The Vocation of the Business Leader* (Vatican City: Pontifical Council for Justice and Peace, 2012), 2–3. See also Francis, *Letter to H. E. Mr. David Cameron, British Prime Minister, on the Occasion of the G8 Meeting*, June 15, 2013.

130. See Francis, *Laudato Si'*, 137–201.

131. Ibid., 141.

132. Ibid., 142.

133. Ibid., 93.

134. This story appeared in several news outlets, see e.g., Shib Shankar Chatterjee, "Thread Barrier and World's Hottest Chilli to Keep Asian Elephants At Bay," *NewsBlaze*, November 16, 2010, http://newsblaze.com/story/20101116124707shan.nb/topstory.html.

135. Francis, *Evangelii Gaudium*, 202.

136. See, for example, "Poverty and Equity Data," The World Bank, *http://povertydata.worldbank.org/poverty/home/*.

137. In Spanish "inequality" is *desigualdad*. In *Evangelii Gaudium* the Pope does not use this word but *inequidad*, which implies an element of injustice. The official English translation of *Evangelii Gaudium* nevertheless rendered it simply as "inequality." The official Vatican translation of the encyclical *Laudato Si'* has learned from the error and uses the word "inequity."

138. See Francis, *Evangelii Gaudium*, 192.

139. See Francis Fukuyama, *Trust: The Social Virtues and the Creation of Prosperity* (New York: Simon & Schuster, 1995), 7–26.

140. See Arthur C. Brooks, *The Road to Freedom: How to Win the Fight for Free Enterprise* (New York: Basic Books, 2012), 30–31, quoting Martin Seligman.

141. Francis, *Evangelii Gaudium*, 202.

142. Ibid., 57.

143. Ibid., 56.

144. See Pierpaolo Donati, *Relational Sociology: A New Paradigm for the Social Sciences* (London: Routledge, 2011); by the same author, *La matrice teologica della società* [The Theological Matrix of Society] (Soveria Mannelli: Rubbettino, 2010).

145. *Gaudium et Spes*, 24, quoting John 17:21–22 (emphasis added).

146. Benedict XVI, *Caritas in Veritate*, 54–55.

147. See Francis, *Laudato Si'*, 92, 120, 137, 138, 142.

148. Ibid., 240.

149. The Latin text of the draft is: "Excogitare licet personas humanas, cum ad imaginem Dei unius et trini creatae sint et ad Eius similitudinem reformatae, aliquam imitationem Eius in se praebere." See Francisco Gil Hellín, ed., *Constitutionis pastoralis Gaudium et Spes: Synopsis historica* [Pastoral Constitution Gaudium et Spes: Historical Synopsis] (Pamplona: EUNSA, 1985), 211–13.

150. For this see Pierpaolo Donati, "Beyond the Market/State Binary Code: The Common Good as a Relational Good," in *Free Markets and the Culture of*

Common Good, ed. Martin Schlag and Juan Andrés Mercado (Heidelberg: Springer, 2012), 61–81; by the same author, "Azione morale, riflessività e soggetto relazionale," *Annales Theologici* 26, no. 2 (2012): 275–304.

151. See Francis, *Evangelii Gaudium*, 51.

152. Benedict XVI, *Caritas in Veritate*, 35.

153. Ibid., 36: "The great challenge before us .... is to demonstrate, in thinking and behavior, not only that traditional principles of social ethics like transparency, honesty and responsibility cannot be ignored or attenuated, but also that in commercial relationships the principle of gratuitousness and the logic of gift as an expression of fraternity can and must find their place within normal economic activity."

154. Francis, *Evangelii Gaudium*, 53.

155. See Oreste Bazzichi, "Postfazione" in San Bernardino da Siena, *Antologia delle Prediche volgari: Economia civile e cura patorale nei sermoni di San Bernardino da Siena*, eds. Flavio Felice and Mattia Fochesato (Siena: Cantagalli, 2010), 217. For sources see San Bernardino da Siena's sermon on commerce in *Antologia*, 151–161; and his "Sermo 43," in *Quadragesimale de Evangelio aeterno*, 379, where he rejects the morality of loans at interest to save paupers because they only increase the economic weight they have to bear.

156. See for instance Hilaire Belloc, *The Servile State* (London: Constable, 1927), 49.

157. Francis, *Address to Representatives of the Confederation of Italian Cooperatives*.

158. For data showing the spread of corruption on an annual basis, see www.transparency.org.

159. Francis, *Meditation: Dirty Bread of Corruption*, November 8, 2013.

160. Francis, Bull *Misericordiae Vultus* (April 11, 2015), 19.

161. Francis, *Laudato Si'*, 125.

4

Contemplation and Business

IN THE PRECEDING PAGES A LOT has been written about Francis's commitment to the poor and his social concerns. It has also been stated that the Church's mission is primarily spiritual and supernatural. We thus end this book meditating on Pope Francis's *preferential option for God*. He prays a lot everyday. However, I am not writing his biography, but only providing some reflections on his public pronouncements. I also want to keep within the general framework of our topic, which is business. Therefore my interest here is to show how spiritual life, contemplation, and prayer are at the root of the renewal of business as a calling to holiness that Francis has in mind.

Pope Francis has repeatedly stated that the economic crisis is a moral-cultural crisis of man. The crisis in which we find ourselves is not solely rooted in economics; it is a deeply rooted cultural crisis affecting Western civilization.[1] Economic factors point to underlying moral issues: poverty, public and private debt, and unemployment are just symptoms of a moral illness. Moreover, not only the West but also the rest of the world is suffering from severe tensions, taking the form of political extremism, terrorism, and war, which ultimately have their roots in gross economic inequalities and moral failures. Thus it is not wrong to speak of a global economic and cultural crisis. Its existence confirms the truth of John XXIII's words in his encyclical *Pacem in Terris*: "The world will never be the dwelling-place of peace, till peace has found a home in the heart of each and every human person, till all preserve within themselves the order ordained by God to be preserved."[2]

Even though formulation of the proper criteria and directives for action have been left to the laity,[3] the task of the Magisterium in this context is still immense. It consists of clarifying the issues and constantly reminding all people of the main principles of Christian teaching, and giving them the spiritual means to live by them. As Pierre Manent writes: "The Catholic Church, mediatrix of the Mediator has no other political task, but it is an urgent one, than making itself a convincing witness of the goodness of God."[4] The Church is the sacrament of the world, a visible instrument for invisible grace. A sacrament consists of word and matter, of teaching and example. The day after he was elected, Francis preached to the cardinal electors:

> We can walk as much as we want, we can build many things, but if we do not profess Jesus Christ, things go wrong. We may become a charitable NGO, but not the Church, the Bride of the Lord. When we are not walking, we stop moving. When we are not building on the stones, what happens? The same thing that happens to children on the beach when they build sandcastles: everything is swept away...[5]

I understand Pope Francis's desire for internal economic, financial, and disciplinary reform, and his desire for a poor Church for the poor, in this context. It is Francis's hope that this reform will make an important contribution to the credibility of the Church's sacramental presence in the economic field. How can the Church's social teaching be acceptable to the faithful and to the world if she does not apply her moral standards to the management of her own material assets?

Francis asks Christians who are active in business for more than simple fulfillment of moral norms and abiding by the teachings of the Church; instead, he asks businesspeople to be radically open to the guidance of the Holy Spirit in their work. Since the beginning of his pontificate he has been repeating the message that the Church, including lay Christians living out vocations in business, must go forth boldly. He has warned against a self-referential Church, closed in on herself and her problems. This would be an "ill Church."[6] He calls on all the baptized to open themselves without fear to the action of the Holy Spirit. The third Person of the Holy Trinity grants us the courage to proclaim the Gospel through our lives and words even if we feel the wind blowing in our faces. The Holy Spirit conveys joy and verve to our task of evangelization: "How I long to find the right words to stir up enthusiasm for a new chapter of evangelization full of fervor, joy, generosity, courage, boundless love and attraction!"[7] Lay Christians are called to give the world the light of truth and the warmth of Christian love from within the very structures of their secular professions.[8] Their vocation places them in all walks of life and in every kind of economic activity, so that they can become holy and evangelize others, not by proselytism but by attracting others through a spirit-filled, sincere, and integrated life. Spirit-filled evangelization is "guided by the Holy Spirit, for he is the soul of the Church called to proclaim the Gospel."[9] We need to fully comprehend what this implies. It is not enough to set out on this path using only our own means, ideas, and horizons, praying for help to put our aims into practice, admirable though they may be. Spirit-filled evangelization requires submitting oneself wholly to the guidance and leadership of the Holy Spirit: He is the Evangelizer, we cooperate with Him. We are His instruments, not He ours. Pope Francis wants us to discover the Holy Spirit as a Person, as an Agent and Teacher, and thus to become one with Christ. "In union with Jesus, we seek what he seeks and we love what he loves."[10] This is possible only in a life transformed by the Holy Spirit implanting the life of Christ in us.

We need to be interiorly free from all idolatry to be able to perceive the inspirations of the Holy Spirit. God creates us for freedom, and his redemption truly liberates us. Freedom is a divine gift, but it requires a struggle for purification on our side. The liberty given to us by the Spirit of the Lord is freedom from the idolatry of money and from the trap of looking exclusively to material possessions to achieve our happiness. True Christian freedom through faith requires us to rely first on God's grace. The peaceful attitude that results from this reliance is free of activism, and helps us to understand that the structures and institutions making up our economic system are unintended byproducts of something much larger: of the desire to give glory to God and to adore Him in all things. Josef Pieper understood culture to be the result of our leisure;[11] that is, of that internal sphere of liberty that goes beyond utility. In the same way, Western civilization is the result of an intention to achieve something other than itself—I would posit that Western civilization, with its characteristic economic, financial and political institutions, is an outgrowth of *contemplation*. In order to achieve a right ordering of the economy, we must once again become contemplatives.

What is contemplation?

In his dialogues, Pope Gregory the Great describes an event in the life of St. Benedict, who one night was praying at the window of the tower he lived in. While he was in prayer, God showed him the whole world of all times past, present, and future in the flash of a single bolt of lightning. Astounded, the fictitious partner in the dialogue asked Gregory how God could make all of the world so small that it fit into a bolt of lightning. God did not shrink the world, answered Gregory, but made Benedict's soul so large in holy contemplation that everything fit into his heart.[12]

The spirit-guided transformation of business Pope Francis has in mind is a fruit of prayer: "How good it is to stand before a crucifix, or on our knees before the Blessed Sacrament, and simply to be in his presence! How much good it does us when he once more touches our lives and impels us to share his new life!"[13] Letting ourselves be touched, healed, and transformed by Christ is a form of contemplation. Contemplation is the awareness of God's loving and merciful gaze that constantly follows and comforts each one of us. It is the highest and simplest form of prayer, in which our intellect and will come to rest in God. However, it demands purification and intellectual humility from us. "Blessed are the pure in heart, for they shall see God."[14] We cannot see God with our eyes of flesh, not even with our intelligence, but only with our heart. And our heart must be pure in order to see God. The heart is the innermost core of our freedom where we choose what our will and intellect should turn to: to truth or lies, to good or evil. Over and over again, our heart needs purification, needs to be turned and opened toward truth and goodness. Only thus can we contemplate God. This attitude of contemplation is a form of wisdom which allows us to understand the world from its very first cause, from God. It helps us comprehend, though often dimly, the reason and meaning of things. Wisdom is not only knowledge but loving participation in God's Providence. Understanding this is so important in our time and age. Thanks to technological progress we know more about how things work and about how the human body functions and the laws governing reality. We know *what* things are. However, we are losing sight of *who* man is and what his life is *for*. We are surprised that the purpose of our life is nothing we can make, but instead is given to us from above. Contemplation is the attitude of receiving truth and sense from God, and once again we need purity and poverty of heart—in order to taste God in wisdom our hearts must be free of idols and falsity. Contemplation is the capacity of receiving truth as it is, not as we would wish it to be, and without trying to produce our own version of it. Contemplation quietly observes and is amazed at what it beholds; it listens and perceives God's message in all things. Contemplation is not compatible with the reduction of reason to its scientific-technical dimension; contemplation desires to know how and why things are, not only how they function or for what they can be used. "We tend to demean contemplative rest as something unproductive and unnecessary, but this is to do away with the very thing which is most important about work: its meaning. We are called to include in our work a dimension of receptivity and gratuity, which is quite different from mere inactivity."[15]

Contemplation seeks the first cause; it is a form of wisdom, and therefore of love. Rather than rendering us passive, authentic contemplation opens us to others. Pope Francis points us to an important insight:

> Whenever we encounter another person in love, we learn something new about God. Whenever our eyes are opened to acknowledge the other, we grow in the light of faith and knowledge of God. If we want to advance in the spiritual life, then, we must constantly be missionaries. The work of evangelization enriches the mind and the heart; it opens up spiritual horizons; it makes us more and more sensitive to the workings of the Holy Spirit, and it takes us beyond our limited spiritual constructs.[16]

A form of contemplation that would enclose us in ourselves and exclude others would be an expression of false piety.[17] On the contrary, contemplation allows us to perceive the whole of Creation; and the whole of Creation leads us to God. The world and human society does not exclude God—together they form a unity. All human goods emerge as the fruits of contemplation. These things are good because our heart is directed toward God, and as St. Augustine constantly points out, if we *enjoy* God, we will *use* created things well.[18]

A contemplative person does not rely exclusively upon his or her own efforts but is open to God and to transcendence. Contemplation is open to the Savior. In an etymological sense, it is *eccentric*, with its center or focus outside of the contemplator. Rémi Brague describes the characteristic element of Western civilization as "*romanitas*" ("romanness," Roman in essence),[19] which can be represented by the symbol of the aqueduct bridging cultural divides in the service of mediation and transmission. The Romans were aware that they were indebted to the Greeks, and that the barbarians, in turn, had received a cultural heritage from them, the Romans. In order to allow water to flow, an aqueduct must be slightly inclined: both ends cannot be on the same level. In the realm of culture, this allows for one culture to give something it has to another that does not have it. Christianity has transformed the notion of *romanitas* into its conception of "sacrament," and elevated it to the dimension of grace. Just as an aqueduct connects one place to another with water, the sacramentality of the Church straddles the chasm between heaven and earth; it is a symbol of a greater yet invisible heavenly dimension. It points beyond itself. The significance and goodness of Western civilization derives from its orientation toward something else, toward Someone utterly other, toward God. I would argue that our Western economic and political institutions have emerged from this loving devotion to God, which has sometimes been expressed in a spontaneous and even playful way.

Take the Franciscans and the other mendicant orders for example: their vow of poverty consecrated them to God, and nevertheless, or rather as a byproduct of this vow, they contributed decisively to overturning the canonical ban on interest as usury, thereby promoting an essential element of the modern economy. As they were not allowed to *own* property, but were permitted to *use* it, they saw that the value of an object clearly resides in its use or utility, not in being possessed. Because they could not possess money, they were obliged to bring it into circulation; they thus discovered the possibility of economic growth through investment. The money for investment was entrusted to a "spiritual friend" who cared for the friars' economic needs—the first money managers. Because these "friends" had to be accountable for the money entrusted to them, the friars perfected double-entry bookkeeping. The Franciscans, in contact with the poor and with workers, realized that the canonical ban on any form of interest excluded craftsmen and small and medium enterprises from access to credit, driving them into the hands of usurers. They thus created the *Montes Pietatis*, the first bank in our modern sense of the word. These financial institutions were the first micro-credit lenders. They charged a small rate of interest to cover the costs of running the *Montes Pietatis*; collateral was taken, but it was not allowed to be the tools or livestock of the farmer or craftsman applying for a loan because he needed these to work and create wealth in order to pay back the loan. Charging interest brought the Franciscans in conflict with the Inquisition, and the pope had to intervene to defend them. He clearly stated that the interest charged by these banks was not to be considered usury.[20]

This loving devotion to God also gave us our Western political institutions. Certain religious orders, in particular the Cistercians, were the only institutions of the Middle Ages (except the Republic of Venice and the northern Italian *comuni*) ruled according to democratic principles. An abbot ruled the monasteries; however, for many questions he had to turn to the chapter of his community that decided by majority of votes. Other issues were deliberated by all the monks in the abbey, and the abbot himself was freely elected. No king or other authority in the medieval world was bound in a similar way. They certainly all had their councils, but as the word "council" implies, their statements were legally speaking advice, and not binding. It took centuries of political strife to achieve the institutions of democratic participation that shape our contemporary political culture. As a curious aside, in the absence of any other model, the French National Assembly formed after the revolution adopted the Cistercian rules of procedure for its deliberations – an unintended homage to the Christian origins of democracy.

The aim of these monastic institutions, however, was not to directly and intentionally construct secular society. The aim was always something greater than that: the service of God. For the monks, "*Nihil operi Dei praeponatur*," nothing is more important than prayer.[21] Perhaps it is due to the openness for God's grace and mercy that we experience in meditation and adoration, that there is also an element of spontaneity and playfulness, and a lot of good humor and joy in the Christian roots of Western civilization. For example, in his rule, Benedict commands not only serious work and prayer, but also the siesta; and we are indebted to his order for the existence of champagne, a beverage that throughout the centuries has served for toasting many happy occasions, private and public.

True renewal stems from the development of living traditions. If a society is not tied to something that came before, it usually turns out to be nothing but a repetition of some past error and a dead end. Out of the Christian tradition of contemplation and of glorifying God, we can draw the spiritual energy and the true innovation we need to renew the political and economic system in a way that maintains continuity with its achievements and cleanses it of its sins. This can be seen in the program of cultural transformation that John Paul II and his successors have called a "New Evangelization."[22] The self-destruction of the West has arisen from a certain resentment toward its past—Christian values are often associated with negative historical events such as the Inquisition or the Crusades, and Christian culture is ridiculed by social liberalism as being the heritage of "dead white men."[23] Christians in Europe and the United States should work together on an endeavor of cultural renewal—the U.S. cannot emerge from the cultural crisis without revitalizing its own cultural roots in Europe, and Europe cannot overcome the crisis without the U.S., the present-day cultural leader of the West.

I am convinced that we can renew a hierarchy of values and overcome the economic crisis only if we rediscover what it means to be contemplative, because our economy and society are byproducts of contemplation, that is, fruits of Christian spirituality. In other words, whoever wants to save the economy for the economy's sake will fail, and whoever wants to make money for money's sake will be unhappy. This would be the "idolatry of money" or the illusory confidence in wealth that Francis rejects: "don't place your trust in money."[24] It leads to rent-seeking and destroys the kind of principled entrepreneurship that puts virtues into practice in order to create happiness and prosperity for all.

When politicians, especially in Europe, say that the public values of Western society are those of the Enlightenment alone and do not include the values of Christianity,[25] they make the same mistake as Kant: they want Christian values without Christ. This is impossible.[26] Pierre Manent has spoken of the "religion of the absence of God that is currently destroying and demoralizing the West."[27] He is right. I rather tend to agree with Viktor Orbán that the West will only recover economically if it returns to Christian values.[28] Charles Taylor has put it in more academic terms: he foresees a decline of the "secular narrative understood as a subtraction story," because the theory that religion is withering away has now become empirically implausible.[29] What he wrote in 2007, we can confirm to be true only a few years later: religion has a future in the West.

How can we renew our hierarchy of values and overcome the economic crisis? I think "love in truth" (*caritas in veritate*), a concept already present in John XXIII's *Pacem in Terris*, is the answer. Charity as a social principle is Christian humanism's most important contribution to society. As Pope Francis describes it, Christian humanism is "the humanism of the 'mind of Christ Jesus' (Phil 2:5)," which does not consist of "abstract provisional sensations of the spirit," but rather of the "warm interior strength that renders us able to live and make decisions."[30] Francis highlights humility, detachment, and beatitude as the concrete sentiments of the Christian heart. The practice of Christian charity in a spirit of detachment will "achieve that integral restoration of the human person which is the aim of Christian humanism."[31] Once again, in these formulations Pope Francis appeals for virtuousness, addressing the challenges with a prophetic vision.

However, the question remains open as to how to approach the cultural and economic problem at the institutional and structural level. How is charity infused into institutions? It cannot be done directly. Asserting a "rule" of charity as a directly applicable social principle would be dangerous, a "rule" typical of authoritarian regimes. Charity can only be infused into society by means of aligning institutions with the principles of Catholic social teaching, including justice, human dignity, solidarity, and subsidiarity, all powered from within by the "wild force" of love.[32] The first step must be to support good institutions that reinforce virtuous practices. We cannot perform virtuous practices, charity among them, without institutions. We cannot be free in the true sense of the word on our own, isolated on an island. We are free only in institutions we have built through joint and coordinated effort. We experience liberty when we are able to relate to others in relationships of mutual respect and harmony. Thus, the Catholic social tradition is called on to protect institutions from internal corrosion and external annihilation by instilling respect for those exercising authority, and educating people to adhere to the rules and laws that direct our actions toward the common good. Without this basic and affirmative step, all our prophetic denunciations and virtuous appeals do not reach their aim of serving society as a whole and the poor in particular. The second step, however, is to preserve our institutions from petrification and sclerosis by opening them to continually adapt to changing circumstances and needs. Sustaining an organization's mission requires accepting relentless change. Every living reality (and every institution made up of living persons is such a reality) must develop in order to preserve its original functionality. In the perspective of the Catholic social tradition, this change and development must be guided by hearts full of compassion and well-informed reason. Let our hearts, or as Francis would say, "the power of tenderness," lead the way. In this sense, Christian humanism, by offering society the living presence of Christ, is a "disturbing element." De Lubac put it beautifully: "Christ is, first and foremost, the great disturber." He awakens us from our sleep. Faith continually disturbs us and upsets "the too beautiful balance of our mental conceptions and social structures."[33] In the Christian worldview, "holiness comes before peace."[34] The communities of Christian life in the middle of a contrasting cultural majority are, as Jacques Maritain has called them, "prophetic minorities" or "shock minorities"[35]—some might experience their contrarian lifestyle as a form of moral disapproval of the mainstream. But Christian moral law pivots around charity, and by doing so, does society an enormous, even vital service. To stay alive, free, and democratic, our liberal democracies need the influence of charity shedding light on those who suffer in the dark, giving voice to those who are inarticulate in their screams of pain, and protecting the legal force of their claims.

Jesus sent his apostles into the world as witnesses of his Resurrection. In his lecture upon receiving the Nobel Prize for literature in 1970, Alexandr Solzhenitsyn quoted a Russian proverb: "One word of truth shall outweigh the whole world."[36] In a world of strife and struggle we realize how important hope is. Without hope life becomes unbearable. Hope, however, needs truth. Hope that is not based on truth is not hope but illusion.

The truth our hope is built on is Christ's Resurrection. Trusting in the "irresistible force" of the Resurrection[37] means entering into a logic of mystery, a reality invisible to human eyes. The reality the pope refers to is that, in the middle of evil, good springs forth, like the shoots of plants that grow among the garbage: "in the midst of darkness something new always springs to life and sooner or later produces fruit. On razed land life breaks through, stubbornly yet invincibly."[38] "Christ's Resurrection everywhere calls forth seeds of that new world; even if they are cut back, they grow again, for the Resurrection is already secretly woven into the fabric of this history, for Jesus did not rise in vain. May we never remain on the sidelines of this march of living hope!"[39] The power of the Resurrection cannot be measured or planned by human programs or measurements. It escapes our control—the Resurrection brought to nothing human efforts to keep Christ in the grave. The "New Evangelization" of society is therefore something mysterious and unpredictable; our efforts are in the hands of God, and always bring fruit, perhaps not in the place and time we expect, perhaps in other parts of the world.[40] Christ's Resurrection has re-created things marred by sin, suffering, and death. Jesus has transformed all of human life, work, and reality, except sin, into a path to God. All normal and ordinary walks of life and earthly activities have become divine paths of holiness and evangelization. Living within the irresistible force of the Resurrection does not mean abandoning an ordinary life of work and family, but it means discovering that God waits for us where we are. There and nowhere else are we called to give witness to Christ.

Where is God, where is Christ today? Where he always has been: in the hearts of his people, on their lips and in their lives, inside a "prophetic and contemplative lifestyle, one capable of deep enjoyment free of the obsession with consumption."[41] We can therefore be confident that God's Spirit is already making "all things new."[42] "Rather than a problem to be solved, the world is a joyful mystery to be contemplated with gladness and praise."[43] The Catholic social tradition will continue to be fruitful also in the realm of business because of the contemplative life of laypeople in the midst of economic life: out of their hearts will come the energy and the spiritual resources to overcome the crisis. "A true missionary, who never ceases to be a disciple, knows that Jesus walks with him, speaks to him, breathes with him, works with him. He senses Jesus alive with him in the midst of the missionary enterprise."[44] This sense of mission comes from a profound life of prayer. "Without prolonged moments of adoration, of prayerful encounter with the word, of sincere conversation with the Lord, our work easily becomes meaningless; we lose energy as a result of weariness and difficulties, and our fervor dies out."[45]

Pope Francis concluded both *Evangelii Gaudium* and *Laudato Si'* with a chapter on spirituality, and we have ended this book with a meditation. Throughout this book I have tried to explain Francis's message on business in a way that presents its authentic force in our cultural context, without diluting his prophetic denunciations and his appeals for virtuousness. We urgently need both of these because our nation is beset by inequalities and many other pressing social concerns. However, I have also tried to point out what Pope Francis has left to the work of others: positively constructing institutions for the common good and rethinking the institutional implementation of Catholic social teaching. The Catholic social tradition defends institutions that serve the common good. Among these are government, businesses, and financial institutions, but also the family, private property, markets, the rule of law, and social security for those in need, among other things. All these must be protected from inner corrosion and outside aggression. They need to develop according to the principles of justice and love. As this book focuses exclusively on Francis, these topics require further study in a subsequent work. I would like to finish with a confession of faith in God's guidance of the Church through her pastors, whose indications and teaching are stimulated by the Holy Spirit, and thus are not only practical exhortations but also intellectual light for our minds. By accepting them, the Catholic social tradition moves forward and brings forth the fruits of the Holy Spirit.

Notes to Chapter Four

1. Cf. Francis, *Address to the Centesimus Annus Pro Pontifice Foundation*, 2013, where he stated: "The current crisis is not only economic and financial but is rooted in an ethical and anthropological crisis."

2. John XXIII, Encyclical Letter *Pacem in Terris* (April 11, 1963), 165.

3. See Paul VI, *Octogesima Adveniens*, 4.

4. Pierre Manent, "L'Église entre l'Humanité Réelle et l'Humanité Rêvée," in *The Global Quest for* Tranquillitas Ordinis: Pacem in Terris, *Fifty Years Later*, ed. The Pontifical Academy of Social Sciences (Vatican City: Libreria Editrice Vaticana, 2013), 109–18, 118.

5. Francis, *Homily for the "Missa Pro Ecclesia" with the Cardinal Electors*, March 14, 2013.

6. Francis, *Carta a Los Participantes en la 105 Asamblea Plenaria de la Conferencia Episcopal Argentina*.

7. Francis, *Evangelii Gaudium*, 261.

8. See Vatican Council II, *Lumen Gentium*, 31.

9. Francis, *Evangelii Gaudium*, 261.

10. Ibid., 267.

11. Cf. Josef Pieper, *Leisure: The Basis of Culture*, trans. Gerald Malsbary (South Bend: St. Augustine's Press, 1998).

12. See Gregory the Great, *Dialogues*, trans. Odo John Zimmerman, in *Fathers of the Church* 39, (New York: Fathers of the Church, Inc., 1959), 104–6.

13. Francis, *Evangelii Gaudium*, 264.

14. Mt 5:8.

15. Francis, *Laudato Si'*, 237.

16. Francis, *Evangelii Gaudium*, 272.

17. See ibid., 281.

18. See e.g., Augustine, *The City of God*, vol. 2, *The Works of Aurelius Augustine, Bishop of Hippo* (Edinburgh: T & T Clark, 1871), XV, 7, p. 58.

19. See Rémi Brague, *Eccentric Culture: A Theory of Western Civilization* (South Bend: St. Augustine's Press, 2002).

20. On Franciscan economic ethics and its influence on economic development, see Giacomo Todeschini, *Franciscan Wealth*; Giacomo Todeschini, *I Mercanti e il tempio: La società cristiana e il circolo virtuoso della ricchezza fra Medioevo ed età moderna* [The merchants and the temple: Christian society and the virtuous circle of wealth between the Middle Ages and the modern age] (Bologna: Il mulino, 2002); Oreste Bazzichi, *Dall'usura al giusto profitto: L'etica economica della Scuola francescana* [From usury to a just profit: Economic ethics in the Franciscan School] (Cantalupa: Effatà, 2008).

21. Benedict, *The Rule of Saint Benedict*, n. 43, p. 101. The expression "opus Dei" here means prayer in liturgy and song.

22. See Francis Cardinal George, *The Difference God Makes*, 23–28.

23. This expression is criticized by Roger Scruton, *Culture Counts: Faith and Feeling in a World Besieged* (New York: Encounter Books, 2007).

24. Francis, "Interview for Televisa, March 6, 2015," in Jorge Mario Bergoglio-Papa Francesco, *Interviste e conversazioni*, 326. My translation.

25. See the Preamble of the Treaty of Lisbon Amending the Treaty on European Union and the Treaty Establishing the European Community, *Official Journal of the European Union* 306/01 (2007/C): 1–231, especially 1–10.

26. Convincingly argued by Alasdair MacIntyre, *After Virtue: A Study in Moral Theory* (London: Duckworth, 1985).

27. Manent, "L'Église," 117–18.

28. For a discussion of Prime Minister Orban's speech at the XIV Congress of Catholics and Public Life, see Hilary White, "Abandonment of Christian Principles Led to Europe's Economic Crisis: Hungarian Prime Minister," *Lifesite News*, November 20, 2012, http://www.lifesitenews.com/news/ abandonment-of-christian-principles-led-to-europes-economic-crisis- hungaria/.

29. See Charles Taylor, *A Secular Age* (Cambridge, Mass.: Harvard University Press, 2007), 423–37, 569–79. The "secular narrative as a subtraction story" is an attempt to interpret modernity as a process of the gradual withdrawal of religion from public, social, scientific, and cultural life that will end in the disappearance of religion altogether.

30. Francis, *Address to the Participants in the Fifth Convention of the Italian Church.*

31. John P. Bequette, *Christian Humanism: Creation, Redemption, and Reintegration* (Lanham: University Press of America, 2007), 168, 171.

32. See Jacques Maritain, *True Humanism* (London: Bles and Scribner's, 1954), 82.

33. Henri de Lubac, *The Drama of Atheist Humanism* (San Francisco: Ignatius Press, 1995), 14.

34. John Henry Newman refers to this phrase of a pastor as shaping his youth. It is also true in the context of Christian humanism. Cf. John Henry Newman, *Apologia pro vita sua* (London: Routledge, 1907), 6.

35. Jacques Maritain, *Man and the State*, ed. Richard O'Sullivan (London: Hollis & Carter, 1954), 126–33.

36. Alexandr Solzhenitsyn, "Nobel Lecture," 1970, *Nobelprize.org,* http:// www.nobelprize.org/nobel_prizes/literature/laureates/1970/solzhenitsyn- lecture.html.

37. See Francis, *Evangelii Gaudium*, 276.

38. Ibid.

39. Ibid., 278.

40. See ibid., 279.

41. Francis, *Laudato Si'*, 222.

42. See Rev 21:5.

43. Francis, *Laudato Si'*, 12.

44. Francis, *Evangelii Gaudium*, 266.

45. Ibid., 262.

Bibliography

Abela, Andrew and Joseph Capizzi. *A Catechism for Business: Tough Ethical Questions and Insights from Catholic Teaching,* 2nd ed. Washington, D.C.: The Catholic University of America Press, 2016.

Acemoglu, Daron and James A. Robinson. *Why Nations Fail: The Origins of Power, Prosperity, and Poverty.* New York: Crown Business, 2012.

Allen, John L. *The Francis Miracle: Inside the Transformation of the Pope and the Church.* Des Moines: Time Books, 2015.

Amihud, Yakov, Haim Mendelson, and Lasse Heje Pedersen. *Market Liquidity: Asset Pricing, Risk, and Crises.* Cambridge: Cambridge University Press, 2012.

Anselm, Reiner. "Zweireichelehre I." In Vol. 36, *Theologische Realenzyklopädie.* Edited by Gerhard Müller, 776–84. Berlin: De Gruyter, 2004.

Aquinas, Thomas. *Super Evangelium S. Matthaei Lectura.* Edited by Raphael Cai. Turin: Marietti, 1951.

———. *Summa Theologiae.* Edited by Thomas Gilby, O.P. 61 vols. Cambridge: Blackfriars, 1964–80.

———. *In Libros Politicorum Aristotelis Expositio.* Edited by Raimondo Spiazzi. Roma: Marietti, 1966.

Augustine. *The City of God.* Vol. 2, *The Works of Aurelius Augustine, Bishop of Hippo.* Edinburgh: T & T Clark, 1871.

———. "Of the Works of Monks." Translated by H. Browne. In Vol. 3, *Nicene and Post-Nicene Fathers, First Series.* Edited by Philip Schaff. Buffalo, N.Y.: Christian Literature Publishing Co., 1887. New Advent website. Edited by Kevin Knight. http://www.newadvent.org/fathers/1314.htm. Accessed March 22, 2017.

———. "Ennarationes in Psalmos." In Vol. 39, *Corpus Christianorum, Series Latina.* Turnholt: Brepols, 1956.

———. "Tractate 6." In *St. Augustine: Tractates on the Gospel of John 1–10.* Translated by John W. Rettig. *The Fathers of the Church* 78. Washington, D.C.: The Catholic University of America Press, 1988.

———. "Sermon 50." In *Sermons II (20–50) on the Old Testament.* Translated by Edmund Hill. Vol. 3.2, *The Works of Saint Augustine: A Translation for the 21st Century.* Edited by John E. Rotelle. Brooklyn, N.Y.: New City Press, 1990.

Banerjee, Abhijit V. and Esther Duflo. *Poor Economics: A Radical Rethinking of the Way to Fight Global Poverty.* New York: Public Affairs, 2011.

Battista Alberti, Leon. *I Libri della Famiglia*. Edited by Ruggiero Romano and Alberto Tenenti. Torino: Einaudi, 1969. Translated into English by Renée Neu Watkinsas, *The Family in Renaissance Florence*. 4 vols. Prospect Heights, Ill.: Waveland Press, 1994.

Bazzichi, Oreste. *Dall'usura al giusto profitto: L'etica economica della Scuola francescana* [From usury to a just profit: Economic ethics in the Franciscan School].Cantalupa: Effatà, 2008.

Beck, Thorsten. "The Role of Finance in Economic Development: Benefits, Risks, and Politics." In *The Oxford Handbook of Capitalism*, edited by Dennis C. Mueller, 161–204. Oxford: Oxford University Press, 2012.

Belda Plans, Juan. *La Escuela de Salamanca* [The School of Salamanca]. Madrid: BAC, 2000.

Bellarmine, Robert. "Controversiarum De Summo Pontifice Liber Quintus (De potestate Pontificis temporali)." In Vol. 2, *Roberti Bellarmini Opera Omnia*. Edited by Justinus Fèvre. Paris: Vivès, 1870.

———. *On Temporal and Spiritual Authority*. Edited by Stefania Tutino. Indianapolis: Liberty Fund, 2012.

Belloc, Hilaire. *The Servile State*. London: Constable, 1927.

Bellocq Montano, Arturo. "What is Catholic Social Teaching in the Mission of the Church?" In *Handbook of Catholic Social Teaching: A Guide for Christians in the World Today*, edited by Martin Schlag, 9–20. Washington, D.C.: The Catholic University of America Press, 2017.

Benedict. *The Rule of Saint Benedict*. Translated by Leonard Doyle. Collegeville, Minn.: The Liturgical Press, 2001.

Benedict XVI. *Christmas Address to the Roman Curia*. December 22, 2005.

———. *Deus Caritas Est*. Encyclical Letter. December 25, 2005.

———. *Address to the Participants in the Plenary Assembly of the Pontifical Commission for Latin America*. January 20, 2007.

———. *Inaugural Address at the Fifth General Conference of the Bishops of Latin America and the Caribbean*. May 13, 2007.

———. *Message for the World Day of Peace 2009*. December 8, 2008.

———. *Caritas in Veritate*. Encyclical Letter. June 29, 2009.

———. *Address in Westminster Hall*. September 17, 2010.

———. *Homily for the Celebration of First Vespers of the First Sunday of Advent for Unborn Life*. November 27, 2010.

———. *Address in the Reichstag Building on His Visit to the Bundestag*. September 22, 2011.

———. *Africae Munus*. Apostolic Exhortation. November 19, 2011.

Bequette, John P. *Christian Humanism: Creation, Redemption, and Reintegration*. Lanham: University Press of America, 2007.

Bergoglio, Jorge Mario-Papa Francesco. *Interviste e conversazioni con i giornalisti: Due anni di Pontificato*. Vatican City: Libreria Editrice Vaticana, 2015. Prior edition published in English as *God is Always Near: Conversations with Pope Francis*. Huntington, Ind.: Our Sunday Visitor, 2015.

Berman, Harold J. *Law and Revolution II: The Impact of the Protestant Reformations on the Western Legal Tradition.* Cambridge, Mass.: Harvard University Press, 2003.

Bernardino of Siena. *Quadragesimale de Evangelio aeterno.* Vol. 4, *S. Bernardini Senensis, Opera Omnia, Quadragesimale de Evangelio aeterno.* Quaracchi: Collegio S. Bonaventurae, 1956.

———. *Antologia delle Prediche volgari: Economia civile e cura pastorale nei sermoni di San Bernardino da Siena.* Edited by Flavio Felice and Mattia Fochesato. Siena: Cantagalli, 2010.

Berry, Christopher J. *The Idea of Commercial Society in the Scottish Enlightenment.* Edinburgh: Edinburgh University Press, 2013.

Böckenförde, Ernst-Wolfgang. "Die Entstehung des Staates als Vorgang der Säkularisation." In *Recht, Staat, Freiheit: Studien zur Rechtsphilosophie, Staatstheorie und Verfassungsgeschichte,* 92–114. Frankfurt: Suhrkamp, 2006.

———. *Der säkularisierte Staat: Sein Charakter, seine Rechtfertigung und seine Probleme im 21. Jahrhundert.* München: Carl Friedrich von Siemens Stiftung, 2007.

Boff, Leonardo and Clodovis Boff. *Introducing Liberation Theology.* Maryknoll, N.Y.: Orbis Books, 2015.

Boo, Juan Vicente. *El Papa de la Alegría* [The Pope of Joy]. Barcelona: Espasa, 2016.

Bracciolini, Poggio. "De avaricia." In *Prosatori Latini del Quattrocento.* Edited by Eugenio Garin. Milano: Riccardo Ricciardi Editore, 1952.

Brague, Rémi. *Eccentric Culture: A Theory of Western Civilization.* South Bend: St. Augustine's Press, 2002.

Brooks, Arthur C. *The Road to Freedom: How to Win the Fight for Free Enterprise.* New York: Basic Books, 2012.

Carpenter, Kenneth E. *The Dissemination of* The Wealth of Nations *in French and in France 1776–1843.* New York: The Bibliographical Society of America, 2002.

Casanova, José. *Public Religions in the Modern World.* Chicago: The University of Chicago Press, 1994.

Chafuen, Alejandro A. *Faith and Liberty: The Economic Thought of the Late Scholastics.* Lanham: Lexington Books, 2003.

Chesterton, G.K. *What's Wrong With the World.* Leipzig: Tauchnitz, 1910.

Chrysostom, John. "De Lazaro." In Vol. 48, *Patrologiae cursus completus. Series graeca.* Edited by J.P. Migne. Paris: Imprimerie Catholique, 1862.

Cierva, Ricardo de la. *Jesuitas, Iglesia y Marxismo 1965–1985: La teología de la liberación desenmascarada* [Jesuits, Church, and Marxism 1965–1985: Liberation theology unmasked]. Madrid: Plaza & Janes, 1986.

Clement of Alexandria. *Who is the Rich Man That is Being Saved?* Edited by Percy Mordaunt Barnard. In *Early Christian Classics* 66. London: Society for Promoting Christian Knowledge, 1901.

Congregation for the Doctrine of the Faith. *Instruction on Certain Aspects of the "Theology of Liberation."* August 6, 1984.

———. *Libertatis Conscientia: Instruction on Christian Freedom and Liberation.* March 22, 1986.

———. *Notification on the Works of Father Jon Sobrino, SJ.* November 26, 2006.

———. *Explanatory Note on the Notification on the Works of Father Jon Sobrino, SJ.* November 26, 2006.

Consejo Episcopal latinoamericano. *II Conferencia General del Episcopado Latinoamericano: Documentos finales de Medellín.*1968. http://www.celam.org/doc_conferencias/Documento_Conclusivo_Medellin.pdf. Accessed March 22, 2017.

———. "La evangelización en el presente y en el futuro del América Latina." In *Documento de Puebla: III Conferencia General del Episcopado Latino-americano.* 1979. http://www.celam.org/doc_conferencias/Documento_Conclusivo_Puebla.pdf. Accessed March 22, 2017.

———. *Documento de Santo Domingo: IV Conferencia General del Episco-pado Latinoamericano.* 1992. http://www.celam.org/doc_conferencias/Documento_Conclusivo_Santo_Domingo.pdf. Accessed March 22, 2017.

———. *Document of Aparecida: V General Conference of the Latin American Episcopate.*2007. http://www.celam.org/aparecida/Ingles.pdf. Accessed April 18, 2016.

Cotrugli, Benedetto. *Il libro dell'arte di mercatura.* Edited by Ugo Tucci. Venezia: Arsenale Editrice, 1990.

Curnow, Rohan M. "Which Preferential Option for the Poor? A History of the Doctrine's Bifurcation." *Modern Theology* 31, no. 1 (2015): 27–59.

De Lubac, Henri. *The Drama of Atheist Humanism.* San Francisco: Ignatius Press, 1995.

De Soto, Domingo. *De iustitia et iure.* Madrid: Instituto de Estudios Políticos, 1968.

Deaton, Angus. *The Great Escape: Health, Wealth, and the Origins of Inequality.* Princeton and Oxford: Princeton University Press, 2013.

Decretum Gratiani. Vol. 1, *Corpus iuris canonici.* Edited by Aemilius Ludwig Richter and Emil Friedberg. Graz: Akademische Druck- und Verlagsanstalt, 1955.

Delgado, Mariano and Michael Sievernich. "Zur Rezeption und Interpretation des Konzils der Metaphern." In *Die großen Metaphern des Zweiten Vatika-nischen Konzils. Ihre Bedeutung für heute,* edited by Mariano Delgado and Michael Sievernich, 15–32. Freiburg: Herder, 2013.

Denzinger, Heinrich. *Enchiridion Symbolorum: A Compendium of Creeds, Definitions and Declarations of the Catholic Church.* Edited by Peter Hünermann. San Francisco: Ignatius Press, 2012.

Donati, Pierpaolo. *La matrice teologica della società* [The Theological Matrix of Society]. Soveria Mannelli: Rubbettino, 2010.

———. *Relational Sociology: A New Paradigm for the Social Sciences.* London: Routledge, 2011.

———. "Azione morale, riflessività e soggetto relazionale."*Annales Theologici* 26, no.2 (2012): 275–304.

———. "Beyond the Market/State Binary Code: The Common Good as a Relational Good." In *Free Markets and the Culture of Common Good*, edited by Martin Schlag and Juan Andrés Mercado, 61–81. Heidelberg: Springer, 2012.

Economic Commission for Latin America and the Caribbean. "Publications." http://www.cepal.org/en/publications. Accessed May 17, 2017.

Ellis, John Tracy. *The Life of James Cardinal Gibbons, Archbishop of Baltimore, 1834–1921.*Westminster: Christian Classics, 1987.

Escrivá, Josemaría. *Conversations with Monsignor Escrivá de Balaguer.* Dublin: Ecclesia Press, 1972.

Extraordinary Synod of Bishops. *The Final Report of the 1985 Extraordinary Synod.* December 8, 1985. https://www.ewtn.com/library/CURIA/SYNFINAL.HTM. Accessed June 9, 2017.

Fazio, Mariano. *El Papa Francisco: Claves de su pensamiento.* Madrid: Rialp, 2013. Translated into English as *Pope Francis: Keys to His Thought.* New Rochelle, N.Y.: Scepter Publishers, 2013.

Ferguson, Niall. *The Ascent of Money: A Financial History of the World.* New York: Penguin Press, 2008.

Fitzgibbons, Athol. *Adam Smith's System of Liberty, Wealth, and Virtue: The Moral and Political Foundations of* The Wealth of Nations. Oxford: Clarendon Press, 1995.

Francis. *Homily for the "Missa Pro Ecclesia" with the Cardinal Electors.* March 14, 2013.

———. *Carta a Los Participantes en la 105 Asamblea Plenaria de la Conferencia Episcopal Argentina.* March 25, 2013. *Address to the Participants in the Plenary Assembly of the International Union of Superiors General.* May 8, 2013.

———. *Address at the Vigil of Pentecost with the Ecclesial Movements.* May 18, 2013.

———. *Address to the Centesimus Annus Pro Pontifice Foundation.* May 25, 2013.

———. *Address to the Students of the Jesuit Schools of Italy and Albania.* June 7, 2013.

———. *Letter to H. E. Mr. David Cameron, British Prime Minister, on the Occasion of the G8 Meeting.* June 15, 2013.

———. *Address to Participants in the Ecclesial Convention of the Diocese of Rome.* June 17, 2013.

———. *Address to the Leadership of the Episcopal Conferences of Latin America.* July 28, 2013.

———. *Press Conference During the Return Flight from Rio de Janeiro.* July 28, 2013.

———. *Address to the Participants in a Conference Sponsored by the Pontifical Council for Justice and Peace Celebrating the 50th Anniversary of* Pacem in Terris. October 3, 2013.

———. *Meditation: Dirty Bread of Corruption.* November 8, 2013.

———. *Evangelii Gaudium*. Apostolic Exhortation. November 24, 2013.

———. *Lenten Message*. December 26, 2013.

———. *Message to the Executive Chairman of the World Economic Forum on the Occasion of the Annual Meeting at Davos-Klosters*. January 17, 2014.

———. *General Audience*. January 29, 2014.

———. *Address to the Italian Pro-Life Movement*. April 11, 2014.

———. *In-Flight Press Conference from Korea to Rome*. August 18, 2014.

———. *Address to Representatives of the Confederation of Italian Cooperatives*. February 28, 2015.

———. *Misericordiae Vultus*. Bull. April 11, 2015.

———. *Laudato Si'*. Encyclical Letter. May 24, 2015.

———. *Address at the Second World Meeting of Popular Movements*. July 9, 2015.

———. *In-Flight Press Conference of His Holiness Pope Francis from Paraguay to Rome*. July 13, 2015.

———. *Address to the Bishops of the United States of America*. September 23, 2015.

———. *Address to the Joint Session of the United States Congress*. September 24, 2015.

———. *Address to the Members of the General Assembly of the United Nations Organization*. September 25, 2015.

———. *Speech to the Christian Union of Business Executives*. October 31, 2015.

———. *Address to the Participants in the Fifth Convention of the Italian Church*. November 10, 2015.

———. *Letter to Cardinal Marc Ouellet, President of the Pontifical Commission for Latin America*. March 19, 2016.

———. *Address at the Conferral of the Charlemagne Prize*. May 6, 2016.

———. *Address to Participants in the International Conference of the Christian Union of the Business Executives (UNIAPAC)*. November 17, 2016.

———. *Address to Participants in the Meeting "Economy of Communion," sponsored by the Focolare Movement*. February 4, 2017.

———. *Pastoral Visit to Genoa: Encounter with representatives of the world of work*. May 27, 2017.

Fuenmayor, Amadeo de, Valentín Gómez-Iglesias, and José Luis Illanes. *The Canonical Path of Opus Dei: The History and Defense of a Charism*. Translated by William H. Stetson. Princeton, N.J.: Scepter Publishers, 1994.

Fukuyama, Francis. *Trust: The Social Virtues and the Creation of Prosperity*. New York: Simon & Schuster, 1995.

George, Francis Cardinal. *The Difference God Makes: A Catholic Vision of Faith, Communion, and Culture*. New York: The Crossroad Publishing Company, 2009.

Gera, Lucio. "Cultura y dependencia a luz de la reflexión teológica," and "Pueblo, religión del pueblo e iglesia," in *Escritos Teológico-Pastoralesde Lucio Gera*. Vol. 1, *Del Preconcilio a la Conferencia de Puebla (1956–1981)*. Edited by Virginia Raquel Azcuy, Carlos M. Galli, and Marcelo González. Buenos Aires: Agape Libros – Facultad de Teología UCA, 2006.

Gil Hellín, Francisco, ed. *Constitutionis pastoralis Gaudium et Spes: Synopsis historica* [Pastoral Constitution Gaudium et Spes: Historical Synopsis]. Pamplona: EUNSA, 1985.

Gregory the Great. *Dialogues*. Translated by Odo John Zimmerman. *Fathers of the Church* 39. New York: Fathers of the Church, Inc., 1959.

——. *Moralia in Iob Libri XXIII-XXXV*. In Vol. 143 B, *Corpus Christianorum*. Edited by Marci Adriaen. Turnhout: Brepols, 1985.

Gregory, Brad S. *The Unintended Reformation: How a Religious Revolution Secularized Society*. Cambridge, Mass.: Harvard University Press, 2012.

Grupo de reflexión "Centesimus Annus." *Diálogos entre Juan Pablo II y Fidel Castro* [Dialogues between John Paul II and Fidel Castro]. Buenos Aires: Editorial de la Ciencia y Cultura, 1998.

Guardini, Romano. *Werke*. Edited by Franz Heinrich. Paderborn: Schöningh, 1989.

Gutiérrez, Gustavo. *Teología de la Liberación*. Salamanca: Ediciones Sígueme, 2009. Translated into English by Caridad Inda and John Eagleson as *A Theology of Liberation: History, Politics, and Salvation*. Maryknoll, N.Y.: Orbis Books, 1973. Reprint 1988 with new introduction by author, 2014.

Gutiérrez, Gustavo and Gerhard Ludwig Müller. *Dalla parte dei poveri: Teologia della liberazione, teologia della chiesa*. Padova: Messaggero di Sant'Antonio; Bologna: EMI, 2013. Translated into English by Robert A. Krieg and James B. Nickoloff as *On the Side of the Poor: The Theology of Liberation*. Maryknoll, N.Y.: Orbis Books, 2015

Haakonssen, Knud, ed. *The Cambridge Companion to Adam Smith*. Cambridge: Cambridge University Press, 2006.

Hanks, Thomas D. "Poor, Poverty (NT)." In Vol. 5, *The Anchor Bible Dictionary*. Edited by David Noel Freedman, 414–24. New York: Doubleday, 1992.

Härle, Wilfried. "Zweireichelehre II." In Vol. 36, *Theologische Realenzyklopädie*. Edited by Gerhard Müller, 784–89. Berlin: De Gruyter, 2004.

Hayek, Friedrich August. *The Constitution of Liberty: The Definitive Edition*. In *The Collected Works of F.A. Hayek* 17. Edited by Ronald Hamowy. Chicago: The University of Chicago Press, 2011.

Himitian, Evangelina. *Francesco: Il Papa della gente* [Francis: The pope of the people]. Milano: BUR, 2013.

Hirschfeld, Mary L. "Reflection on the Financial Crisis: Aquinas on the Proper Role of Finance." *Journal of the Society of Christian Ethics* 35, no. 1 (2015): 63–82.

Hittinger, Russell. "Introduction to Modern Catholicism." In *The Teachings of Modern Roman Catholicism on Law, Politics, and Human Nature*, edited by John Witte Jr. and Frank S. Alexander, 1–38. New York: Columbia University Press, 2007.

Hobbes, Thomas. *Leviathan*. Edited by J. C. A. Gaskin. Oxford: Oxford University Press, 2009.

Hugh of St. Victor. *Didascalicon: I doni della promessa divina. L'essenza dell'amore. Discorso in lode del divino amore*. Milano: Rusconi, 1987.

Illanes, José Luis. "Teología de la liberación: Análisis de su método." [Liberation theology: an analysis of its method] *Scripta Theologica* 17, no. 3 (1985): 743–88.

Isensee, Josef. "Die katholische Kritik an den Menschenrechten: Der liberale Freiheitsentwurf in der Sicht der Päpste des 19. Jahrhunderts." In *Menschenrechte und Menschenwürde*, edited by Ernst-Wolfgang Böckenförde and Robert Spaemann, 138–174. Stuttgart: Klett-Cotta, 1987.

Ivereigh, Austen. *The Great Reformer: Francis and the Making of a Radical Pope.* New York: Holt, 2014.

Ivern, Francisco. "L'analisi marxista." In *Pedro Arrupe: Un uomo per gli altri*, edited by Gianni La Bella. 797–807. Bologna: Il Mulino, 2007.

John XXIII. *Mater et Magistra.* Encyclical Letter. May 15, 1961.

———. *Pacem in Terris.* Encyclical Letter. April 11, 1963.

John Paul II. *Laborem Exercens.* Encyclical Letter. September 14, 1981.

———. *Redemptoris Mater.* Encyclical Letter. March 25, 1987.

———. *Sollicitudo Rei Socialis.* Encyclical Letter. December 30, 1987.

———. *Christifideles Laici.* Apostolic Exhortation. December 30, 1988.

———. *Centesimus Annus.* Encyclical Letter. May 1, 1991.

———. *Veritatis Splendor.* Encyclical Letter. August 6, 1993.

———. *Discorso ai Rappresentanti del Mondo Accademico e della Cultura nell'Ateneo della Capitale.* September 9, 1993.

———. *Tertio Millennio Adveniente.* Apostolic Letter. November 10, 1994.

———. *Evangelium Vitae.* Encyclical Letter. March 25, 1995.

———. *Vita Consecrata.* Apostolic Exhortation. March 25, 1996.

———. *Ecclesia in America.* Apostolic Exhortation. January 22, 1999.

———. *Address at the Fifteenth World Youth Day.* August 19, 2000.

———. *Novo Millennio Ineunte.* Apostolic Letter. January 6, 2001.

Kaletsky, Anatole. *Capitalism 4.0: The Birth of a New Economy.* London: Bloomsbury, 2011.

Kaye, Joel. *Economy and Nature in the Fourteenth Century: Money, Market Exchange, and the Emergence of Scientific Thought.* Cambridge: Cambridge University Press, 1998.

Kempshall, Matthew S. *The Common Good in Late Medieval Political Thought.* Oxford: Clarendon Press, 1999.

Kolb, Robert. "Two-Kingdoms Doctrine." In Vol. 5, *The Encyclopedia of Christianity.* Edited by Erwin Fahlbusch, Jan Milic Lochman, Jaroslav Pelikan, John Samuel Mbiti, and Lukas Vischer, 569–75. Grand Rapids: Eerdmans-Brill, 2008.

Kvalbein, Hans. "Poor/poverty." In *New Dictionary of Biblical Theology.* Edited by T. Desmond Alexander and Brian S. Rosner, 687–90. Leicester: Inter-Varsity Press, 2003.

La Bella, Gianni. Introduction. *Pedro Arrupe: Un uomo per gli altri* [Pedro Arrupe: A man for others]. Edited by Gianni La Bella. 7–48. Bologna: Il Mulino, 2007.

Langholm, Odd. *Economics in the Medieval Schools: Wealth, Exchange, Value, Money & Usury According to the Paris Theological Tradition, 1200–1350.* Leiden: E.J. Brill, 1992.

————. *The Merchant in the Confessional: Trade and Price in the Pre-Reformation Penitential Handbooks.* Leiden: Brill, 2003.

Lapide, Pinchas. *Il discorso della montagna: Utopia o programma?* Brescia: Paideia, 2003.Translated into English as *The Sermon on the Mount: Utopia or Program for Action?* Maryknoll, N.Y.: Orbis Books, 1986.

Le Bras, Gabriel. "Usure." In Vol. 15.2, *Dictionnaire de Théologie Catholique.* Edited by A. Vacant, E. Mangenot, and E. Amann, 2315–390. Paris: Letouzey & Ané, 1950.

Leo XIII. *Rerum Novarum.* Encyclical Letter. May 12, 1891.

Locke, John. *The Second Treatise of Government.* In *Two Treatises of Government and A Letter Concerning Toleration.* Edited by Ian Shapiro. New Haven: Yale University Press, 2003.

MacIntyre, Alasdair. *After Virtue: A Study in Moral Theory.* London: Duckworth, 1985.

Manent, Pierre. "L'Église entre l'Humanité Réelle et l'Humanité Rêvée." In *The Global Quest for* Tranquillitas Ordinis: Pacem in Terris, *Fifty Years Later,* edited by The Pontifical Academy of Social Sciences, 109–18. Vatican City: Libreria Editrice Vaticana, 2013.

Manns, Frédéric. "Ricchezza e povertà nel giudaismo intertestamentario." In Panimolle, S.A., ed. *Ricchezza – Povertà nella Bibbia* [Wealth – Poverty in the Bible].Vol. 59, *Dizionario di spiritualità biblico-patristica,* 73–97. Roma: Borla, 2011.

Mara, Maria Grazia, ed. *Ricchezza e povertà nel cristianesimo primitivo* [Wealth and poverty in early Christianity]. Roma: Città Nuova, 1991.

Maritain, Jacques. *Man and the State.* Edited by Richard O'Sullivan. London: Hollis & Carter, 1954. Reprint Washington, D.C.: The Catholic University of America Press, 1998.

————. *True Humanism.* London: Bles and Scribner's, 1954.

Marx, Reinhard. *Das Kapital: Ein Plädoyer für den Menschen.* München: Pattloch, 2008.

McCann, Dennis P. "Option for the Poor: Rethinking a Catholic Tradition." In *The Preferential Option for the Poor,* edited by Richard John Neuhaus, 35–52. Grand Rapids: Eerdmans, 1988.

Methol Ferré, Alberto and Alver Metalli. *Il Papa e il Filosofo* [The Pope and the philosopher]. Siena: Cantagalli, 2014.

Milanovic, Branko. *Global Inequality: A New Approach for the Age of Globalization.* Cambridge, Mass.: The Belknap Press of Harvard University Press, 2016.

Mueller, Dennis C. Introduction. "The Good, the Bad, and the Ugly." In *The Oxford Handbook of Capitalism,* edited by Dennis C. Mueller, 1–14. Oxford: Oxford University Press, 2012.

Nazianzen, Gregory. "On St. Basil." In *Funeral Orations by Saint Gregory Nazianzen and Saint Ambrose.* Translated by Leo P. McCauley et al. *The Fathers of the Church* 22. Washington, D.C.: The Catholic University of America Press, 1953.

Newman, John Henry. *Apologia pro vita sua.* London: Routledge, 1907.

Noonan, John T., Jr. *The Scholastic Analysis of Usury*. Cambridge: Harvard University Press, 1957.

Novak, Michael. *The Spirit of Democratic Capitalism*. New York: Touchstone, 1982.

Olivi, Peter John. *Usure, compere e vendite: la scienza economica del XIII secolo* [Usury, buying, and selling: the economic science of the 13th century]. Edited by Amleto Spicciani, Paolo Vian, and Giancarlo Andenna. Novara: Europía, 1998.

———. *Traité des contrats*. Edited by Sylvain Piron. Paris: Les Belles Lettres, 2012.

———. *A Treatise on Contracts*. Translated into English by Ryan Thornton and Michael Cusato, OFM. St. Bonaventure, N.Y.: Franciscan Institute Publications, 2016.

Palmieri, Matteo. *Vita civile*. Edited by Gino Belloni. Firenze: Sansoni, 1982.

Panimolle, S.A., ed. *Ricchezza – Povertà nella Bibbia* [Wealth – Poverty in the Bible]. Vol. 59, *Dizionario di spiritualità biblico-patristica*. Roma: Borla, 2011.

Paul VI. *Address During the Last General Meeting of the Second Vatican Council*. December 7, 1965.

———. *Populorum Progressio*. Encyclical Letter. March 26, 1967.

———. *Octogesima Adveniens*. Apostolic Letter. May 14, 1971.

———. *Evangelii Nuntiandi*. Apostolic Exhortation. December 8, 1975.

Pellegrini, Marco. *Religione e Umanesimo nel primo Rinascimento da Petrarca ad Alberti* [Religion and humanism in the early Rennaissance: From Petrarch to Alberti]. Firenze: Casa editrice Le Lettere, 2012.

Pereña, Luciano. "La Escuela de Salamanca y la duda indiana." In *Francisco de Vitoria y la Escuela de Salamanca: La ética en la conquista de América*, edited by Demetrio Ramos, 292–344. Madrid: CSIC, 1984.

Pesch, Heinrich. *Liberalismus, Sozialismus und christliche Gesellschaftsordnung*. Vol. 2, *Die sociale Frage beleuchtet durch die "Stimmen aus Maria-Laach."* Freiburg: Herder, 1899.

Pieper, Josef. *Leisure: The Basis of Culture*. Translated by Gerald Malsbary. South Bend: St. Augustine's Press, 1998.

Piketty, Thomas. *Capital in the Twenty-First Century*. Cambridge, Mass.: Harvard University Press, 2014.

Pius XI. *Quadragesimo Anno*. Encyclical Letter. May 15, 1931.

Pleins, J. David. "Poor, Poverty (OT)." In Vol. 5, *The Anchor Bible Dictionary*. Edited by David Noel Freedman, 402–14. New York: Doubleday, 1992.

Pontifical Council for Justice and Peace. *Compendium of the Social Doctrine of the Church*. Vatican City: Libreria Editrice Vaticana, 2005.

———. *The Vocation of the Business Leader*. Vatican City: Pontifical Council for Justice and Peace, 2012.

Rahner, Hugo. *Church and State in Early Christianity*. San Francisco: Ignatius Press, 1992.

Rahner, Karl. "Über die Einheit von Nächsten- und Gottesliebe." In Vol. 12, *Sämtliche Werke*. Edited by Johann Friedrich Herbart. Freiburg: Herder, 2005.

Ratzinger, Joseph. "Market Economy and Ethics." In *Church and Economy in Dialogue: A Symposium in Rome*, edited by Lothar Roos, 13–16. Cologne: Bachem, 1986.

———. *Principles of Catholic Theology: Building Stones for a Fundamental Theology*. San Francisco: Ignatius Press, 1987.

Reno, R. R. "Thy Will be Done." *First Things*. August–September 2015: 3–7.

Rhee, Helen. *Loving the Poor, Saving the Rich: Wealth, Poverty, and Early Christian Formation*. Grand Rapids: Baker Academic, 2012.

Rhonheimer, Martin. *Christentum und säkularer Staat* [Christianity and the secular state]. Freiburg: Herder, 2012. A shorter version of this book is translated into English by William F. Murphy as "Christianity and Secularity: Past and Present of a Complex Relationship," in *The Common Good of Constitutional Democracy: Essays in Political Philosophy and on Catholic Social Teaching*. Washington, D.C.: The Catholic University of America Press, 2013.

Rivas Rebaque, Fernando. *Defensor pauperum: Los pobres en Basilio de Cesarea: homilías VI, VII, VIII y XIVB* [Defender of the poor: The poor in Basil of Cesarea: Homilies VI, VII, VIII, and XIVB]. Madrid: BAC, 2005.

Roos, Lothar. "Tugendethik und Ordnungsethik: Papst Franziskus und die Soziallehre der Kirche." *Die Neue Ordnung* 70, no.6 (2016): 424–34.

Rubin, Sergio and Francesca Ambrogetti. *Pope Francis: Conversations with Jorge Bergoglio— His Life in His Own Words*. New York: Penguin Group, 2013. Translated into Spanish as *El Jesuita. La historia de Francisco, el Papa argentino*. Barcelona: Vergara, 2013.

Ruggie, John Gerard. *Just Business: Multinational Corporations and Human Rights*. New York: W.W. Norton, 2013.

Scannone, Juan Carlos. *Teologia de la Liberación y Doctrina Social de la Iglesia* [Liberation theology and the social doctrine of the Church]. Buenos Aires: Guadalupe-Cristiandad, 1987.

———. *Quando il popolo diventa teologo: Protagonisti e percorsi della teología del pueblo*. Bologna: EMI, 2016.

Schlag, Martin. "The Encyclical *Caritas in Veritate*, Christian Tradition and the Modern World." In *Free Markets and the Culture of Common Good*, edited by Martin Schlag and Juan Andrés Mercado, 93–109. Heidelberg: Springer, 2012.

———. *Cómo poner a dieta al cannibal: Ética para salir de la crisis económica*. Madrid: Rialp, 2015.

———. "Catholic Social Teaching on the Economy: Pope Benedict XVI's Legacy." In *Free Markets with Solidarity and Sustainability: Facing the Challenge*, edited by Martin Schlag and Juan Andrés Mercado, 178–196. Washington, D.C.: The Catholic University of America Press, 2016.

———. "The Preferential Option for the Poor." In *The Development of Catholic Social Teaching*, edited by Gerard Bradley and Christian Brugger. Notre Dame: Notre Dame University Press, forthcoming.

———, ed. *The Handbook of Catholic Social Teaching: A Guide for Christians in the World Today*. Washington, D.C.: The Catholic University of America Press, 2017.

Schumpeter, Joseph A. *Capitalism, Socialism and Democracy*. New York: Harper, 2008.

Scotus, John Duns. *Ordinatio III*. In Vol. 19, *Opera Omnia*. Edited by Commissio Scotistica. Civitas Vaticana: Typis Vaticanis, 2007.

———. *Ordinatio IV*. In Vol. 13, *Opera Omnia*. Edited by Commissio Scotistica. Civitas Vaticana: Typis Vaticanis, 2011.

Scruton, Roger. *Culture Counts: Faith and Feeling in a World Besieged*. New York: Encounter Books, 2007.

Sedmak, Clemens. *A Church of the Poor: Pope Francis and the Transformation of Orthodoxy*. Maryknoll: Orbis Books, 2016.

Sen, Amartya. *The Idea of Justice*. London: Penguin Books, 2010.

Shiller, Robert J. *Finance and the Good Society*. Princeton: Princeton University Press, 2013.

Siedentop, Larry. *Inventing the Individual: The Origins of Western Liberalism*. London: Penguin Books, 2015.

Skidelsky, Robert and Edward Skidelsky. *How Much is Enough? Money and the Good Life*. London: Penguin Books, 2013.

Smith, Adam. Vol. 1, *An Inquiry Into the Nature and Causes of the Wealth of Nations*. Edited by R. H. Campbell and A. S. Skinner. Indianapolis: Liberty Fund, 1979.

Sobrino, Jon. *Jesucristo liberador: Lectura histórico-teológica de Jesús de Nazaret*. Madrid: Trotta, 1991. Translated into English by Paul Burns and Francis McDonagh as *Jesus the Liberator: A Historical-Theological Reading of Jesus of Nazareth*. Maryknoll, N.Y.: Orbis Books, 1993. Reprint 2003.

Solzhenitsyn, Alexandr. "Nobel Lecture." 1970. *Nobelprize.org*. http://www.nobelprize.org/nobel_prizes/literature/laureates/1970/solzhenitsyn-lecture.html. Accessed March 23, 2017.

Stark, Rodney. *The Victory of Reason: How Christianity Led to Freedom, Capitalism, and Western Success*. New York: Random House, 2005.

Suda, Max Josef. *Die Ethik Martin Luthers* [The Ethics of Martin Luther]. Göttingen: Vandenhoeck & Ruprecht, 2006.

Taylor, Charles. *A Secular Age*. Cambridge, Mass.: Harvard University Press, 2007.

The 32nd General Congregation of the Society of Jesus, December 2–March 7, 1975. "Decree 4." In *Documents of the 31st and 32nd General Congregations of the Society of Jesus*. Edited by John Padberg, S.J. St. Louis: Institute of Jesuit Sources, 1997. http://onlineministries.creighton.edu/CollaborativeMinistry/our-mission-today.html. Accessed March 22, 2017.

Todeschini, Giacomo. *I Mercanti e il tempio: La società cristiana e il circolo virtuoso della ricchezza fra Medioevo ed età moderna* [The merchants and the temple: Christian society and the virtuous circle of wealth between the Middle Ages and the modern age]. Bologna: Il mulino, 2002.

———. *Franciscan Wealth: From Voluntary Poverty to Market Society*. Translated by Donatella Melucci. St. Bonaventure: Franciscan Institute Publications, 2009.

Treaty of Lisbon Amending the Treaty on European Union and the Treaty Establishing the European Community. *Official Journal of the European Union* 306/01 (2007/C): 1–231.

Utz, Arthur Fridolin. *Kommentar zu Thomas von Aquin, Summa Theologiae II-II, qq 57–79, Recht und Gerechtigkeit, Band 18 der deutsch-lateinischen Ausgabe der Summa Theologiae, übersetzt von den Dominikanern und Benediktinern Deutschlands und Österreichs.* Heidelberg: Gemeinschaftsverlag F. H. Kerle, 1953.

Valero, Urbano. *El proyecto de renovación de la Compañía de Jesús (1965–2007)* [The project of the renewal of the Society of Jesus (1965–2007)]. Bilbao: Mensajero – Sal Terrae, 2011.

Vatican Council II. *Lumen Gentium.* Dogmatic Constitution. November 21, 1964.

———. *Gaudium et Spes.* Pastoral Constitution. December 7, 1965.

Vega, Joseph de la. *Confusion de Confusiones: Portions Descriptive of the Amsterdam Stock Exchange.* Translated by Hermann Kellenbenz. Eastford, Conn.: Martino Fine Books, 2013.

Verstraeten, Johan. "Re-thinking Catholic Social Thought as Tradition." In *Catholic Social Thought: Twilight or Renaissance?*, edited by Jonathan Boswell, Francis P. McHugh, and Johan Verstraeten, 59–77. Leuven: Leuven University Press, 2000.

Veyne, Paul. Vol. 1, *A History of Private Life: From Pagan Rome to Byzantium.* Cambridge, Mass.: Harvard University Press, 1987. Reprint 2012 as *The Roman Empire.*

Vitoria, Francisco de. "Relectio De potestate Ecclesiae prior." In *Obras de Francisco de Vitoria: Relecciones teológicas*, edited by Teofilo Urdanoz, 242–327. Madrid: BAC, 1960.

Von Balthasar, Hans Urs. *The Moment of Christian Witness.* San Francisco: Ignatius Press, 1969. Reprint 1994.

White, Hilary. "Abandonment of Christian Principles Led to Europe's Economic Crisis: Hungarian Prime Minister." *Lifesite News*, November 20, 2012. http://www.lifesitenews.com/news/abandonment-of-christian-principles-led-to-europes-economic-crisis-hungaria/. Accessed March 23, 2017.

Wittreck, Fabian. *Geld als Instrument der Gerechtigkeit: Die Geldlehre des Hl. Thomas von Aquin in ihrem interkulturellen Kontext.* Paderborn: Schöningh, 2002.

The World Bank. "Poverty and Equity Data." http://povertydata.worldbank.org/poverty/home/. Accessed March 23, 2017.

Wood, Diana. *Medieval Economic Thought.* Cambridge: Cambridge University Press, 2002.

Ziesler, John. "Righteousness." In *The Oxford Companion to the Bible.* Edited by Bruce M. Metzger and Michael D. Coogan, 655–56. Oxford: Oxford University Press, 1993.

Zimmermann, Jens. *Hermeneutics: A Very Short Introduction.* Oxford: Oxford University Press, 2015.

Zingales, Luigi. *A Capitalism for the People: Recapturing the Lost Genius of American Prosperity*. New York: Basic Books, 2012.

———. "Does Finance Benefit Society?" Working Paper. The National Bureau of Economic Research, 2015. http://faculty.chicagobooth.edu/luigi. zingales/papers/research/finance.pdf. Accessed March 23, 2017.

Subject Index

Abortion, vii, 7, 36, 97n146, 97n148
Almsgiving, 21, 118, 122, 134
Anglo-Saxon countries, 24, 43n73, 54, 59, 62, 72–73, 77–78, 87
Argentina, 5, 53–54, 56–57, 61, 79–80, 83–86, 102–103, 111, 170
Avarice. *See* Greed

Bible, 8, 13–14, 18–19, 24, 33, 39n21, 40n38, 46n122, 69, 126–128, 131, 146, 186
Business: and Catholic theology, 1, 24–25, 33; and contemplation, 156–169; Francis's message on: vii–viii, 12, 30, 37, 70–71, 108–148; goal of, 18, 30, 34, 75–77, 113–114, 136–138; infusing with charity, 27, 143–144, 146, 168–169; as a vocation, 103, 113, 133, 149n23, 153n117, 156–159. *See also* Ethics, business

Capital: 9, 31–32, 35–36, 74, 80, 106, 108, 131; social capital, 140
Capitalism: 9, 24–25, 30–32, 49, 54, 62, 64–65, 73–77, 79–81, 87–88, 92n57, 100, 108, 111–112, 153n106; Anglo-American tradition of, *See* Anglo-Saxon countries; "crony," 28, 54, 83, 85, 147; financial, 30–31, 44n100, 106, 108, 112
Caritas in Veritate, 7, 39n20, 43n75, 43n84, 44n87, 44n89, 44n92, 47n125, 47n128, 117, 149n1, 154n146, 155n152, 165, 174, 183

Catholic social doctrine, *See* Catholic social teaching
Catholic social teaching: viii, 1–2, 7, 9, 15, 17, 21, 23, 26–28, 39n23, 49, 51, 65–67, 80, 82–83, 85, 122, 134, 136, 166, 169; and Francis, 113, 119, 131; principles of, 7–12
Catholic social thought: vii, 2–9, 21–22, 28, 37n2, 60, 65, 88; tradition of, 23–24, 75, 130, 141
Catholic social tradition: 2, 37n2, 51, 166, 168–169. *See also* Catholic social thought, tradition of
CELAM (Consejo Episcopal Latino-americano—the Latin American Bishops' Conference), 62, 65, 69–70, 94n90–94, 95n95–98, 176
Charity: 28, 60, 65, 91n37, 119, 136, 165; and business, 27, 37; and Catholic social teaching; 7–8, 27, 67, 117, 142; social: 7, 9, 11, 118, 135, 146, 165–67. *See also* Almsgiving
Children, 36, 77, 97n146, 100, 123, 148, 157
Chrematistic cycle, 35
Christ, vii, viii, 8–9, 14, 19, 24, 29, 36, 63–65, 104, 111, 113, 115–117, 119, 121–124, 126, 128–129, 136, 138, 142, 157–158, 160, 165, 167–168
Church Fathers, 13–15, 20–21, 23, 33, 118, 126
Civil society. *See* Society, civil
Collectivism, 15, 54, 113
Commerce, 23–24, 33, 44, 108, 132, 155n155

Commercial society, 21, 33, 43n73,
  73
Common good, 9, 16–18, 21, 41n53,
  55, 68, 80, 100, 102–103, 108, 110,
  112, 126, 133–135, 137, 145, 147,
  166, 169
Communism, 15–16, 24–25, 40n43,
  75, 85–86, 111
Community, 17–19, 68, 77, 90n16,
  103, 118, 126, 135, 153, 163;
  Christian, 2, 20, 77, 100, 127–128,
  163, 167
*Compendium of the Social Doctrine
  of the Church* (CSDC), 7, 12,
  39n19, 40n32–34, 40n42, 49,
  93n77, 149n10, 150n33, 182
Competition, 10–11, 23, 33, 73, 81,
  88, 106, 108, 139, 145–147
Congregation for the Doctrine
  of the Faith (CDF), 64, 66, 74,
  92n66, 93n70, 93n73, 176
Conscience, 10, 15, 34, 60, 70, 75, 86,
  112, 118, 120, 129, 135, 139
Consumer: 106–108, 145, 147; credit,
  76, 130; goods, 133
Consumerism, 36, 81, 85, 129,
  131–132, 153n106
Consumption, 59, 109, 131, 140,
  153n106, 168
Contemplation, ix, 148, 156,
  159–162, 164–165, 168
Conversion, 29, 54, 63, 67, 100
Cooperatives, 44n97, 146–147,
  152n103, 155n157
Corporation, 65, 73, 77, 81, 84–85,
  101, 106, 137
Corruption, 11, 28, 54–55, 85, 88,
  109, 112, 147–148, 155n158–159
Cronyism. *See* Capitalism, "crony"
Cultural context: viii, 20, 24, 26, 34,
  51, 55–56, 72, 87–88, 169; Latin
  American, 57, 71–72, 79, 81, 87;
  Western, 25, 66, 78, 111, 127, 145,
  170
Cultural transfer, viii, 55–56, 72–73,
  87–88, 127, 162

Cultural transformation, 37, 56, 65,
  101, 110, 116–117, 125, 136, 139,
  159, 164, 167–168
Culture: 5, 21, 67–68, 71–74, 110,
  117, 125, 159; Christian and
  Catholic, 1, 76–77, 117, 164; crisis
  of, 7, 156, 164; "throwaway", 111,
  131–133; of work, 82, 101, 140

Debt: 35–36, 65, 84, 130–131, 156;
  public 131, 153n107
Democracy, 4, 9, 12, 24, 33, 58, 81,
  132, 163, 167. *See also* Inclusion
Dependence theory, 64–66, 92n56
Developed countries, 31, 84, 87, 129,
  140
Developing countries, 45n104, 61,
  84, 106
Development: of Church doctrine
  and theology, 3, 8–9, 14, 16, 35,
  38n8, 48, 56, 61–62, 67, 75, 125,
  164–166; economic, 27–28, 36,
  45n102, 45n107, 71, 102, 109,
  121, 135, 139, 170n20; integral
  human: 21–22, 28, 43n75, 60,
  79, 110, 112, 133, 136–140, 146,
  153n117; international, 9, 28,
  45n105, 55, 92n56
Dignity: 9–10, 18, 21–22, 26,
  52, 86–87, 98, 118, 120–121,
  130–131, 134–135, 138–140, 144,
  148, 149n1, 166; of work, 30, 80,
  102–103, 105, 112, 121, 148
Dualism, 3, 26

Ecology: 36, 52, 97n148, 99, 103, 131;
  integral: 137
Economic cycle, 31, 34, 150n28
Economic theory, ix, 11, 21, 23, 54,
  75, 105, 107, 110, 130
Economy, the: vii–viii, 1, 4, 7, 11–12,
  23, 31, 49, 53–54, 56–57, 72–77,
  80, 84, 87, 98, 103–107, 109–114,
  127, 135, 137, 139–140, 143–145,
  147–148, 159, 164–165. *See also*
  Development, economic; Ethics,

economic; Freedom, economic; Institutions, economic; Law, economic; Order, economic, Politics and economics, Value, economic

Economy of communion, 77, 95n114

Economy, liquid. *See* Liquidity

Education, 22, 31, 58, 61, 66, 82, 111, 118, 120, 139, 166

Employment, 22, 71, 81, 84, 103, 106, 133, 135, 140, 146, 156

Entrepreneur, 31, 76–77, 85, 88, 103–104, 108, 133, 135, 145, 165

Equality of opportunity, 66, 74, 82–83, 137–139. *See also* Inequality; Inequity

Ethics: business, viii, 76, 110, 112, 130, 134–135, 139–140; economic, 23, 25, 28, 71, 76–77, 82, 88, 110, 130, 135, 140, 147, 169n1; finance, 31–32, 36; individual, 7, 19, 125; institutional, 11–12, 40n31; social, 7, 21, 27, 68, 70, 155n153

Europe, 11, 24, 27, 44n96, 61–62, 74, 78–79, 84, 101, 122, 141, 164–165, 171n28

European Union: 170n25

Evangelii Gaudium, 41n44, 41n53, 43n76, 43n78, 44n98, 52, 90n16, 90n19, 90n20, 90n24, 90n33, 90n35, 95n99–100, 96n136, 97n147, 99, 149n4, 149n9, 151n66, 151n70–71, 152n82, 152n97, 152n100, 152n104, 153n115–116, 153n125, 154n135, 154n138, 154n141, 155n151, 155n154, 169, 170n7, 170n9, 170n13, 170n16, 171n37–40, 170n44, 178

Exchange: 17, 22–23, 26, 29, 31, 34–35, 54, 88, 130, 140; stock, 44n96

Exclusion, 53, 59, 64, 66, 70, 85, 101–102, 110, 112, 121, 128–129, 133, 137–139, 161

Exploitation, 21, 23–24, 27, 59, 63–65, 74–77, 79–81, 88, 90n36, 144. *See also* Institutions, extractive

Family, 6, 22, 87, 113, 132, 138–139, 168–169; supporting, 21, 30, 86, 118, 120–121, 125, 130

Faith: Christian, 1, 6–7, 12, 64, 117, 123, 126–127; and church doctrine, 48, 50, 60, 64, 69, 78, 93n66; and culture, 1, 52, 55–56, 125; and the poor, 2, 54, 63, 90n33, 119–120; and reason, 6, 26, 35; social dimension of, 3, 5–6, 21–22, 59, 70–71, 124, 127–128, 136, 167; virtue of, 59, 124, 159, 161, 169

Finance: viii, 12, 28–37, 40n31, 44n96, 44n100, 45n102–106, 70, 81, 104, 107, 130, 186; Islamic 47n124

Financial capitalism. *See* Capitalism, financial

Financial markets. *See* Markets, financial

Fraternity, 27, 86, 124, 144, 146, 155n153. *See also* Charity, social

Freedom: 106, 135–136, 140, 160; Christian, 5, 87, 100, 159; economic, 8, 22, 25, 105, 154n140; interior, 14, 19, 129–130, 135, 159; religious, 25, 78; as value, 7, 9, 25–26. *See also* Markets, free

Gaudium et Spes, 5–6, 38n14, 51, 61, 89n11, 91n43, 100, 128, 143, 149n2, 153n123, 154n145, 154n149, 179, 185

Gift: 142, 146; logic of, 27, 144, 155n153. *See also* God, gifts and grace of

Great Depression, 9, 75, 79–80

Greed, 10, 21, 29–30, 32–34, 37, 43n71, 46n116, 107, 125, 130, 139, 145, 148

God: vii, 1–4, 6, "absence of", 165; and the Bible, 8, 10, 13–15; devotion to, 59, 126, 157, 160, 162–164; and Francis, 57, 114–118, 122, 128–129, 141–143, 156, 161; gifts and grace of, 80–81, 97n146,

103, 118, 121–122, 129, 159, 164; glory of, 29, 46n113, 121, 159; and justice, 137; knowledge of, 51–52; man in image of, 142; and neighbor, 36, 60, 65; Providence and wisdom of, 4, 38n6, 41n43, 42n65, 69, 100, 103, 118, 138, 160, 168–169; and the world, 157, 165

Gospel, vii–viii, 8, 14, 38n6, 56, 60, 77, 100, 104, 111, 117, 122–124, 134, 158; social, 49. *See also* Prosperity gospel

Government, 5–6, 10, 59, 71, 75, 78–79, 84, 91n36, 101–102, 106–107, 110–111, 126, 133, 136, 140, 146, 169; Argentine, 80

Grace, 4, 8, 38n6, 121, 157, 159, 162, 164. *See also* Holy Spirit

Gratuitousness, 27, 144, 155n153, 161

Happiness, 10, 22, 29, 74, 87, 100, 112, 118, 120, 122, 131, 139, 159, 164–165

Health care: 22, 54, 66, 110–111, 118, 139

Hermeneutics, 49–53, 56, 63, 67, 89n7, 92n53, 99

Holy Spirit, 8, 118, 124, 158–159, 161, 168–169

Holy Trinity, 26, 142–143, 158

Hunger, 22, 59, 97n146, 120, 123; of elephants, 137

Idolatry (of money), 30, 54, 59, 77, 90n35, 102, 111, 129–130, 141, 159–160, 165

Immigration, vii, 27, 66, 79, 87, 97n146, 101

Inclusion, 28, 68, 71, 112, 133, 135, 139. *See also* Institution, inclusive

Inculturation, 55–56

Individual rights. *See* Rights, individual

Individualism, 26, 60, 81, 88, 123, 128

Inequality, vii–viii, 31, 53, 113, 120, 133, 138–139, 141, 151n78, 154n137, 156, 169

Inequity, 85, 138, 154n137

Institutions: 8–11, 37, 55, 70, 73, 79, 85, 133, 146; ecclesial, viii, 3, 113, 116, 163–164; economic, 10, 13, 16–18, 26, 28, 31, 54, 73, 82, 143, 159; ethics of, 11–12, 40n31; extractive, 54, 75, 79, 81–83; financial, 31, 45n106, 130, 135, 159, 163, 169; and the good, 166, 169; inclusive, 33, 54–55, 79, 81–84, 87–88, 148; political 28, 54, 68, 79, 81, 110, 125, 162–163

Israel, 13–14, 19

Jesuits. *See* Society of Jesus

Jesus. *See* Christ

Jobs, 11, 71, 85, 103, 105, 144

Joy, 6, 8, 19, 28, 42n64, 53, 103, 129, 141, 158, 164, 168

Jubilee year, 13–14, 148

Injustice: 10–11, 48, 58–59, 65, 77, 99, 110, 124, 128, 137–138, 144, 151n59, 154n137; social, 10, 36, 49, 86, 123, 139

Justice: 3, 7–8, 23, 58–59, 65, 87, 118, 138, 140, 166; and business, 34, 96n134, 136–137, 144; and charity, 8–9, 135–136, 169; Church as advocate for, 6, 86, 91n39, 98, 129; commutative, 26; distributive, 13, 26, 81, 87, 128, 135, 138–139; price, *See* Price, just; social, vii–viii, 6, 9, 11, 26, 59–60, 80–81, 113, 134; and truth, 23, 128; virtue of, 14, 37, 141, 144; wage, *See* Wage, just

Kingdom of God, 3, 8, 38n6, 62, 122, 129

Labor: 8, 10–11, 22, 41n51, 60, 75, 86–87, 105, 121, 138; child, 36; forced, 79

Laity, 5–6, 33, 91n39, 93n66, 100–101, 113, 124–125, 133, 157–158, 168

Latin America, 48, 56, 61–62, 66, 72, 74, 82–86, 88, 98; bishops of, 62, 65, 69–70, 89n5; pope from, 28, 49, 54, 71–72, 84–86; and U.S. liberal capitalism; 65, 72, 74, 76, 78–81, 83, 84–88

Laudato Si', 47n126, 52, 89n13, 89n15, 95n99–10, 99, 105, 108, 110, 137, 149n6, 149n21, 150n26, 150n29, 150n34–37, 150n41–44, 150n47–56, 151n57, 153n109–113, 153n122–124, 154n130–133, 154n147, 155n161, 169, 170n15, 171n41, 171n43, 178

Law: 4–5, 8, 16, 19, 38n6, 78, 102, 106, 108, 140, 160, 166; canon: 24, 50, 116, 122; civil or human, 14–16, 40n41; divine, 3, 6, 14–15, 69; economic, 6, 23, 76, 145; moral, 3, 5, 75, 167; natural: 4, 7, 16–18, 35; Roman: 13–14

Law, rule of, 9–10, 24, 82, 87, 96n118, 110, 112, 135, 148, 169

Leadership, 36–37, 101, 106, 136–137, 154n129, 158, 164

Liberalism: 62, 76, 78–79, 81, 88, 96n118, 164; neo-: 78, 80–81, 87

Liberality, 125–126

Liberation theology, 48–49, 60–71, 92n57, 94n83

Liberty, 74, 78, 84, 87, 110, 136, 159, 166

Life, right to, 87, 132–133

Liquidity, 11, 31–32, 35, 45n101

Liturgy, vii, 50, 60, 122, 128, 170n21

Love: 9, 104, 161, 169; Christian, 7–8, 22, 26–27, 36, 116–117, 123, 158, 161, 165–166; of country: 57, 84; of the Earth, 129; of God; 1, 8, 36, 60, 91n37, 117, 122, 129; of money; 33: of neighbor, 36, 60, 116–117, 124, 128–129, 134, 136, 161; for the poor and suffering, 54, 60,

62–63, 66–67, 70, 114, 116–117, 126, 144, 148. *See also* Charity

Markets: 1, 11–12, 22–28, 36, 40n31, 54, 76, 81, 83–85, 88, 102, 106–110, 131, 134–136, 139–141, 143–146, 154; "deified," 88, 141; financial: 28, 31–32, 73, 85, 88, 141; free: ii, 22, 24–25, 31, 39n24, 54, 73, 76, 79–80, 82–83, 88, 107–108, 114, 120, 135, 139–140, 147

Market economy, 26, 28, 71, 76, 95n113, 133, 148

Marxism, 19, 48–49, 58, 62, 64, 69, 75–76, 81, 92n56, 94n88, 114

Material prosperity, 21–22, 54–55, 74, 102–103, 133, 139, 165, 186

Materialism, practical, 9, 121, 129, 148

Mediation, 63–64, 68, 138, 162

Medieval, 14–15, 17–18, 21, 23, 33–36, 40n38, 41n45, 43n84, 125, 163, 170n20

Mercy, vii, 8, 19, 28, 121, 139, 148, 160, 164

Migration. *See* Immigration

Misery, 18, 20, 22, 42n66, 54, 57, 59, 61, 65, 115, 120–121, 139

Money: 12; attraction of, 29, 165; changers in Bible, 24; history of, 29, 33–37, 162–163; importance of, 30, 122, 130; investing, 21, 35, 145, 162; proper use of, 30, 103, 109, 118, 125, 129–130; versus real value, 23, 34, 74, 106–107, 111, 124. *See also* Finance; Idolatry (of money); Trust, in money; Wealth, placing confidence in

Monism, 2

Narrative, 25, 55, 165, 171n29

New Testament, 14, 19–20

Offices of the Christian: 9–10, 127; priestly, 11; prophetic, 3, 11; regal: 3, 10

Old Testament, 3, 10, 13–14, 18
Opportunity. *See* Equality, of opportunity
Ordoliberalism, 76
Order: business, 137; economic, 12, 73–76, 88, 108, 159; moral, 74, 157; social, 3, 4, 8–9, 12, 16–17, 24, 38n4, 65, 73–74, 100, 129, 133
Orders, religious: 100, 102, 124–125, 162–164; Jesuit, 57–61, 123

Pauperism, 116, 122, 125, 155n155
Peace: 8–9, 16–17, 22, 44n85, 117, 119, 136, 157, 159, 167; justice and, 86
People of God, 53, 68, 114, 116, 128
Peripheries, 86, 92n56, 101, 104, 118
Philanthropy: 77
Politicians, 3, 71, 98, 106, 147, 165
Politics: 3–4, 6, 20, 32, 91n39, 129, 149; Argentine: 68, 79–86; and the Church, 68, 98, 129, 157; and economics, 80, 106, 133–134, 164; modern democratic: 17, 19, 28, 54–55, 82, 110, 125, 162–163; partisan: 6, 31, 60–61, 85. *See also* Institutions, political; Power, political
Poor, the: and capitalism, 71, 74, 76, 112, 133, 135, 145; and Catholic social teaching, 10, 67, 98, 119, 136, 139; and the Church Fathers, 15–16, 20–21, 23–24, 42n57, 42n67, 126; empathy for, 65, 77, 81; and the Franciscans, 162–163; and the government, 76, 102; and the New Testament, 19, 41n55; and the Old Testament, 13, 18–19; and Pope Francis, 48, 54–55, 57–61, 66, 80, 84–85, 90n33, 104–105, 110, 116–119, 123, 133–135, 139–141, 148, 156–167; serving, viii, 2, 8, 105, 141, 166. *See also* Inclusion; Preferential option for the poor

Post-modernism, 25
Potestas indirecta, 3–5, 38n8
Poverty: and the Bible, 18–20; causes of, 31, 64–67, 97n148, 133, 139, 156; chosen versus objective, 19, 59, 119–125, 148, 162; and Church Fathers, 20; and Francis, 1954, 57–58, 77, 102, 111, 113–117, 119; reducing, viii, 10, 31, 87, 133, 138–139; of spirit, 19, 116, 123, 152n91, 160
Power: 14, 41n43, 48, 59, 105, 110, 124; civil, 3–4, 91n36; economic, 10, 22, 29, 55, 65, 74, 82–84, 105, 107, 128; lack of, 68, 145; papal, 4, 6; political, 2, 4, 10, 29, 74, 82–84; spiritual, 115–116, 128, 136, 144, 166–168
Powers, separation of, 2–4, 6, 9, 82
Preferential option for the poor, 58, 62–63, 66–68, 70, 93n69, 93n76, 94n80, 114, 119, 126, 134–135
Prices: just, 22–23, 34; lowering, 46n113, 106, 108, 145; raising, 83–84, 101, 145
Private property: 8, 12–18, 25, 40n31, 40n41, 41n51–53, 122, 126–128, 140, 162, 169; right to, vii, 10, 12–13, 16–17, 73, 81
Profit: 11–12, 18, 21, 31–34, 43n82, 77, 81, 101, 104, 108–109, 125, 137, 141, 144
Prophetic dimension: of the Christian, 10, 101, 127, 167–169; of the Church, 10, 48, 64; of liberation theology, 65, 70; of the Old Testament, 3, 10, 14; of Pope Francis: 11–12, 53, 59, 88, 110, 127–128, 147, 166–167;
Prosperity, *See* Material prosperity
Prosperity Gospel, 66

Reason, 4, 6, 8, 15, 26, 118, 142–143, 160–161, 167
Reciprocity, 78, 117, 144

Reformation: 2–4, 38n6, 153n106
Relationships: commercial, 1, 14, 26–27, 36, 83, 144, 155n153; between faith and society, 5, 78, 125; between Francis and media, 53, 58; with God, 2, 13, 142; between human beings, 11, 26, 132, 141–144, 166;
Rent-seeking, 32, 88, 103, 131, 165
Renaissance, 34, 46n119, 125
Rerum Novarum, 8, 10, 17, 39n26, 40n33, 59, 75, 80, 181
Resources: human, 124, 153; material, 20, 105, 120; natural, 41n51, 87, 109, 137; spiritual, 168; utilizing wisely, 22, 30, 82, 145, 147; wasting, 109, 132
Resurrection, 8, 128, 167–168
Rich, the, 10, 15, 18–21, 42n63–66, 59, 68, 85, 101, 103–104, 117, 119, 131, 139, 145
Righteousness, 8, 18, 39n22, 42n66, 132
Rights: of the Church, 4, 98–99; individual, 17–18, 70, 132; natural human, 7, 9–10, 17, 67, 78, 84, 100, 132–133, 138; property, vii, 10, 12–13, 16–18, 41n52, 73, 81–82; of the State 41n52; workers' 8, 75, 86, 90n36. *See also* Life, right to

Sacrament, 60, 157, 160, 162
Salvation, 4, 33, 60, 64–65, 98, 128, 138
Salamanca, School of, 4, 34, 38n8, 46n118, 174
Second Vatican Council, v, 4–6, 39n17, 48, 50–52, 58, 61, 78, 89n12, 100, 124, 127–128, 142–143
Sexual revolution, 7
Sexuality, 132
Sick, the, 20, 22–23, 53, 97n146, 123, 126
Sin: avoiding, 43n82; capital (or deadly) 33, 46n116, 139; and Christ, 121, 164, 168; conse-

quences of, 15–16, 18, 138; and Pope Francis, 37, 77 –78, 100, 110–111, 120, 130, 148, 151n59; structure of, 10, 120
Social market economy, 11, 69, 71, 76, 92n57
Socialism, 9–10, 62, 64, 66, 75–76, 92n57, 111
Society: ii, 1, 9–11, 13, 17–18, 20, 24–26, 32, 34, 65, 68–70, 72, 74, 76, 78, 80–82, 84–85, 91n39, 98, 105, 109, 111–112, 124–125, 130–134, 136–138, 140, 142, 146–147, 149n1, 161, 164–167; American: 74, 87–88; commercial: 21, 33, 43n73, 73; civil, 3, 5–6, 134; evangelization of, 5, 27, 168; order of, 3, 7, 9, 17, 24, 129, 133
Society of Jesus, 56–61, 90n32, 90n34, 91n39
Solidarity, ii, 9, 26, 39n24, 41n53, 70, 80, 124, 134–137, 143, 146, 166
Speculator (or speculation), 11, 29, 85, 88, 104, 141
Spirituality, 21, 33, 49, 51, 56–57, 60, 69, 100, 131, 143, 148, 156, 165, 169. *See also* Poverty, of spirit
Subsidiarity, 9, 166
Summa Theologiae, 40n43, 41n45–46, 43n74, 43n83, 44n95, 46n113–114, 152n91, 173, 185

Technocratic paradigm, 106, 110
Technology, 32, 82–83, 87, 105, 110, 145, 160
Theology: viii, 12, 20–21, 66, 69–70, 86, 88, 96n143, 114, 116, 119, 123, 143; and business, 1; detached from reality, 123; Franciscan School, 16; medieval, 35; moral, 7, 13–14, 17, 34, 118. *See also* Liberation theology; Theology of the people
Theology of Liberation. *See* Liberation theology

Theology of the people: 48–49, 61, 64, 66–69, 85, 94n80, 94n83, 101, 114, 116, 134

Thrift: 74, 108, 131

Trust: in God, 117, 121, 167; in money, 11, 14, 165; as social virtue: 26, 59, 139–140, 143, 154

Truth: and charity, 27, 36, 136, 142, 158, 165; Church's mission of, 37, 51, 93n66, 119, 128, 149n1; criteria for finding, 28, 69, 89n14; and hope, 167; value of, 7–9, 23, 160

Unborn, 6, 93n79, 113

Unemployment. *See* employment

United States (U.S.), 37, 55, 62, 72–73, 76, 82–84, 86–87, 96n144, 97n146, 111, 141, 164

Usury, 10, 24, 35, 46n121–122, 76, 130, 162–163

Value, economic, 22, 26, 33–34, 75, 77, 107, 137, 162

Values, moral and spiritual: 5–9, 12, 19, 22–24, 37, 53, 68, 72–74, 78, 80–81, 86–87, 105, 108, 110, 112, 129, 133, 140, 164–165

Violence, 19, 48, 58, 61, 65, 68, 78, 87, 92n64, 97n146

Virtue: cardinal, 37, 118; as a good, 14; individual, 28, 110; related to money, 19, 21, 88, 121–126, 135, 140, 153n106, 165–166, 169; social, 9–11, 136; theological, 113, 122–123

Wage, just, 8, 22–23, 30–31, 34, 42n66, 91n36, 151n59

Wealth: 12, 21–22, 24, 29, 33–34, 54, 59, 73–75, 79, 84, 110, 122, 129–130, 137, 151n59, 151n76; in Bible, 18–20, 42n64–66, 43n82; creating, 28, 31, 36, 77, 82, 87, 102–103, 120, 133, 163; placing confidence in, 43n72, 103, 121, 165; sharing, 15, 20, 81, 87

Wealth of Nations: 73, 95n105, 110, 150, 184

Work: 17, 20, 32, 41n51, 101–105, 108, 112–113, 118, 121, 133, 139–140, 148, 153n106, 153n117, 158, 160–161, 163–164, 168–169; culture of, 82, 101; dignity of, 102–103, 121; pastoral, 51, 57, 69, 87, 94n80, 100, 161

Worker: 8–10, 15, 30, 42n66, 60, 75, 80, 86, 101, 103–104, 163. *See* Rights, workers'

World, the: 5, 7, 14, 36, 54, 59, 63, 65, 72, 77, 100–101, 123, 126–127, 129, 142, 157–161, 167–168; Anglo-Saxon: 54, 73, 87; of business: 70, 104; our modern: 5, 103, 139; of the poor, 65; spirit of the, 122, 129; this present: 30, 61, 63, 100, 139, 159; Western: 25, 31, 73, 121–122, 146; of work, 149n24

Worldliness, spiritual: 22

World War II: 11, 85

Index of Names

Acemoglu, Daron, 79, 81, 83, 96n121, 173

Allen, John L., 49, 89n6, 173

Ambrose of Milan, 21, 152n93, 181

Arrupe, Pedro, v, 56–60, 90n28–30, 91n39, 96n127, 180

Aristotle, 15, 33, 35, 41, 125

Augustine of Hippo, 14–16, 20, 24, 40n38–40, 42n69, 43n83, 161, 170n18, 173

Basil of Caesarea, 21, 42n67, 43n71, 50, 89n9, 152n93, 181, 183

Bellarmine, Robert, 4, 38n9, 38n11, 174

Benedict of Nursia, 46n113, 159, 164, 170n21, 174

Benedict XIV, 35

Benedict XVI [Ratzinger, Joseph], vii, viii, 3–4, 6–7, 25–27, 36, 38n4, 38n10, 39n16, 39n20, 39n24, 43n75, 44n87–92, 47n125, 47n128, 49–51, 61, 67, 76, 89n5, 89n9, 91n41–43, 93n79, 95n113, 96n119, 98–99, 116–117, 127, 131, 142–144, 149n1, 149n3, 152n97, 154n146, 155n152, 174, 183

Bernardino of Siena, 130, 145, 152n102, 155n155, 175

Boff, Clodovis, 62–63, 91n47, 92n55–58, 92n60, 92n64, 93n67, 175

Boff, Leonardo, 62–63, 91n47, 92n55–58, 92n60, 92n64, 93n67, 175

Clement of Alexandria, 21, 43n72, 175

de Soto, Domingo, 34, 46n120, 176

de Tocqueville, Alexis, 132

Duns Scotus, John, 16, 41n47, 184

Escrivá, Josemaría, 152n90, 177

Fazio, Mariano, 55, 90n18, 149n18, 177

Francis of Assisi, 30, 114

Gera, Lucio, 48, 67, 94n86–87, 178

Gibbons, James Cardinal, 59, 90n36, 141, 150, 177

Gregory the Great, 33, 46n115, 159, 170n12, 179

Guardini, Romano, 110, 150n56, 179

Gundlach, Gustav, 75

Gutiérrez, Gustavo, 62, 64–65, 91n44, 92n57–62, 93n76, 94n90, 95n107, 179

Hayek, Friedrich August von, 78, 96n118, 179

Hirschfeld, Mary L., 24, 44n94, 179

Ignatius of Loyola, 58

Ivereigh, Austen, 38n12, 52, 80, 90n17, 90n20, 94n85, 96n122, 96n125–126, 96n135, 109, 150n25, 180

Job, 42n56

John Chrysostom, 15, 21, 41n44, 175

John Paul II, vii, viii, 1, 7, 9, 24, 37n1, 39n18, 40n32, 40n34, 41n54,

43n79, 44n86, 49–51, 55, 66–67, 80, 88, 89n4, 90n22–23, 93n74, 93n78, 96n125, 96n131, 114–115, 127, 131, 149n12, 151n74, 164, 179–180
John XXIII, 9, 51, 64, 92n54, 115, 157, 165, 170n2, 180,

Kant, Immanuel, 165

Leo XIII, 5, 8, 10, 17, 39n26, 40n33, 41n52, 181
Locke, John, 17, 41n51, 181
Lombardi, Federico, 52
Luther, Martin, 3, 38n6, 184

Machiavelli, Niccolò, 125
Mandeville, Bernard, 125
Manent, Pierre, 157, 165, 170n4, 171n27, 181
Maritain, Jacques, 167, 171n35, 181
Marx, Reinhard Cardinal, 76, 95n111, 181
Marx, Karl, 64, 75
Menem, Carlos, 84–85
Methol Ferré, Alberto, 49, 67, 85, 94n81, 96n120, 96n133, 96n140, 181
Müller, Gerhard Ludwig Cardinal, 38n6, 64, 74, 92n57, 95n107, 173, 179

Nell-Breuning, Oswald von, 75
Newman, John Henry, 171n34, 181

Paul VI, 22, 39n17, 43n75, 43n77, 51, 58, 60, 89n12, 91n38, 100, 149n13, 170n3, 182
Pesch, Heinrich, 75, 95n110, 182

Piketty, Thomas, 32, 45n107, 182
Pius IX, 91
Pius XI, 9, 11, 75, 95n108, 153n126, 182

Quadragesimo Anno, 9, 75, 85, 95n108, 153n126, 182

Rahner, Karl, 91n37, 183
Robinson, James A., 79, 81, 83, 96n121, 96n128, 96n132, 173

Scalfari, Eugenio, 52–53
Scannone, Juan Carlos, 49, 67, 69, 94n80, 94n82, 94n84, 94n87, 94n89, 183
Shaw, Enrique, 103, 149n23
Siedentop, Larry, 78–79, 95n116, 184
Smith, Adam, 17, 73–76, 95n105, 108–110, 146, 150n40, 153n107, 177, 179, 184
Sobrino, Jon, 62–63, 65, 92n66, 93n66, 176, 184
Solzhenitsyn, Alexandr, 167, 171n36, 184

Taylor, Charles, 165, 171n29, 184
Mother Teresa of Kolkatta, 119
Thomas Aquinas, 15–16, 29, 33, 35, 40n43, 41n45, 43n74, 43n83, 44n93–95, 46n113–114, 152n91, 173, 179, 185

Utz, Arthur, 15, 40n43, 185

Vitoria, Francisco de, 4, 38n8, 182, 185
Von Balthasar, Hans Urs, 91n37, 185
von Mises, Ludwig, 78